World in Motion

GLOBALIZATION AND THE ENVIRONMENT SERIES

Series Editors

Richard Wilk, Department of Anthropology, 130 Student Building, Indiana University, Bloomington, IN 47405, USA, or wilkr@indiana.edu

Josiah Heyman, Department of Sociology & Anthropology, Old Main Building #109, University of Texas, 500 West University Avenue, El Paso, TX 79968, USA, or jmheyman@utep.edu

This AltaMira series publishes new books about the global spread of environmental problems. Key themes addressed are the effects of cultural and economic globalization on the environment; the global institutions that regulate and change human relations with the environment; and the global nature of environmental governance, movements, and activism. The series will include detailed case studies, innovative multi-sited research, and theoretical questioning of the concepts of globalization and the environment. At the center of the series is an exploration of the multiple linkages that connect people, problems, and solutions at scales beyond the local and regional. The editors welcome works that cross boundaries of disciplines, methods, and locales and span scholarly and practical approaches.

Books in the Series

Power of the Machine: Global Inequalities of Economy, Technology, and Environment, by Alf Hornborg (2001)

Confronting Environments: Local Environmental Understanding in a Globalizing World, edited by James Carrier (2004)

Communities and Conservation: Histories and Politics of Community-Based Natural Resource Management, edited by J. Peter Brosius, Anna Lowenhaupt Tsing, and Charles Zerner (2005)

Globalization, Health, and the Environment: An Integrated Perspective, edited by Greg Guest (2005)

Cows, Kin, and Globalization: An Ethnography of Sustainability, by Susan A. Crate (2006)

Global Visions, Local Landscapes: A Political Ecology of Conservation, Conflict, and Control in Northern Madagascar, by Lisa L. Gezon (2006)

Globalization and the World Ocean, by Peter Jacques (2006)

Rethinking Environmental History: World-System History and Global Environmental Change, edited by Alf Hornborg, John McNeill, and Joan Martínez-Alier (2007)

The World's Scavengers: Salvaging for Sustainable Consumption and Production, by Martin Medina (2007)

Saving Forests, Protecting People? by John W. Schelhas and Max J. Pfeffer (2008)

Capitalizing on Catastrophe: Neoliberal Strategies in Disaster Reconstruction, edited by Nandini Gunewardena and Mark Schuller (2008)

World in Motion: The Globalization and the Environment Reader, edited by Gary M. Kroll and Richard H. Robbins (2009)

World in Motion

The Globalization and the Environment Reader

Edited by
Gary M. Kroll and Richard H. Robbins

ALTAMIRA
PRESS

A Division of
ROWMAN & LITTLEFIELD PUBLISHERS, INC.
Lanham • New York • Toronto • Plymouth, UK

ALTAMIRA PRESS

A division of Rowman & Littlefield Publishers, Inc.
A wholly owned subsidary of The Rowman & Littlefield Publishing Group, Inc.
4501 Forbes Boulevard, Suite 200
Lanham, MD 20706
www.altamirapress.com

Estover Road
Plymouth PL6 7PY
United Kingdom

British Library Cataloguing in Publication Information Available

World in motion : the globalization and the environment reader / [edited by]
Gary M. Kroll and Richard H. Robbins.
 p. cm.
 Includes bibliographical references and index.
 ISBN-13: 978-0-7591-1025-0 (cloth : alk. paper)
 ISBN-10: 0-7591-1025-5 (cloth : alk. paper)
 ISBN-13: 978-0-7591-1026-7 (pbk. : alk. paper)
 ISBN-10: 0-7591-1026-3 (pbk. : alk. paper)
 1. Human ecology—Philosophy. 2. Nature—Effect of human beings on. 3.
Human beings—Effect of environment on. 4. Globalization—
 Environmental aspects. 5. Sustainable development. I. Kroll, Gary,
 1970– II. Robbins, Richard H. (Richard Howard), 1940–
 GF21.W67 2009
 338.9′27—dc22   2008026708

Printed in the United States of America

∞ ™ The paper used in this publication meets the minimum requirements of
American National Standard for Information Sciences—Permanence of Paper for
Printed Library Materials, ANSI/NISO Z39.48-1992.

Contents

Preface

Richard Wilk
Indiana University

This book is being published at a time that seems to be a turning point in public debate about globalization and the environment. With the reluctant entry of the US government into the Bali agreements on climate change in December of 2007, we may finally see the beginning of an era where the major world powers agree that the earth's environment is in trouble, and that we must begin to act in a globally-coordinated way to face the challenges of packing seven billion or more human beings onto the planet.

In assembling this reader, Gary Kroll and Richard Robbins have issued an impassioned and broad call to action, not on a narrow agenda of climate change or species conservation, or any of the other on an immensely long list of urgent single environmental issues, each of which could occupy an army of scientists, lobbyists, and activists. Instead their book weaves these different issues together to show how they are all closely related facets of the growth system of global capitalism, a project which Robbins has also pursued in his outstanding textbook "Global Problems and the Culture of Capitalism." While conventional environmental science often divides up issues like water, wildlife conservation, forestry, transportation, conflict and consumer culture, this book shows that they are all deeply connected.

This new enterprise of connecting all the parts of the global environmental crisis together requires a host of new intellectual tools. It requires an acute sense of history and even prehistory, knowledge of human nature and culture, and tools from the full range of social sciences from sociology and psychology to cognitive science and experimental economics. We need to be able to read, understand and synthesize complex data in evolutionary science, demography, climatology and many other sciences. The academic disciplines invented in the nineteenth century which we have inherited are simply not up to the task. The selections in this book reflect both the diversity of approaches which we need to understand the full breadth of global environmental problems, and the necessary willingness to transcend disciplinary jargon, to speak a common language.

So this is an extremely readable and accessible volume, and its scholarship and intellectual muscle is largely hidden below the surface, in the cumulative impact of the readings, in clever juxtapositions, and in the way themes are interconnected. The editors recognize that our understanding of problems and our progress towards solutions are unsettled and still very much in a formative stage, and they do not bludgeon the reader with pronouncements and political postures or edicts on how things must be. They are not in the business of manufacturing artificial 'pro and con' positions on issues– there is no attempt to achieve the strange kind of media 'balance' where the statement of scientific consensus on an issue like global climate change is matched with an industry-funded denial, as if the two kinds of statement were equal 'facts.' There is no need to manufacture issues where there is so much legitimate uncertainty, where we need debate and creative thinking, and there is no end of real ethical conflict over the means and ends in the stakes of environmental change.

One way this reader is quite different from anything published before on the connection between globalization and the environment is the way it is firmly centered not on animals, forests, or climate, but on *people*. Kroll is a historian and Robbins is an anthropologist; both have spent much of their careers trying to understand the diversity of human cultures. All of the chapters and readings in this collection begin from the assumption that the environmental crisis created by human beings cannot be solved without the willing participation of those same people, and that participation requires understanding the basis of their action. In far too many environmental stories, people appear only in the characters of greedy and selfish exploiters, hapless deluded victims, happy but doomed eco-savages, or heroic scientists. Anyone who has followed the literature on parks and conservation over the last thirty years has seen how hard it has been for conservationists and scientists to come to grips with the diversity and complexity of the real human communities which live in and around the natural environments which are being 'preserved.' There have been plenty of cultural misunderstandings on all sides, and a host of failed projects and parks plagued by diminishing biodiversity and unsustainable economic situations.

We see the same kinds of issues arise over and over in the contexts of debates over climate change, water resources, pollution, mining and a host of other environmental issues. You simply cannot reduce these problems to simple moral dramas of good and evil, or science against society, and expect to reach workable solutions, because every specific case is embedded in complex cultural and historical human systems. When it comes to electricity use or Sport-Utility vehicles, you cannot simply legislate change without consent—you have to understand why people use so much energy in their homes, why they love their bloated cars, why they feel like they need huge garages and 100 liters of bottled water a year. Human problems require humane solutions founded in cultural understanding.

More than anything, this reader is a work of profound optimism. Having taught about global environmental issues myself for a number of years, I know that students can find the flood of information about dire world problems discouraging, even overwhelming. I don't think there is anyone who works on these issues who does not sometimes feel like the problems are huge mountains and all we are doing is carrying away grains of sand one at a time with tweezers. But it is important to remember that the whole concept of global environmentalism is in its infancy, we are really the pioneers at the very dawn of a new era. More to the point, every single chapter in this book presents an avenue of attack, a way of thinking through and addressing pressing global problems. There is no single correct way of going about changing things and solving global problems. Start anywhere!

Acknowledgments

Any academic work, particularly an edited volume such as this one, is truly a collaborative effort. Thanks must go to Richard Wilk and Josiah Heyman whose vision and efforts have made the Globalization and the Environment series possible. We thank also the authors of the articles in the collection, as well as their representatives. At AltaMira, Rosalie Robertson, Sarah Walker, Jack Meinhardt, Doug English, and Marissa Marro worked overtime to help with the final product. And special thanks must go to Chris Jordan, whose photos grace the pages and, along with his other work (available at www .chrisjordan.com), help provide visual urgency to the issues discussed in the book. And thanks to Amy, Rebecca, Zoey, Tracie, Lynn and Mirren for tolerating our self-imposed isolation while working on the volume.

Chris Jordan, Sand & Gravel Yard

Introduction
Globalization and the Environment: A Primer

Richard H. Robbins

> Humanity has the ability to make development sustainable—to ensure that it meets the needs of the present without compromising the ability of future generations to meet their own needs.
>
> —*Our Common Future* (1986)

> "Sustainable," we think, has now to be understood ideologically, as the effects that the majority of people can be persuaded to find tolerable, as the necessary environmental consequence of an ever more necessary growth process.
>
> —Elaine Hartwick and Richard Peet (2003)

We live in a society that considers trade and consumption the source of all well-being. It is a society built on the foundation of perpetual economic growth, in which we are required to produce and buy more this year than last and more next year than this in perpetuity. In fact, failure to grow can bring our entire economic edifice and the society it supports crashing down around us. To ensure this does not occur, we have evolved an economic and cultural strategy designed to encourage and, in many ways, guarantee a flourishing economy. This strategy goes by various terms, including "liberalism," "neoliberalism," or "market capitalism" (Korten 1995: 70). It represents also what is loosely termed "globalization." The major principles or assumptions of this strategy are:

1. Perpetual economic growth, as measured by gross national product (GNP), is the source of well-being and progress.

1

2. Free markets, unrestrained by government, produce the most efficient and socially optimal allocation of resources.
3. Economic globalization, achieved by removing barriers to the free flow of goods and money anywhere in the world, is generally beneficial to almost everyone.
4. Privatization, which shifts functions and assets from governments to the private sector, improves efficiency.
5. The major function of government is to provide the infrastructure necessary to promote commerce and enforce the rule of law with respect to property rights and contracts.

These principles, translated into government policy, have become the standard recipe, the "Washington consensus" as it became known, to be applied by national and global governance institutions regardless of national or cultural differences (Korten 1995; Hartwick and Peet 2003: 189). This view of well-being has sometimes been readily adopted by national leaders, but it has also sometimes been imposed on countries by such institutions as the International Monetary Fund (IMF), the World Bank, or the World Trade Organization (WTO).

There is little doubt that the application of these policies or their approximation has resulted in remarkable, though uneven, global economic growth and prosperity. In the past two centuries, in spite of occasional downturns, the societies of the world have produced more wealth than was produced in all the human history that preceded it. Overall, in dollar terms calculated in 1990 international dollars, the wealth of every person on earth has increased thirteen times; in Western Europe it has increased forty times, and in Western offshoots (e.g., United States and Australia) some sixty-five times. And the greatest increase in the world economy occurred from 1950 to 1973 when global wealth, measured by gross domestic product (GDP), almost doubled, growing at a rate of 5 percent a year.

The problem is that maintaining growth comes with costs to our environment as well as our society. Economists generally refer to these costs as "market externalities," assuming that these side effects are somehow peripheral to the maintenance of growth. Environmental destruction represents one of the "negative externalities" of the market. Here are some examples of these environmental externalities:

- Global warming from the burning of fossil fuels—petroleum, coal, and gas—is threatening to raise global temperatures from two to six degrees over the next century, leading to massive climate changes and coastal flooding.
- Twenty-two pounds of carbon dioxide are spewed into the atmosphere

Table A.   Level and Rate of Growth of GDP: World and Major Regions, A.D. 0–1998

Region	0	1000	1820	1998	0–1000	1000–1820	1820–1998
	Level of Growth (1990 international dollars)				*Annual average compound growth rate*		
Western Europe	11.1	10.2	163.7	6,961	−0.01	0.34	2.13
Western offshoot (U.S., Australia, etc.)	0.5	0.8	13.5	8,456	0.05	0.35	3.68
Japan	1.2	3.2	20.7	2,582	0.10	0.23	2.75
Latin America	2.22	4.6	14.1	2,942	0.07	0.14	3.05
Eastern Europe and the former USSR	3.5	5.4	60.9	1,793	0.05	0.29	1.92
Asia (excluding Japan)	77.0	78.9	390.5	9,953	0.00	0.20	1.84
Africa	7.0	13.7	31.0	1,939	0.07	0.10	1.96
World	102.5	116.8	694.4	33,726	0.01	0.22	2.21

Adapted from Maddisen 2003: 28.

for every gallon of gasoline burned; the people of the United States consume 840 million gallons a day.

- Seventy-three different kinds of pesticides were discovered in the groundwater from which we drink, made up of more than one hundred active pesticide ingredients that are suspected carcinogens and are implicated in birth defects and genetic mutations.
- Three million tons of toxic chemicals are emitted into the air, land, and water from factories in the United States.
- More than half a million trees are destroyed to produce 88 percent of the Sunday paper we read.
- The average college student produces 640 pounds of solid waste per year, including 320 pounds of paper and 500 disposable cups.
- Forty billion dollars a year in health care costs and lost economic productivity can be attributed to pollution.
- Every sixty minutes a species of plant or animal life becomes extinct.
- Over 25 million acres of arable and pasture land, the source of 98 percent of the world's food, are critically degraded and abandoned each year.[1]

Such environmental changes will affect virtually everyone. Nevertheless, the environmental externalities of economic growth will disproportionately affect the poorer among us. For example, death rates for the world's poor from global warming–related illnesses, such as malnutrition and diarrhea, will rise by 2030. Hundreds of millions of Africans and tens of millions of Latin Americans who now have water will be short of it in less than twenty years. By 2050, more than 1 billion people in Asia could face water short-ages. By 2080, water shortages could threaten 1.1 billion to 3.2 billion peo-ple, depending on the level of greenhouse gases that cars and industry spew into the air, and by 2080, between 200 million and 600 million people could be hungry because of global warming's effects.

While most people and virtually all climate scientists recognize the dan-gers posed to the environment and the lives dependent on it, there is dis-agreement regarding what to do about it. Neoliberals claim that the solution to our environmental and social problems lies in maintaining and even accel-erating economic growth and global economic expansion. More money, they claim, will lead to new solutions and new technologies that will solve envi-ronmental as well as social problems. Critics of globalization, on the other hand, suggest that unrestrained growth will result in, among other things, even greater deforestation, the acceleration of harmful climate change, and further degradation of farmland and water supplies. This issue is likely one of the most important of the twenty-first century. *Do we need to support and accelerate growth and assume that more money and newer technologies will alleviate environmental damage, or do we seek to transform our eco-nomic and social lives to reduce those activities that lead to environmental destruction?*

The readings in this volume provide perspective on this vital question. Assuming that continued growth will help solve environmental problems is clearly the easier alternative; we just need to continue what we are doing. Transforming our economic and social lives is more difficult, considering that the scope of such a transformation could require a change at least as great as occurred during the industrial revolution. Consequently to better understand the effects of globalization on our environment, we need to criti-cally examine each of the five major premises of neoliberal economics and the different arguments regarding how globalization affects our lives.

PRINCIPLE 1: PERPETUAL ECONOMIC GROWTH, AS MEASURED BY GROSS NATIONAL PRODUCT (GNP), IS THE SOURCE OF WELL-BEING AND PROGRESS

Arguably the GNP, or GDP[2] as it is now called, is the single most important measure in our culture. The GDP is simply the total of money spent or invested in goods and services by households, governments, and businesses. The GDP emerged from the long-standing efforts of national governments to measure the progress of their economies. In the seventeenth and eigh-teenth centuries, for example, governments were interested in taxable wealth, which at that point was largely agricultural. In the nineteenth century a nation's measurable wealth was taken to include its manufacturers and, finally, the cost of things. This was a significant jump. It meant that to have any worth, something had to have a price. Thus such things as family or community activities and the natural habitat, because they were outside the price system, had no value (Cobb et al. 1995).

In 1932, when the United States was in the throes of the Great Depression, the U.S. Commerce Department asked Simon Kuznets, a young economist, to develop a uniform way of representing national accounts. Kuznets's efforts gave birth to what was to become the GNP. Progress was to be measured in terms of how much money people spent.

The problem is, as Eric A. Davidson (2000) has put it, "you can't eat GNP." That is, what counts for the calculation of GNP needn't represent a positive contribution to the life of the nation or its citizens. The GNP includes money paid for marriage licenses, but it also includes lawyers' fees for divorce and the separate residences divorce produces. It includes spending on food but also on diet drugs and programs, as well as medical treatment for obesity. It includes the costs of producing weapons as well as the costs for cleaning up the damage they produce. The conversion of forest into wood products is counted completely as economic growth without depreciating the environmental loss that it entails. Cleaning up the environmental damage we create, if it creates profits for someone, is counted as growth. Manufacturing that contributes to the degradation of water resources counts toward GNP, as does the sale of bottled water to a populace wary of its publicly funded water supplies. Standing forests have no value in the national accounts until they generate revenue. As Clifford Cobb, Ted Halstead, and Jonathan Rowe (1995) put it,

> By the curious standard of the GDP, the nation's economic hero is a terminal cancer patient who is going through a costly divorce. The happiest event is an earthquake or a hurricane. The most desirable habitat is a multibillion-dollar Superfund site. All these add to the GDP, because they cause money to change hands. It is as if a business kept a balance sheet by merely adding up all "transactions," without distinguishing between income and expenses, or between assets and liabilities.

Neoliberal economists generally argue that environmental problems, rather than being caused by economic growth as measured by GDP, can be solved by growth. They point to research which suggests that while countries in the initial stages of economic growth may experience increased environmental degradation, once per capita income reaches a certain point, the environment improves (Chu 1999). The problem is that, even if the research is useful (and there much evidence that it is not; Harbaugh et al. 2002), estimates of per capita income at which the environment improves range from about $4,000 to $13,000. Since more than half the world's population earns $5,000 per capita or less, billions must try to survive in increasingly devastated environments.

There are, fortunately, other ways to measure the consequences of our way of life. Redefining Progress, a nonprofit public policy institute, proposes that we assess the state of a society through the genuine progress indicator (GPI). The GPI takes household consumption as a base figure and then adjusts it by adding factors such as the value of housework and parenting, value of volunteer work, and so on, while subtracting for such things as cost of environmental pollution, crime, noise, family breakdown, loss of leisure time, all factors that would contribute to GNP. Subtracting items that diminish our quality of life, rather than adding them, as does the GNP, we find that as GNP has risen over the past few decades, the GPI has declined.

An even more direct measure of environmental quality is the notion of the ecological footprint developed by Mathis Wackernakel and his associates. In the opening selection of the reader we have included a description of how

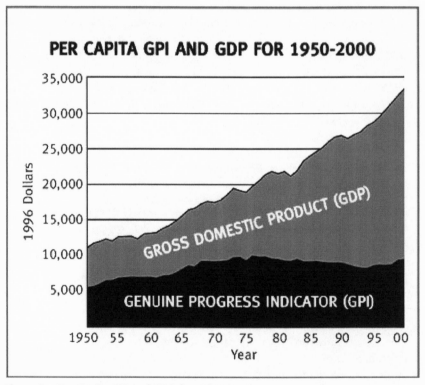

Figure A.   Per Capita GPI and GDP for 1950–2000

the idea of footprint works and how it can be applied. Clearly if environmental health were as much a priority as economic health, measures such as the ecological footprint should become as central a measure to our well-being as the GDP.

PRINCIPLE 2: FREE MARKETS, UNRESTRAINED BY GOVERNMENT, PRODUCE THE MOST EFFICIENT AND SOCIALLY OPTIMAL ALLOCATION OF RESOURCES

Neoliberal advocates don't like regulations placed on economic activities by nation-states. They argue that the market—the process of people buying and selling goods and services—left to its own devices without interference from government will ultimately solve environmental problems. A clean environment, they reason, is a commodity, just like television sets, computers, or soap, and if people desire the commodity, the market will supply it. On the other hand, if governments try to dictate environmental policy, their actions will distort the workings of the market and negatively impact economic growth and subsequently efforts to clean up the environment.

Automobiles are a prime example of the conflicted relationship between economic growth and the environment and whether to adopt market or government solutions to environmental problems. Automobiles are wonderful economic instruments. The sale of automobiles generates wealth, as does the sale of gasoline, the building of roads, the repair of automobiles, the sale of parts, the growth of tourism, the growth of military budgets to protect energy supplies, and so on. Yet while automobiles generate enormous economic growth, they also produce negative market externalities such as the production of carbon gases that produce global warming, the destruction of habitats to build roads, medical problems stemming from automobile pollution, and violent conflict over scarce energy supplies. While these externalities may seem abstract, they are not so to the people suffering from them. Thus villagers in Nigeria, as Alicia Fentiman describes in "The Anthropology of Oil" (in chapter 2), who benefit little from the wealth produced by automobiles, have had their environment, their livelihoods, and the social fabric of their society destroyed by the extraction of oil from their land.

The tension between economic growth and the environment is particularly acute in countries experiencing rapid growth, such as China. In 1963 China produced a total of three automobiles; by 1990, it produced 81,055; in 2000, 612,000; and by 2005 over 1 million. While the automobile has created more wealth in China, it has also become the leading cause of urban air pollution. Since China, with well over a billion people, wants to emulate the United States, where there are as many automobiles as driver's licenses, the prospect for environmental destruction is enormous. The Chinese government could, of course, adopt environmental policies to minimize the environmental externalities of automobiles. The government could set rules insisting that automobile manufacturers use only the latest, cleanest technology; or they could set gasoline mileage standards. However, when the automobile industry in China began to expand, car manufacturers in China imported older technologies, largely because the Chinese government was reluctant to impose regulations and sacrifice growth (Gallagher 2000).

Another problem with the market solution to environmental destruction is that environmental problems often go beyond national borders. As the article "Phaeton's Reins: The Human Hand in Climate Change" (in chapter 10) reveals, the pollution of the earth's atmosphere goes well beyond individual country contributions to environmental problems. Will people fund solutions for pollution that they are not responsible for? Will they pay for a cleaner environment if it is not theirs, even if their activities are creating the problem?

Even if the market could offer clean environments as commodities, as economists claim, what happens to populations who can't afford the commodity? That is, for the market to respond to a demand, the demand must be backed up by money. Left to the market, the world would be divided into those who can afford a clean environment and those who can't. In fact, that is the situation that we are approaching, as poor nations and areas are exposed to far greater environmental hazards than are rich ones. The article on environmental justice (in chapter 13) in the Pacific provides a glaring example of what happens to those without the economic resources to "buy" a safe and clean environment.

PRINCIPLE 3: ECONOMIC GLOBALIZATION, ACHIEVED BY REMOVING BARRIERS TO THE FREE FLOW OF GOODS AND MONEY ANYWHERE IN THE WORLD, IS GENERALLY BENEFICIAL TO ALMOST EVERYONE

"Free trade" is another term commonly associated with globalization. Its goal is to remove national boundaries and barriers to the free flow of goods, services and capital between nations. Traditionally these barriers consisted of tariffs or taxes on goods from other countries that might compete with domestic industries. Or they may consist of subsidies (government payments) to local industries or businesses to give them an advantage in competing with foreign businesses or organizations. Today the major watchdog of free trade is the World Trade Organization (WTO). The establishment of the WTO goes back to 1944 when U.S. President Franklin D. Roosevelt gathered the government financial leaders of forty-four nations to a meeting at the Mt. Washington Hotel in Bretton Woods, New Hampshire. Out of that meeting came the plan for the International Bank for Reconstruction and Development (World Bank), the International Monetary Fund (IMF) to control currency exchange, and the framework for a worldwide trade organization that would lead to the establishment in 1948 of the General Agreement on Tariffs and Trade (GATT) to regulate trade between member countries. Although GATT was not as comprehensive an agreement as many traders would have liked, its scope was widely enlarged on January 1, 1995, with the establishment of the World Trade Organization (WTO).

Neoliberals argue that free trade stimulates economic growth and helps alleviate poverty. Since economic prosperity provides people with more money, they argue, citizens can use that money to create a demand for a cleaner environment. The problem is that governmental attempts to protect the environment often conflict directly with economic activities and the free trade agenda. That is, in addition to tariffs, taxes on imports, or government subsidies to domestic business, government attempts to protect the environment often run afoul of the WTO. For example, when researchers discovered that dolphin populations were endangered by tuna fishing, the U.S. government reacted by issuing rules to protect dolphins and banning the importation of tuna from countries whose fishing fleets did not follow those rules. Mexico claimed that this law violated articles of the WTO and appealed to the WTO to rescind the rules or permit retaliatory tariffs to be applied to U.S. exports. The WTO ruled that the laws protecting dolphins were unnecessary barriers to trade.

By joining a multilateral organization such as the WTO, IMF, or World Bank, or entering trade agreements with other countries that can supersede the laws of national governments, countries have, in effect, ceded control of their environments to these organizations whenever an environmental regulation (or any other regulation) is judged to be a barrier to free trade. The WTO does have a provision (Article 20) ensuring that nothing in the agreement "shall be construed to prevent the adoption or enforcement by any contracting party of measures . . . necessary to protect human, animal, or plant life or health, or relating to the conservation of exhaustible natural resources." However, in every instance in which an environmental rule was challenged as a barrier to trade, the WTO dispute settlement panel ruled in favor of trade and against the environment (Hartwick and Peet 2003: 201–2).

Tellingly, while the United States has been willing to cede control of its economy to multilateral organizations such as the WTO, it refuses to cede control over the environment to multilateral agreements. Thus the United States is one of the few countries that refuse to join the Kyoto Accord to reduce carbon emissions and refuse to ratify the Basal Convention that prohibits trading in toxic waste. Yet if the environment is worth saving, it seems reasonable for the United States, certainly the largest producer of carbon emissions and toxic waste, to support global environmental regulatory agencies similar in scope and power to the WTO. By not joining in such regulation, the United States is again prioritizing economic growth over environmental safety.

PRINCIPLE 4: PRIVATIZATION, WHICH SHIFTS FUNCTIONS AND ASSETS FROM GOVERNMENTS TO THE PRIVATE SECTOR, IMPROVES EFFICIENCY

Privatization takes functions that were performed by government and transfers them to private, generally corporate control. The neoliberal argument is that corporations are more efficient and innovative than government agencies or monopolies. Thus services traditionally handled by governments such as water and sewage, power, transportation, and communication, along with government-run industries in socialized economies, are best turned over to or sold to private interests. Neoliberals argue privatization not only makes production and service functions more efficient, but also better able to make environmental improvements. They argue that, first, private enterprises make more efficient use of resources, are more concerned with waste reduction, and are better able to restructure organizations to gain more efficiency. Second, they say that private enterprises have increased access to capital and greater motivation for investment in cleaner technologies. In state-run enterprises, they say, environmental improvements must compete with other government budgetary priorities. Third, private enterprise is better able to institute advanced environmental management techniques and can better gain access to markets for environmentally friendly goods and services. Finally, there is greater "regulatory freedom" with private enterprises. Environmental regulatory instruments are often ineffective in economies dominated by the public sector, neoliberals claim, because of reluctance to enforce environmental requirements on public entities, whereas if enterprises are privatized, there is a separation between regulators and those being regulated.

However, in practice, the environmental advantages of privatization are difficult to document. For example, privatization of state resources often produces new pollution-producing enterprises (e.g., mines, oil drilling operations, lumber operations). In the former Soviet Union, the growth of private vehicles and the privatization of commercial fleets resulted in more vehicular emissions and less enforcement. Privatization of public transport services resulted in increased numbers of vehicles and increased emissions. Often privatization agreements contain exceptions from environmental compliance, as in Kazakhstan where a steel mill was able to negotiate a seven-year time frame for environmental compliance. In addition, private corporations can often escape responsibility for environmental disasters, as they did at Love Canal in New York state or in Bhopal, India.

But the monetary temptation for corporations to seek control of public utilities is enormous. Private water management is estimated to be a $200 billion business, and the World Bank, which has encouraged governments to sell off their utilities to reduce public debt, projects it could be worth $1 trillion by 2021. In May 2000 *Fortune* magazine predicted that water is about to become one of the world's great business opportunities, and that it promises to be to the twenty-first century what oil was to the twentieth.

Although the potential for profit is great, so are the possibilities for negative environmental externalities. Following the 1989 privatization of water in England and Wales, twenty water courses dried up in a few years because of overextraction. In 1998, Suez-Lyonnaise des Eaux subsidiary Essex & Suffolk Water was convicted for illegal overextraction of water at five sites in Suffolk over a three-year period. "The company admitted 27 charges of illegal extraction and asked for 233 other offences to be considered" (Public Service International Research Unit 2000).

Several multinational corporations are developing projects to transport huge quantities of water from northern areas to "thirsty" countries such as Saudi Arabia and Morocco and to southern California. Agricultural seeds, long considered community assets, are being privatized or patented by biotech companies, thus giving control of nature to traders (Bollier 2002). But by opening nature to corporate control, we are allowing corporations to select those seeds and crops that create the most profit, rather than those that are most environmentally sound. In her article, "Pepsico for Peace" (in chapter 8), Vandana Shiva notes how control of seeds develops crops that require high dosages of pesticides and fertilizers, while producing crop uniformity that threatens the ecological stability of agriculture and makes crops more susceptible to pests, prompting still greater use of pesticides.

PRINCIPLE 5: THE MAJOR FUNCTION OF GOVERNMENT IS TO PROVIDE THE INFRASTRUCTURE NECESSARY TO PROMOTE COMMERCE AND ENFORCE THE RULE OF LAW WITH RESPECT TO PROPERTY RIGHTS AND CONTRACTS

For neoliberals the most significant function of government is to advance trade and do whatever it takes to maintain economic growth. The problem they face, however, is that in countries with democratically elected governments citizens may demand more than that, particularly when it comes to environmental issues. Thus, in the United States, after the publication in 1962 of Rachel Carson's *Silent Spring*, voters demanded governmental action to ensure clean air and water, along with the preservation of other environmental resources. These demands for a cleaner environment led to the passage of the Clean Air Act of 1970 and Federal Water Pollution Control Act of 1972. Both pieces of legislation, along with virtually every other attempt to pass environmental regulations, have been vigorously opposed by corporate interests. Democratic governments all over the world, then, face a dilemma: *how do they respond to citizen demands to protect the environment while, at the same time, respond to pressure from corporate interests not to pass legislation that might affect corporate profits and economic growth?*

Generally speaking, governments have adopted three strategies to address this dilemma. The first is to pay lip service to environmental concerns by emphasizing sustainable growth. The idea of sustainable growth gained popularity as a result of the report issued in 1987 by a commission headed by Norwegian Prime Minister Gro Harlem Brundtland (World Commission on Environmental Development 1987). The Brundtland report, *Our Common Future,* defined sustainable development as development that "meets the needs of the present without compromising the ability of future generations to meet their own needs." The problem is, as already noted, whenever economic growth clashes with environmental concerns, economic growth almost always wins. Furthermore, as Hartwick and Peet (2003: 209) note, the idea of sustainability itself may serve as ideological tool as the greatest negative environmental impact that a majority of citizens can be convinced is necessary to maintain growth. As they put it,

> Sustainability in this sense has a number of meanings that range from keeping growth going using state intervention, through swapping pollution rights in the market, to minimizing pollution effects so that public concern does not result in organized political action (unorganized action can be dismissed as deranged anarchism). (Hartwick and Peet 2003: 209)

A second strategy that governments can adopt to avoid responding to public demands for environmental protection is to displace regulatory power to unelected and largely remote global governance institutions such as the WTO. By assigning the legal right to decide cases in which environmental protection conflicts with economic growth to dispute panels of the WTO, governments can absolve themselves of failing to respond to citizen environmental demands. Allowing multilateral institutions such as the WTO to dictate environmental policy may explain the reluctance of some governments, such as the United States, to enter into multilateral agreements addressing the environment, such as the Kyoto Accord or the Basel Convention. What would occur if two multilateral bodies, one designed to protect the global economy, the other to protect the global environment, disagreed with each other? That may explain why efforts to form a global environmental mechanism (GEM) as proposed by Daniel C. Esty and Maria H. Ivanova (2003), have been so difficult to implement. Yet the failure of governments to support the development of a GEM as vigorously as they have supported the WTO is indicative of global governmental priorities.

Finally, the third governmental strategy to avoid taking significant environmental action that conceivably could endanger continued economic growth is to free corporations and the mass media to spin environmental events and news to allay public fears and interests regarding the environment. Beginning in the 1970s, corporations, as Sharon Beder (2002) documents in her book *Global Spin: The Corporate Assault on Environmentalism*, began spending huge amounts on public relations campaigns to convince the public that they were environmentally conscious, while, at the same time, spending additional millions trying to minimize governmental regulations and countering scientific findings regarding the deterioration of the environment and its consequences on human health. Nowhere was this clearer than in the debate over global warming. Scientists are virtually unanimous in their judgment that global warming is occurring, it is due largely to human activities (see chapter 10), and it may have serious environmental and economic consequences.[3] Yet the media and some governmental spokespersons in the United States convey the impression that the conclusions about global warming are uncertain and that global warming is still being debated in the scientific community. Yet a study by Naomi Oreskes (2004) of 928 papers on climate change in refereed scientific journals found that not one disagreed with the general consensus that global warming is occurring and is the result of human activity. Yet another study (Boykoff and Boykoff 2004) of global warming reporting in over 3,500 stories from the major media outlets (*New York Times, Washington Post, Wall Street Journal,* and *Los Angeles Times*) found that in the interest of "balanced reporting," 53 percent of the stories gave roughly equal treatment to the view that global warming is caused by human activity and the view that it is the result of natural fluctuations. Thirty-five percent emphasized the role of human activity but presented both sides of the debate, and 6 percent emphasized the doubts about the claim that human activity causes global warming. Thus skeptics, financed largely by oil, coal, and gas corporations, who cannot gain an outlet through the normal scientific channels, are given equal weight thus creating the implication that there is *no* consensus in the scientific community. Because the media thrive on controversy, it is in their interest to make it appear that there is no consensus.

Corporations in the United States probably have been granted greater legal rights to utilize their financial power to influence public perceptions than in most other countries. This is attributable to a Supreme Court ruling in 1886 by a single judge in a case involving a dispute between Santa Clara County, California, and the Union Pacific Railroad in which the court ruled that corporations can use their economic power in a way they never before had. Relying on the Fourteenth Amendment, added to the Constitution in 1868 to protect the rights of freed slaves, the Court ruled that a private corporation is a natural person under the U.S. Constitution and consequently has the same rights and protection extended to persons by the Bill of Rights, including the right of free speech (Hartmann 2002). Thus corporations were given the same "rights" to influence the government in their own interest as were extended to individual citizens, paving the way for corporations to use their wealth to dominate public thought and discourse.

By controlling public awareness of environmental issues, the media, corporations, and governments, and often religious institutions help foster the ideology that human beings were put on earth to dominate nature, a view used by advertisers to sell large SUVs (see chapter 6 in this volume) and present, as Sydee and Bader note (chapter 15), in the patriarchal capitalism that equates the domination of nature with the domination of women.

The selections in this reader should help inform you about the relationship between globalization and the environment. It is generally not a favorable relationship, as you can judge yourself by taking an inventory of the environmental damage you confront directly every day. Is the damage worth the benefits that we enjoy as a consequence of continued economic expansion? If not, what sort of changes are required in our culture and lifestyle to halt the damage?

REFERENCES

Beder, Sharon. 2002. *Global Spin: The Corporate Assault on Environmentalism.* White River Junction, Vt.: Chelsea Green.

Bollier, David. 2002. *Silent Theft: The Private Plunder of Our Common Wealth.* New York: Routledge.

Boykoff, Jules, and Matthew Boykoff. 2004. "Journalistic Balance as Global Warming Bias." *Fairness and: Accuracy in Reporting.* www.fair.org/index.php?page = 1978.

Chua, Swee. 1999. "Economic Growth, Liberalization, and the Environment: A Review of the Economic Evidence." *Annual Review of Energy and the Environment* 24: 391–430.

Emanuel, Kerry. 2007. "Phaeton's Reins." *Boston Review,* January-February. http://bostonreview.net/BR32.1/emanuel.html.

Esty, Daniel C., and Maria H. Ivanova. 2003. "Toward a Global Environmental Mechanism." In James Gustave Speth, ed., *Worlds Apart: Globalization and the Environment.* Washington: Island.

Gallagher, Kelly Sims. 2006. *China Shifts Gears: Automakers, Oil, Pollution, and Development*. Cambridge: MIT Press.

Harbaugh, William, Arik Levinson, and David Molloy Wilson. 2002. "Reexamining the Empirical Evidence for an Environmental Kuznets Curve." *Review of Economics and Statistics* 84: 541–51.

Hartmann, Thom. 2002. *Unequal Protection: The Rise of Corporate Dominance and the Theft of Human Rights*. New York: Rodale.

Lovei, Magda, and Bradford S. Gentry. 2002. *The Environmental Implications of Privatization: Lessons for Developing Countries*. World Bank Discussion Paper no. 426. Washington, D.C.: World Bank.

Oreskes, Naomi. 2004. "The Scientific Consensus on Climate Change." *Science* 306: 1686.

Public Service International Research Unit. 2000. *Undermining Democracy and the Environment*. www.psiru.org/reports/2000-03-W-Htrans.doc.

Speth, James Gustave. 2003. *Worlds Apart: Globalization and the Environment*. Washington, D.C.: Island.

World Commission on Environment and Development. 1987. *Our Common Future*. Oxford: Oxford University Press.

1

The Ecological Footprint

All living organisms must necessarily consume resources and produce waste; it's one of the fundamental processes that connects human beings to the wider ecology of the planet. The cumulative resources used and wastes produced of an organism, a house, town, city, or nation can be conceptualized as an "ecological footprint." The concept has become a key reference point in measuring environmental behavior and ecological sustainability. From a human perspective, footprints can vary widely and are dependent on social, cultural, and economic structures. So people from overdeveloped countries almost invariably have a much greater footprint than those living in less developed countries. But what is truly interesting about people in overdeveloped countries is not necessarily the size of their ecological footprints, but rather the footprints' invisibility. Most of us are barely conscious of the myriad ways our daily activities ripple out across the natures and the peoples of the world. In the hope that awareness leads to action, this volume attempts to highlight some of these invisible connections.

An ecological footprint analysis (EFA) can help shed some light on these connections. Over the last ten years these studies have synthesized staggering quantities of global data to assess the sustainability of nations' consumption and production behavior. Redefining Progress (a public policy institute that advocates "smart economics") sponsors one of these studies. Its 2005 update, printed below, notes that "we would need 1.39 earths to ensure that future generations are at least as well off as we are now." The report does more than just paint a gloomy picture of the global environment; it provides the latest empirical information to support that picture, and suggests new directions in theory and methodology for future researchers. As economic globalization pushes forward at breakneck speed, scientists and social scientists are trying to catch up to measure the effect on the global environment.

Jason Venetoulis and John Talberth, *Ecological Footprints of Nations 2005 Update*[1]

OVERVIEW

Ecological footprints measure a population's demands on nature in a single metric: area of global biocapacity. By comparing humanity's ecological footprint with the earth's available biological capacity, ecological footprint analysis (EFA) suggests whether or not our use of crop lands, forest lands, pasture lands, fisheries, built space, and energy lands can be sustained. In previous *Footprint of Nations* reports, Redefining Progress (RP) documented that humanity's ecological footprint has breached the limits of environmental sustainability. We revealed that nature has been utilized beyond its capacity to renew and regenerate indefinitely, a finding consistent with an extinction rate estimated to be as great as one thousand times the natural level, a runaway greenhouse effect, widespread degradation of forest and crop land, collapsing fisheries, and increasing scarcity of all natural resources.

The footprint provides an excellent framework for measuring the extent (area) of humanity's use or appropriation of natural resources and services within in the context of sustainability. The originators, and fellow global leaders in the field, have done much in the way of making continuous advances to EFA (Wackernagel et al. 2005). This report presents a new EFA methodology, Footprint 2.0. Our hope is that Footprint 2.0 contributes to the process of improving EFA by adding to the depth of the concept and subtleties to the methodology.

Footprint 2.0 (EF 2.0) was developed by a team of researchers at RP. In summary, EF 2.0 differs from EF 1.0 by (1) including the entire surface of the Earth in biocapacity estimates, (2) reserving a portion of biocapacity for other species, (3) changing assumptions about carbon sequestration rates, and (4) using net primary productivity (NPP) as the basis for footprint equivalence factors.

Using Footprint 2.0, RP's 2005 edition of *Footprint of Nations* indicates that the situation is significantly worse than what EF 1.0 has shown. For the first time, we have found that footprints associated with crop land, built space, marine and inland fisheries are not sustainable. EF 1.0 shows sustainability on all these accounts. We also found that on a global level, humanity is exceeding its ecological limits by 39 percent—nearly double the amount of ecological overshoot found in our 2004 report using the old approach. This suggests that at present rates of consumption, we would need 1.39 earths to ensure that future generations are at least as well off as we are now.

At the country level, United Arab Emirates, Kuwait, and the United States of America exceeded their biological capacities by the most. On a continental basis, western Europe and North America had the greatest ecological footprints and ran negative ecological balances (footprint biocapacity) while

Africa, Latin America, and other regions had relatively smaller footprints and ran positive ecological balances. Footprint 2.0 also appears to be more sensitive to carbon cycle overshoot and increased built space. We found that nations with higher shares of their energy met by fossil fuels and a more urbanized land base are contributing the most to global ecological deficits.

In addition to introducing the new approach, describing the latest *Footprint of Nations* results using EF 2.0, this report offers some thoughts for future research that may prove fruitful in EFA's ongoing development.

WHAT IS ECOLOGICAL FOOTPRINT ANALYSIS?

Pioneered by William Rees and Mathis Wackernagel in 1996, the ecological footprint approach has become one of the most widely referenced sustainability analysis tools around the globe. Ecological footprint analysis is used to calculate the land area needed to sustain human consumption and absorb its ensuing wastes. Comparing the footprint of a given population in a discrete area with the amount of biologically productive space available to that population provides a way to estimate whether or not a population's consumption is sustainable.

When a population's footprint is smaller than available biocapacity, it is sustainable. When it is larger, that population is said to be engaging in unsustainable ecological overshoot or running a negative ecological balance. In addition to its heuristic value, the power of EFA lies not in the absolute values it yields, but in its ability to compare resource demands of different populations in a common currency of global productivity (Ferguson 1999).

To calculate a nation's footprint, we use official statistics tracking consumption and translate that into the amount of biologically productive land and water area required to produce the resources consumed and to assimilate the wastes generated on an annual basis. Because people use resources from all over the world and affect faraway places with their pollution, the footprint is the sum of these areas wherever they are on the planet. Ecological footprint calculations are based on five assumptions:

1. It is possible to keep track of most of the resources people consume and many of the wastes people generate. Much of that information can be found in existing official statistics.
2. Most of these resource and waste flows can be converted into the biologically productive area that is required to maintain these flows.
3. These different areas can be expressed in the same unit (hectares or acres) once they are scaled proportionally to their biomass productivity. In other words, each particular acre can be translated to an equivalent area of world-average land productivity.

4. Since each standardized acre represents the same amount of biomass productivity, they can be added up to a total representing humanity's demand.
5. This area for total human demand can be compared with nature's supply of ecological services, since it is also possible to assess the area on the planet that is biologically productive.

Ecological footprints and biocapacity are expressed in "global acres." Each unit corresponds to one acre of biologically productive space with world average productivity.

THE FOOTPRINT 2.0 APPROACH

Because the footprint embodies a vast amount of information in a single quantitative measure and attempts to operationalize well-known concepts of carrying capacity and sustainability, its popularity is burgeoning in academic, government, nonprofit, education, and business circles. At its simple best, the footprint has great heuristic value that resonates with people's conception of ecological sustainability.

Beyond the ideal, footprint analysis still has a number of serious shortcomings, such as not including water, toxins, other species, or two-thirds of the earth, and counting carbon emissions as forest area, when the carbon cycle includes the entire planet. Critiques of EFA's assumptions, methods, and data have been well presented in the literature (Van den Bergh and Verbruggen 1999). These and other independent insights, as well as the rising need and demand for accurate sustainability analysis tools, provided much of the impetus for development of Footprint 2.0. Though not addressing all the possible shortcomings, we would suggest that the new approach makes several intuitive steps that improve footprint analysis conceptually and methodologically.

Footprint 2.0 was developed by Jason Venetoulis, Christopher Gaudet, Karl Tupper, Dahlia Chazan, and Christen Cutil at RP in 2004–2005. An initial draft of proposed changes was reviewed by independent academics before the results were tabulated.[2] For a full discussion of the new approach, see Venetoulis and Talberth (2006).

In summary, Footprint 2.0: includes the entire surface of the earth in biocapacity estimates. EF 1.0 only includes about one-third. Other species have been given thoughtful consideration in the footprint literature (Chambers et al. 2000), yet EF 1.0 does not provide a corresponding algorithm. In contrast, Footprint 2.0 deducts 13.4 percent of biocapacity for the needs of other species. Footprint 2.0 also incorporates new carbon sequestration model results. Last but not least, the basis of the EFA equivalence factors are changed from potential of land to provide food for humans to the relative net primary productivity.

Net primary productivity (NPP) is the amount of energy left after subtracting the respiration of primary producers from the total amount of energy that is fixed biologically. NPP provides the basis for maintenance, growth, and reproduction of all consumers and decomposers. NPP is a measure of the total food resource available on the planet (Vitousek et al. 1986). Because human beings appropriate NPP to fuel production and consumption activities and because these activities, in turn, affect NPP availability in the future, NPP is particularly relevant in sustainability analyses. In fact, it has been suggested that human appropriation of NPP is "a more explicit measure of the intensity of human pressure on ecosystem use than the ecological footprint, which focuses more explicitly on demand" (UNEP 2005). Drawing from both, the combination of NPP and footprinting provide the basis for the significant changes represented in EF 2.0. Allow us to elaborate.

EF 1.0 uses potential agricultural productivity as estimated by the global agricultural ecological zone (GAEZ) suitability indexes as a basis for making final biocapacity estimates. GAEZ excludes portions of the earth where productivity is assumed to be negligible—de facto nil. Footprint 2.0 takes a first step toward including these areas in EFA by adding them to biocapacity estimates. Footprint 2.0 also shifts the basis of biocapacity estimates from agricultural potential to NPP by using NPP as measured by Amthor et al. (1998) as the basis (denominator) for equivalence factors.

Footprint 2.0 estimates the equivalence factors for each biome using the ratio of NPP for major biomes to the global average. FP 2.0's equivalence factors for each biome as well as biocapacity estimates are presented on the following page. We would suggest that using NPP as a basis for equivalence factors has three main advantages over agricultural productivity: (1) all of the earth's surface can now be included in EFA; (2) NPP better matches the relative ecological values of various terrestrial and aquatic ecosystems (i.e., crop land is now more valuable than built space), and (3) NPP provides a basis for real-time mapping of biocapacity through satellite-based measurements.

Footprint 2.0 also attempts to take a first step toward making formal accommodation for other species. As noted elsewhere, EF 1.0 takes an explicit anthropocentric stance. As a consequence, the portion of the Earth's biocapacity needed to sustain the diversity of nonhuman life is not removed from the realm of sustainable human appropriation. The unintended result is that footprinting has failed to adequately capture the world's biological diversity crisis, indicating that lands we use to meet our demands for food, fiber, timber, and fish are all managed sustainably, while all remaining lands are ignored, suggesting that they have no ecological significance.

As a first, tentative step toward addressing this concern, Footprint 2.0 formally sets aside a portion of the planet's biocapacity (NPP) for needs of nonhuman species and, more broadly, nonhuman ecosystem functions. While there are a number of techniques—some involving high resolution satellite

Global Footprint Accounts: EF 1.0 and EF 2.0
(All figures in global hectares per capita, 2001 data)

Biome	Biocapacity		Footprint		Ecological Balance	
	EF 2.0	EF 1.0	EF 2.0	EF 1.0	EF 2.0	EF 2.0
Crop land	0.461	0.527	0.521	0.527	-0.060	0.000
Forest land	1.775	0.833	0.464	0.189	1.311	0.644
Pasture land	1.197	0.267	0.470	0.091	0.726	0.176
Built space	0.020	0.100	0.046	0.100	-0.026	0.000
Less Productive Land	0.779	-	0.000	-	0.779	-
Marine and inland fisheries	0.873	0.132	1.045	0.138	-0.173	-0.006
Open ocean	2.337	-	0.000	-	2.337	-
Energy land	8.265	-	19.357	1.142	-11.092	-1.142
Total	15.707	1.859	21.903	2.187	-6.197	-0.328

Figure 1.1. World Biocapacity Estimates for EF 2.0 (All figures in global hectares per capita, 2001 data)

mapping—available for estimating the location and amount of NPP that should be reserved for other species, our second change takes an easier route and simply removes surface based on global gap analysis. Existing gap studies suggest that if approximately 13.4 percent of the terrestrial land on earth were protected, 55 percent of all species that are significantly threatened with extinction would meet targets for survival (Rodrigues et al. 2003). In regions "with high levels of species richness and endemism . . . larger percentages of their territory [require protection]" (Rodrigues et al. 2003).

We use the gap estimate from biocapacity a fixed amount of the earth's as a starting point and deduct 13.4 percent of each EFA biome from biocapacity. We would suggest that this is a conservative estimate of the amount of aquatic and terrestrial space actually needed to ensure the well-being of present and future generations of all life. Nonetheless, it is an adjustment that recognizes the critical importance of providing for other species within the EFA framework.

The final change incorporated into the new footprint approach concerns the largest portion, and the only unsustainable factor reported by EF 1.0 – energy. For every ton of carbon emitted, EF 1.0 apportions a 1.05 hectare footprint based on the carbon uptake potential of relatively young forests in 1980 and 1990.

On the biocapacity side of the footprint equation, no energy land is presented in final accounts. As such, EF 1.0 fails to acknowledge the role that most of the earth plays in the carbon cycle. Footprint 2.0 offers changes that we hope can begin to address these concerns.

According to global carbon models, the total combined carbon sequestration of earth is estimated to be 3.0 gigatons of carbon (Gt C) annually with oceans sequestering an estimated 2.3 Gt C (IPCC 2004). Net terrestrial uptake is estimated to be 0.7 Gt C annually. Terrestrial uptake potential is actually higher, but land use changes (e.g., deforestation) have decreased this potential. Of the earth's 51 billion hectares, oceans cover about 36.7 billion and land covers 14.4. The footprint per ton of carbon estimate used in footprint 2.0 is the weighted average of net sequestration potential of the land and sea or 0.06 tons of carbon per hectare per year.

The result is that Footprint 2.0 adds 8.27 hectares to the final global biocapacity estimates by including the entire earth in energy footprint calculations and increases the footprint per unit of energy. For every ton of carbon emitted, EF 2.0 assigns a footprint of 16.65 hectares. EF 1.0 reports 1.05 t/ha/yr footprint and no biocapacity. An extended discussion of the changes is presented in Venetoulis and Talberth (2006).

THE RESULTS: FOOTPRINT 1.0 AND 2.0

The combined changes to the standard footprint approach discussed in the previous section affect biocapacity estimates and size of the footprint. For the first time, they show a footprint that exceeds biocapacity in other categories besides energy. The table below summarizes our results and provides a comparison of EF 1.0.

Biocapacity estimates rise from about 1.9 global hectares (gha) per capita under EF 1.0 to 15.71 gha under EF 2.0. As compared with EF 2.0, energy land is the greatest addition (8.27 gha per capita) since EF 1.0 assigns no biocapacity to this function. EF 2.0 also adds 3.11 gha per capita to biocapacity for less productive lands and open oceans where EF 1.0 assigns none. Footprint 2.0 increases the size of the average ecological footprint, as well as the share attributable to each biome. EF 2.0 indicates a footprint of nearly 22 gha per person, over ten times the footprint size calculated by EF 1.0. EF 2.0 also has significantly larger footprints associated with forest land, pasture land, and marine and inland fisheries. The new equivalence factors explain most of this difference. Conversely, EF 2.0 shows a smaller built space footprint because built space is relatively less productive based on NPP estimates.

Both approaches show a negative ecological balance, or overshoot. EF 2.0: −6.20 gha per capita; EF 1.0: −0.33. On a per planet basis, if you will, EF 1.0 shows a footprint of 1.18 planets. That is, humanity's ecological footprint would require biocapacity the size of another planet that is 18 percent the size of the earth (at average biocapacity levels) to be sustainable. EF 2.0 shows a footprint of 1.39 planets, a 21 percent increase over EF 1.0.

While the global footprint accounts are dominated by energy, EF 2.0 also

World Biocapacity Estimates for EF 2.0
(All figures in global hectares per capita, 2001 data)

Biome	Area (ha/cap)	Equivalence Factor	Other Species (-13.4%)	Biocapacity (global ha/cap)
Crop land	14.80	2.12	0.22	0.46
Forest land	36.10	3.29	0.54	1.77
Pasture land	29.80	2.42	0.49	1.20
Built space	2.00	0.50	0.04	0.02
Less productive land	66.10	1.04	0.75	0.78
Marine and inland fisheries	21.30	2.67	0.33	0.87
Open ocean	343.60	0.48	4.85	2.34
Energy land	8.27	n/a	n/a	8.27
Average	-	2.00	-	-
Total	16.60	-	7.21	15.71

Figure 1.2. Global Footprint Accounts: EF 1.0 and EF 2.0 (All figures in global hectares per capita, 2001 data)

reveals ecological overshoot for crop land, built space, and marine and inland fisheries.

This is the first time global footprint analysis has been able to capture unsustainable use of these biomes. Fisheries in past EFA studies have been reported to be at the maximum but sustainable: fish footprint equaled 0.14 gha/capita as does biocapacity associated with fisheries. EF 2.0 shows the footprint associated with fisheries at 1.04 gha/capita in 2001, which is about 16 percent larger than the sustainable rate. This appears to better correspond with research in the field (Pauly et al. 2001). Built space and crop land are also reported in deficit using Footprint 2.0, where EF 1.0 shows sustainability.

While these changes may mark improvements in EFA, we still see the need for improvement in the use of sustainability criteria in EF 2.0. For example, neither approach fully captures precipitous declines in the world's forests over the past hundred years. And because EF 2.0 has not yet assigned a footprint to open oceans and less productive lands, our use of these biomes also appears to be within ecological limits. The differences between approaches are worth further consideration in that they may represent the best measure, to date, of our ecological footprint.

On a per capita basis, and as illustrated by figure 1.3, EF 2.0 and EF 1.0 footprints diverge to a considerable extent. With EF 1.0, there is a rise in the footprint (from 2.61 to 2.79) between 1961 and 1973, then a fairly steady

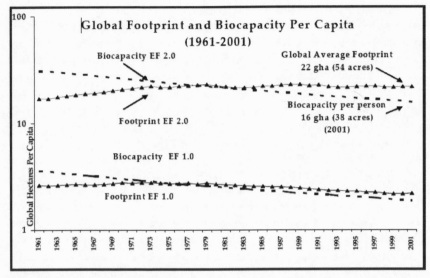

Figure 1.3.   Global Footprint and Biocapacity Per Capita (1961–2001)

decline through 2001 (from 2.79 to 2.19). This could be due to several factors, including rising population or increases in yield factors. EF 2.0 shows per capita footprint increasing over the first twenty years and then becoming fairly stable within the range of 21 to 23 gha per capita thereafter. In the final tally, Footprint 2.0 shows humanity overshot sustainable biocapacity levels by about 8 global hectares per capita. Overshoot of renewable biocapacity suggests a draw down in natural capital to fill the gap. In the ensuing years, this means that there could be less natural capital (to provide renewable biocapacity services) for more people without changes in policy, markets, consumption patterns, and technology.

In terms of global totals, both EF 1.0 and EF 2.0 show similar results in biocapacity through the period. Global ecological footprints have risen steadily under both approaches, but more steeply under EF 2.0. Ecological overshoot began in the late 1970s. Thereafter, overshoot has increased to about 18 percent with EF 1.0 and 39 percent with EF 2.0

Footprint 2.0 also appears to be more sensitive to carbon emissions overshoot and levels of built space. We found that those nations with higher shares of their energy met by fossil fuels and a more urbanized land base are contributing the most to global ecological deficits. Nations with more modest consumption, on the other hand and greater shares of their land base in forests, pasture, crop land, or fisheries tended to have smaller overall footprints with a higher percentage dedicated to food.

Under EF 2.0, nations that use relatively less fossil fuel energy, have larger land masses, and have greater shares of their biological capacity in pasture, forest, or marine and inland fisheries have smaller footprints and are more likely to run positive ecological balances and those with relatively higher fossil fuel use and greater shares of biological capacity devoted to built space are more likely to have larger footprints and run negative ecological balances. This is because EF 2.0 appears to be sensitive to the footprint associated with carbon emissions, puts greater emphasis on the ecological value of pasture land, forest land, and marine and inland fisheries and deemphasizes the ecological value of built space.

African, Asian-Pacific, Latin American, and Caribbean regions tend to fall into the former group and, as a whole, run positive ecological balances. In these regions, the footprint is smaller than biocapacity, indicating that resource use may be sustainable. In contrast, nations in the Middle Eastern, Central Asian, North American, and European regions tend to fall into the latter group and, as a whole, run negative ecological balances. Here, footprints are generally larger than biocapacity indicating that resource use has overstepped ecological limits.

The five nations with the largest per capita ecological deficits (negative ecological balances) are the United Arab Emirates (-213), Kuwait (-146), the United States (-89), Belgium and Luxembourg (-62), and the Netherlands (-56). Nations with the largest per capita ecological surpluses (positive ecological balances) are Mongolia (163), Nambia (97), Gabon (96), Mauritania (68), and Papua New Guinea (65).

As was noted in the 2004 *Footprint of Nations* report, wealthier nations tend to run negative ecological balances, largely because of the high degree of correlation between affluence (expenditures) and fossil fuel consumption. In regions with more modest energy consumption, on the other hand, a higher percentage of their footprint is associated with food. In the Asia Pacific, African, Latin American, and Caribbean regions, the energy footprint is 80 percent or less, while in Europe, North America, the Middle East, Europe and Central Asia the energy footprint share is 90 percent or greater.

Differences between regions are also revealed by comparing the breakdown of the footprint, excluding energy. In Central Europe the footprint associated with crop land is the largest of all categories, while in the rest of Europe fisheries appear to be taking up the largest percentage. In North America and Latin America, the extraction of forests makes up the largest footprint category.

Wealthier countries (despite technological advantages) were found to have larger footprints on a per capita basis as compared to fellow global citizens who consume less. For example, footprints per capita in Africa in 2001 were 7.5 gha (18.5 acres). In North America the average was 95 gha (234 acres).

In the UAE the average footprint was 235 gha (578 acres). The amount of biocapacity available per person on a sustainable basis globally estimated with EF 2.0 is about 16 gha (30 acres).

FUTURE REFINEMENTS TO ECOLOGICAL FOOTPRINT ANALYSIS

The footprint provides an excellent framework for measuring the extent (area) of humanity's appropriation of natural resources and services within the context of sustainability. Since its inception, there has been continuous valuable advances in footprinting (Wackernagel et al. 2005). Our hope is that Footprint 2.0 adds to the concept and methodology on its way to becoming a genuine, scientifically robust, sustainability research tool.

While not yet having the opportunity to consider unforeseen problems with EF 2.0, we would suggest that the most important improvements in EFA still needed are (1) establishing and incorporating sustainable thresholds; (2) refining the technique to better account for other species and land not included; and (3) developing a theoretical basis and methodology for dealing with water, other climate changing gases, and toxins. These are discussed at length in Venetoulis and Talberth (2006).

Additional refinements to EFA now being explored by RP include calculating the footprint of additional greenhouse gases, addressing the effects of environmental toxins, modeling the footprint of water consumption, and establishing sustainability criteria for fisheries, forests, and water.

While carbon dioxide makes up the largest share of climate changing gasses from anthropogenic sources, analyses that link methane (CH4), nitrous oxide (N_2O), and fully fluorinated compounds (PFCs, HFCs, and SF6) to appropriation of biocapacity would represent a significant step forward in making EFA more comprehensive and meaningful with respect to the effects of climate change.

At first glance it appears very difficult, if not impossible, to convert the impacts associated with uranium, lead, arsenic, mercury, and other toxics into an area-based measure such as footprint. Footprinting is, after all, a quantitative indicator, not qualitative. Still, the relationship between concentrations of these toxins in a biome and its NPP may shed light on techniques to expand the scope of EFA to address these critical environmental concerns. Likewise, developing a defensible footprint for water consumption that captures aquifer depletion, loss of ecologically sustainable in-stream flows, and degradation of water quality would represent a significant improvement in accounting for vital ecosystem services performed by lakes, rivers, streams, and underground water reserves. RP is seeking support and partners to continue to refine EFA to address these critical issues over the next year, in anticipation of its *Footprint of Nations 2006* report.

REFERENCES

Amthor, J. S. 1998. "Terrestrial Ecosystem Responses to Global Change: A Research Strategy." *ORNL Technical Memorandum 1998/27*. Ecosystems Working Group of the Oak Ridge National Laboratory, Oak Ridge, Tennessee.

Chambers, N., C. Simmons, and M. Wackermenagel. 2000. *Sharing Nature's Interest: Using Ecological Footprints as an Indicator of Sustainability*. U.K.: Earthscan.

Ferguson, Andrew R. B. 1999. "The Logical Foundations of Ecological Footprints." *Environment, Development, and Sustainability* 1: 149–56.

Ferng, Jiun-Jiun. 2005. "Local Sustainable Yield and Embodied Resources in Ecological Footprint Analysis: A Case Study on the Required Paddy in Taiwan." *Ecological Economics* 53: 415–30.

Haberl, H., et al. 2004. "Human Appropriation of Net Primary Production And Species Diversity in Agricultural Landscapes." *Agriculture, Ecosystems, and Environment* 102, no. 2: 113–18.

Intergovernmental Panel on Climate Change (IPCC). 2004. "Inter-annual and Decadal Variability of Atmospheric CO_2 Concentrations." In *The Special Report on Land Use, Land-Use Change, and Forestry*, www.grida.no/climate/ipcc/land_use/020.htm#table1-2.

Lélé, Sharachchandra, and R. B. Norgaard. 2005. "Practicing Interdisciplinarity." *Bioscience* 55, no. 11: 967–75.

Pauly, D., and R. Watson. 2001. "Systematic Distortions in World Fisheries Catch Trends." *Nature* 414: 534–36.

Rees, W., and M. Wackernagel. 1996. *Our Ecological Footprint*. Gabriola Island: New Society Publishers.

Rodrigues et al. 2003. "Global Gap Analysis: Towards a Representative Network of Protected Areas." *Advances in Applied Biodiversity Science* 5: 73–74.

United Nations Environmental Program (UNEP). 2005. *Convention on Biological Diversity: 2005, Indicators for Assessing Progress towards the 2010 Target: Ecological Footprint and Related Concepts*. New York: UNEP.

Van den Bergh, J. C. J. M., and H. Verbruggen. 1999. "Spatial Sustainability, Trade, and Indicators: An Evaluation of the Ecological Footprint." *Ecological Economics* 29, no. 1: 61–72.

Venetoulis, Jason, and John Talberth. 2006. "Net Primary Productivity as the Basis for Ecological Footprint Analysis." Forthcoming.

Vitousek, P. M., P. R. Ehrlich, A. H. Ehrlich, and P. A. Matson. 1986. "Human Appropriation of the Products of Photosynthesis." *Bioscience* 36: 368–73.

Wackernagel, M., C. Monfreda, D. Moran, P. Wermer, S. Goldfinger, D. Deumling, and M. Murray. 2005. *National Footprint and Biocapacity Accounts 2005: The Underlying Calculation Method*. Oakland, Calif.: Global Footprint Network.

Wright, D. H. 1990. "Human Impacts on the Energy Flow through Natural Ecosystems and Implications for Species Endangerment." *Ambio: A Journal of the Human Environment* 19: 189–94.

I
ENVIRONMENTS

Chris Jordan, Oil Filters

2

Energy

All life depends on the consumption of energy. Most of this life-sustaining energy is provided by the sunshine that falls down on the earth to catalyze an almost alchemical process that we call photosynthesis. This is how human life evolved; it operated within the constraints of what some call "the muscle cluster," a reference to the historical fact that all human economies relied on the power of muscles fueled by solar energy captured in plant life. In the eighteenth century, Europeans invented ingenious techniques for utilizing the energy stored up in "fossil" fuels—coal is nothing more than a kind of battery that, eons ago, was charged by the sun's rays. The industrial revolutions of Britain, Europe, and the United States were underwritten by this "coketown cluster." And just as coal defined the warp and weft of nineteenth-century European imperialism, so too did oil seep into the fabric of most people living in twentieth-century industrialized nation-states. At its heart, oil ushered in a revolution of movement. Inhabitants of societies living in the "motown cluster" were able to move machines, trade goods, and their bodies at previously unimaginable speeds. One of the most basic freedoms that many industrialized societies enjoy—the freedom of movement—is literally enabled by ancient solar energy captured in a miraculous carbon liquid.

While there is nothing new about global trade, our recent era of globalization is fundamentally based on the promise of oil. The world of multilateral trade agreements written with the promise of market integration and structural adjustments is fundamentally about the movement of goods, capital, and labor across geopolitical boundaries. It seems that only now there is a dawning popular consciousness that this movement requires energy, much of it in the form of oil. In order to secure this ever-increasing demand for oil, governments joined hands with massive corporations to form blocs of power that would startle the likes of Rockefeller and Carnegie. These institutions have become masters in the extraction, refining, distribution, and marketing of oil, and they have utilized the miraculous logic of industrial capitalism to create a commodity for purchase—gas at a pump for instance—that erases awareness of the social and environmental costs entailed in oil production.

The commodity chain of oil production creates a tangled web of social and environmental costs. Here we will focus on the social and environmental impact of oil extraction in the Nigerian delta. British and American firms have been extracting high quality crude from the Niger delta oil fields since the 1960s and the region is now the fifth largest supplier of U.S. oil. While the industry has brought great wealth to some in Nigeria, especially those in the north, the people of the Niger delta, where the oil is extracted, have had to endure some of the most pernicious externalities of the production system. Here, Alicia Fentiman trains her anthropological eye on a small fishing community whose cultural and economic existences have been greatly degraded by the industry.

Alicia Fentiman, "The Anthropology of Oil: The Impact of the Oil Industry on a Fishing Community in the Niger Delta"[1] (1996)

The aim of this article is to examine the impact of oil on the lives of people in a small fishing community in the Niger delta.[2] This data is intended to contribute to the scarce literature available on the Niger delta and help shed light on the various ways in which oil has affected the institutions of at least one ethnic group. Although it is a detailed descriptive study of one community, the basic problems and tensions discernible in the case study apply to much of the Niger delta.

ETHNOGRAPHIC BACKGROUND

My focus is on the village of Oloma, a rural fishing community on the island of Bonny in the eastern Niger delta. Ethnically, the village population consists almost entirely of the Ibani-Ijo. The population of Bonny Island is centered in Bonny Town with a number of satellite villages, of which Oloma is one, and several fishing ports dispersed throughout the meandering creeks and waterways. The island is situated in the tidal mangrove swamps of the eastern Niger delta. It is bounded by other Ijaw communities, such as those of the Elem Kalabari to the west, the Okrikans to the north, and the Andoni, Opobo, and Ogoni to the east. Bonny is located approximately fifty kilometers southeast of the industrial and commercial center of Port Harcourt. Tributaries of the Bonny River dissect the flat surface of the island, creating swamps and creeks that are bordered by mangrove trees. Much of the land is uninhabitable; fresh water resources are scarce.

HISTORICAL OVERVIEW

Traditionally, the Ibani were fisherfolk dependent on the creeks, waterways, and swamps of the Niger delta for their livelihood. Fish were found in abundance, and salt was evaporated from the sea water trapped in the roots of the mangrove tree. The Ibani traded their fish and salt to the Ibo hinterland in exchange for agricultural produce. This interzonal dependency created the initial trade routes between the Ijo fisherfolk and the hinterland agriculturists. This internal trade network was well established before European contact and provided the mercantile infrastructure on which the success of Bonny's European trade was founded.

Bonny's coastal location certainly contributed to her involvement in the burgeoning trade that followed the advent of European adventurers in Bonny as early as the fifteenth century.[3] Bonny had a pivotal role as the fulcrum of a two-way trade between the Ibo hinterland and the Ibani, on the one hand, and the Ibani and the European traders on the other. Food, livestock, and, most importantly, slaves that came from the hinterland markets were brought to Bonny to be traded. The growing European demand for slaves ensured the role of Bonny traders as middlemen in the West African–European trade. This lasted until the nineteenth century.

In the nineteenth century, the slave trade was abolished and Bonny's merchants turned their attention to palm oil. The palm oil trade flourished because this new commodity was easily traded along the old channels involving the same personnel. Fortuitously, palm oil became at the same time an important export item because of the Industrial Revolution in Europe. Palm oil was in great demand as a lubricant for machinery as well as for making soap and candles. Bonny prospered during the palm oil trade, with the Bonny and Kalabari areas becoming known as the Oil Rivers.

However, in the twentieth century, the prosperity of Bonny began to decline.[4] The major factor was the discovery of coal in commercially viable quantities farther inland. A new mainland port was built by the British colonial administration to exploit the new coal fields. In 1913, Port Harcourt, a new industrial city located fifty kilometers up Bonny River, was opened. Bonny's pivotal trading role was bypassed. "Business gradually moved away from Bonny and Bonny only saw ships passing their way up river. In 1916, there was a great exodus and Bonny faded away to join the ranks of other ports of the past" (Earl 1962: 31). Bonny also lost its leading position with the colonial government as the center for the administrative, commercial, and religious headquarters of the Niger delta. By 1930, Bonny was observed to be in a "state of decay and utter stagnation" (Webber 1931: 52), and in 1938 moves were made to abolish the third-class township that was accorded to Bonny.

Bonny became an economically depressed area and its isolation from the mainland further contributed to her decline. The creation of Port Harcourt provided the Ibani with two alternatives; one was to remain in Bonny and return to the subsistence economy of fishing; the second option was to migrate to Port Harcourt and compete for jobs in the urban sector.

REVIVAL OF BONNY DISCOVERY OF OIL

Although Bonny declined as a port in the first half of the century, the discovery of crude oil in commercial quantities led to Bonny's revival. Evacuation and production facilities to process the crude oil and move it to world markets were needed. At first, a temporary export station was built at Port Harcourt; however, it proved unsatisfactory because only small tankers could visit Port Harcourt and even then they could load only half their capacity. Bonny became the ideal alternative because of its strategic location and its ability to cater to both inshore and offshore loading facilities. By 1961, the Shell Petroleum Development Company completed the first phase of the Bonny terminal. Further terminals were added throughout the 1960s.

The establishment of the oil terminal in Bonny had a tremendous impact on the infrastructure of Bonny Town. There was an influx of people who migrated there, and by 1963 the population had risen to 7,740 people. Skilled jobs, however, were given predominantly to Europeans, whereas the unskilled jobs were given to Nigerians. A study conducted in Bonny on the spatial organization of the oil terminal revealed that most migrants to Bonny were from Rivers State, but were not necessarily Ibani indigenes.[5] A large proportion of Bonny people works outside Bonny due to the lack of employment opportunities within the town and environs (Green 1982: 11).

The educational system in Bonny Town was revived. In 1966, Shell helped to fund new departments in the Bonny secondary school. In 1977, the Finima Girls Secondary School was opened, which provided further education for females. In addition, a teacher training college was reestablished, and it once again became an important educational center.

Money generated from the oil industry contributed to new commercial developments in Bonny. New buildings were constructed, such as a post office, a divisional office, Pan African Bank, a police station, and maritime clearing and forwarding houses. In addition, a new hospital was built. Transportation from Bonny Town to Port Harcourt was improved, thus ensuring better communication between Bonny and the mainland. An intermittent supply of electricity was provided by Shell to the main town, but the peripheral Bonny villages still went without. Indeed, the surrounding fishing villages did not enjoy the benefits that the inhabitants of Bonny Town experienced. Although it may appear that Bonny Town improved with the new opportunities that were a result of the oil industry, there were many detrimental aspects associated with the establishment of the oil industry in Bonny, which often go unrecorded. The lives of the average Bonny person, especially those residing in the fishing villages, have deteriorated because of the impact of oil.

CASE STUDY, BONNY: THE SEEN AND UNSEEN EFFECTS OF OIL

What of the effect of such changes on a fishing community? The environmental impact of oil in and around Oloma is clearly visible. Throughout the surrounding creeks and waterways, the intrusion of oil and oil excavation are markedly evident. The canalization and dredging of creeks by oil companies have significantly altered the landscape. A flow station is located at the end of the creek. Sea trucks pass daily to and from the flow station; the gas flares emit light twenty-four hours a day. Pipes meander throughout the swamps, and signboards scattered throughout the area alert the villagers to danger. These are the visible effects of oil. The presence of oil is all pervading.

However, there is another aspect of the impact of oil that often goes unrecorded. This is the way in which the culture of the people has been affected. The institutions, central to the identity of the Ibani fishing community, need to be discussed to understand the overall effect of oil. The community has experienced both environmental and cultural degradation. The former is seen, the latter unseen.

In the course of my research, I frequently asked, How has Oloma changed? All respondents mentioned that the oil industry has affected their economic livelihood and that oil has interfered with many aspects of their lives. The following interview with a senior male elder vividly portrays the various ways oil has affected the lives of the people of Oloma. He was asked what impact oil has had on the inhabitants of Oloma.

It wasn't until Shell started dredging the creek that everything started to go badly. For example, erosion of land. Before, there was a beautiful sandy beach; but look, it no longer exists. In the back of my house there was a big playground called ogbo-ngelege, but that land has eroded, and now our houses are eroding. Our traditional livelihood is fishing, but there are no more fish. We now buy tinned fish or stock fish. The chemicals from oil spillage have ruined the fish as well as the esem (periwinkles) and mgbe (mangrove oysters). We receive nothing from Shell. For example, no electricity, no piped water, no health facilities, nothing to make us happy. They were supposed to build a fish pond, but look around you, there is nothing. They destroyed our land and dredged our creek. Behind Ayaminima, the neighboring village, there used to be a small creek that was used when there was a storm and during the rainy season when the Bonny River was rough. But now Shell has closed it; they dredged it and filled it up with all their oil pipes. They put up a sign and did not think that many of our people are illiterate. Even if they could read English, the paint has worn off and the message alerting people of danger is no longer visible. Our people are told not to go there, so now we have to go to the main creek every time to get to Bonny. This has caused great problems because the sea becomes very rough and dangerous during the rains, and we no longer have an alternative route. Shell promised to fill in our embankment; they came this year and look what the rains have done. It is already washing away. They put a sign on our soil saying that Oloma is part of their development project; but we have suffered. This is not development, but underdevelopment. They don't care about us. Some of the mangrove trees used for firewood spark and blow up. It used to be the village's major energy source; now women are scared and are going into the bush to find fuel; this is not traditional, and it takes so long. Land where we have our shrines to the gods has been taken away. Parasu, a sacred area near Oloma where we performed Owu (masquerades and sacrifices), has been lost. We were forced to give the government our sacred land and our farmland. Economic trees such as mango, coconut, banana, plantain, paw-paw, and palm fruit have been taken away by the government for the oil industry. At the end of our creek there is a houseboat and flow station; the gas flares scare our fish and the noise of the sea trucks scares our gods and our fish. Sometimes we fish at night depending on the tide, and the sea trucks travel very fast up and down our creek, causing many of us to capsize in our canoes and lose our gear. Those of us who fish often find our nets destroyed and our traps broken; it is so hard to find fish. What are we to do?

Such a view highlights many issues that are associated with the impact of oil on the community. Every aspect of people's lives has been influenced by oil—their economic, political, social, and ritual institutions have all been affected. Indeed, the very institutions that make them culturally unique are eroding at an alarming pace.

CHANGES IN THE FISHING ECONOMY

A model of the economy of the past would show that the major economic activity of the inhabitants of the eastern Niger delta was fishing. In Oloma, there was little farming because the soil was poor and inadequate. Although most families farmed small plots of land, they did not yield enough for subsistence. However, fish were plentiful and salt was abundant. As a result, the Ibani fishermen and women were able to barter their fish and salt with the hinterland markets in exchange for agricultural produce.

The fishing economy was unique in many ways and was structured very differently from any agricultural economy. Most obviously, the private ownership of land was unimportant for the village's prosperity. Instead, the Oloma villagers' economic livelihood was dependent on common assets: the creeks, waterways, and fishing ports that were owned by the village as a whole rather than by individuals. Therefore, there was communal ownership of the productive resources. The village claimed exclusive rights of access to certain waterways and creeks. This system united village members across lineage boundaries. It was thus important for it to remain a united community in order to protect its holdings from competing neighboring villages. The fishing grounds were not susceptible to demarcation as farmlands were; they were used by all members of the village without reference to lineage differentiation (see Alagoa 1970; Horton, 1969).

However, the fishing economy in Oloma has dramatically changed. There are two prime reasons for this: one has been outward migration to urban areas in search of education and wage labor and the other is oil. It was reported:

> [In the past] it was not unusual to see young and old beaming with smiles as they return home with canoe load of fishes of various description. That was the days of yore when fishing was really a worthwhile venture in this part of the country (Niger Delta). . . . Fishing has become a very poor economic activity due mainly to rural-urban migration of able-bodied youths and oil pollution (Tide, February 27, 1982).

Migration from Oloma to Port Harcourt and other urban centers is frequent. The lack of young men in the community was observed while conducting fieldwork. A census survey revealed that the composition of the village consisted primarily of women, children, and the elderly. Men often migrated to Port Harcourt and other mainland towns in search of wage labor. The men who resided in the village commented that they can no longer rely solely on fishing as an economically viable occupation as they had done in the past. They therefore must leave the village. Those who remain behind encounter many obstacles, often attributable to the oil industry. Fishing as a way of life is becoming more and more difficult. Some of the problems they encounter are described below.

Damage by sea trucks: One of the major obstacles to traditional fishing methods in the creeks and waterways is a result of the constant movement of sea trucks traveling to and from the flow station located at the end of the creek. Fishing lines, nets, and traps are often torn; the sea trucks continually destroy property despite protests from the community. The operators of the sea trucks show little concern for the fishermen, fisherwomen, and children. Although there are speed restrictions, they are seldom enforced. Canoes are often capsized by the waves from the sea trucks. The noise the trucks generate is attributed by the local community as a prime reason for scaring away the fish, which is evidenced by low fish yields.

Oil pollution: Despite arguments that overfishing and overpopulation are responsible for low fish yields, the community believes oil pollution has affected their fishing economy. In Oloma, fewer people reside in the community than in the past and fewer people are fishing. As mentioned above, migration to urban areas has become the sought-after choice and necessity by many. This is consistent with remarks made in the local Bonny magazine, *Ogolo.*

> Bonny people, like other rivering people, depend mainly on their water resources for their livelihood. But in the operation of the oil companies, all waste products are dumped into the rivers. The water is polluted, fish are killed, and the fishermen are forced to find alternative sources of livelihood, which in Bonny is very difficult. Gradually people migrate out of the community to other areas to seek beneficial employment, which has led to increasing depopulation of Bonny (Green 1982: 10–11).

However, those who are left behind in the communities still try to survive by fishing; there are no alternatives. They are responsible for feeding their households but are finding it increasingly difficult to make ends meet. The catches are low, and more and more time is spent gathering shellfish. A greater burden has fallen on the women because of the massive outward migration of men. Each day, women spend hours in the mangrove swamps gathering shellfish such as winkles and mangrove oysters. As one fisherwoman remarked, "My life is my paddle; without my paddle we do not eat." It is, however, becoming increasingly difficult to find enough food. The community feels that chemicals and oil are affecting the fish production.

Oil spillage: This is a frequent occurrence in the Niger delta, and many communities, in addition to Oloma, in the oil- producing areas have provided descriptive accounts of the impact of oil spillage on their fishing economy. However, scientific data examining the impact of oil pollution on the aquatic life is scarce. A symposium, The Mangrove Ecosystem of the Niger Delta, held in Port Harcourt in 1980, gathered scholars in different disciplines to discuss and share information on the changes in the environment; oil was shown to be a major factor contributing to the destruction of marine life. It was shown that crude oil contains compounds that are toxic to marine organisms and contribute to extensive mortality in finfish, shellfish, oysters, and birds. This was observed in the Apoi and Ojobo areas.

A study of the Bonny River examined oil pollution and the brackish environment. An experiment that examined the effect of crude petroleum oil and refined oils on aquatic organisms confirmed that crude oil and refined petroleum products in high concentrations were toxic to marine life. By comparing different types of fish and shellfish, it showed that some species were more resilient than others. Data revealed that shrimp were more susceptible to pollutants, followed by oysters and fish. Periwinkles were the most tolerant. Tainting of the flesh confirmed that the effect of oil spillage was lingering. Even small, continual spills affected the productivity of the water. It also showed that pollutants had a pronounced effect on the growth and reproductive capacity of organisms (Onuoba 1985: 131).

A recent spillage in Nembe in 1995 illustrates the problems with which oil producing communities must contend when there is a spillage. An oil spill had occurred from an Agip oil pipeline. For several days, the oil flowed freely into the creeks and mangrove forest. The area went up in flames one night when a woman on a late-night fishing trip mistakenly set off the fire with her lantern. The fire destroyed much of the aquatic life in the area. In addition, farm crops were destroyed (*Newswatch* 1995: 12).

A problem that many communities face during oil spillages is that many of the oil companies are unwilling to pay compensation because they believe that they are caused by sabotage. The communities, however, stress that many of the spillages are "legitimate": caused by poorly maintained and faulty equipment, not sabotage. It is therefore necessary to monitor the areas regularly and to act immediately during spillages. The mangrove fauna and flora are also affected by oil spillages; it was shown that there can be short- and long-term effects to the mangrove from offshore spillage (Odu and Imevbore 1985: 133). Mangrove is an essential part of the Oloma people's economy. Mangrove wood is used for fuel and for making various items such as fish traps, trays, and hats. In Oloma, women complained that chemicals from the oil have absorbed into the mangrove wood, which they use for fuel, and that once ignited, it explodes and causes serious burns.

Gas flaring and pollution: Large quantities of methane gas are associated with oil. During oil production, this gas is burned off at flow stations above the oil wells. This introduces sulfur dioxide and oxides of carbon and nitrogen into the atmosphere. The impact of this on the environment has not been substantiated. However, some suggest that it may contribute to global warming.

Land filling: Another factor responsible for disturbing the way of life in Oloma is land filling. Nearby creeks and waterways have been filled in because of oil operations. This has affected the accessibility to surrounding villages and has taken from the Oloma villagers an alternative route to reach Bonny Town. The Oloma community complained about the landfill because they relied on a specific water route to reach Bonny Town during the rainy season, which has subsequently been filled in. The alternative route was preferred during the rainy season because the Bonny River becomes dangerous.

Canalization also damages the environment. Oil companies create canals to either drain an area for drilling and pipe laying or create channels to transport drilling and other oil production equipment to the site. The channels alter the ecology of the area; they can also alter the flood pattern of the delta by resulting in perennial flooding of the otherwise well-drained plains as was observed in many areas in the Niger delta (Ekoriko 1996: 31).

Erosion: The community believes that the continual movement of sea trucks up and down the creek and the dredging of the land and waterways have significantly contributed to land erosion. In Oloma, several households lost their property due to erosion. Recollections by villagers mention the sandy beach area that used to be in front of the village; it has eroded away, and a sand-bank was designed to prevent further erosion. An embankment was promised for several years, and finally in 1984 a contractor constructed one that washed away during the rainy season. The community feels this was done in a substandard way. Interviews with the contractor at the time of the job revealed that his company had won the contract with the cheapest bid, and he admitted that the job was not going to be sufficient to endure the rainy season. As he rightfully predicted, the embankment gave way, and it became a hazard to the community. Instead of benefiting and improving the situation, it worsened the situation. Gaps in the embankment became dangerous for children and adults walking on the sandbags. One child fell in the gap and broke his leg.

Dredging: Indigenous fishing methods such as dragging a net along the creek bottom are difficult to practice because the creeks have been dredged during oil exploration, and the water is now too deep to stand in, making this form of fishing obsolete. Dredging also destroys valuable freshwater and mangrove vegetation, which can cause an imbalance in the ecosystem because aquatic organisms depend on them for food and shelter during part or all of their life cycles (Wilcox and Powell 1985). In addition, during the dredging process, oil is spilled into the water and the burning of fuel releases carbon, sulfur, and nitrogen oxides into the aquatic environment (Odu and Imevbore 1985: 142).

Oloma and social change: Under the Land Decree Act of 1978, many communities throughout the Niger delta lost valuable farmland. In addition, oil production contributed to the contamination of the land. Although Oloma suffered in many ways when areas of their land were taken away, they have suffered more by losing the access and rights of way to their creeks and waterways. Further, the destruction and contamination of their productive resources have contributed to vast changes in the economic, political, and social structure of the community. As members of the community are forced to migrate because their resources are destroyed, various changes are taking place within these institutions.

RITUAL, BELIEF, AND OIL

Another institution affected by oil in Oloma is the villagers' belief system. The stability and continuity of village life are maintained by participation in a series of ritual practices. These activities are a means by which the community retains their social identity and social stability in times of radical changes. Both rural villagers and urban migrants adhere to such practices and the beliefs associated with them. The principal type of ritual activity is the masquerades of the owu-ogbo society, which displays elaborate masquerades in honor of the water spirits. The owu-ogbo society is central to the social cohesion of the Oloma people. It is a time-honored institution and the practice of the masquerade was brought to Bonny by the Oloma descendants. The Oloma people are known throughout the delta for their expertise in the owu-ogbo plays. Traditionally, when the Ibani engaged predominantly in fishing, the fishermen would return to Oloma during a period called Fongu-Mini, the break in the rains in August, to be reunited with their families. The masquerade serves two essential purposes. First, it honors the water spirits on whom the fishing economy is thought to be dependent. It is believed that by performing masquerades, the fisherfolk will be rewarded with a successful fishing season. Second, the masquerades are used as a means to unite all village members no matter where they may be.

The rationale of the masquerades is derived from the belief that they represent the imitation of the movements of the water spirits. It is believed that fishermen would spy on the spirits in the water and then return to the village and imitate the dances and songs learned from them. There are several types of masquerades performed in Oloma. Each masquerade headpiece is different, and each represents a specific spirit. The person who plays the part of the masquerade is possessed by the spirit he is imitating. The masquerade society is strictly male. Although the owu-ogbo society has undergone many changes due to the impact of Christianity and migration, community members still return to Oloma every holiday season to participate in the masquerades. The masquerades provide a means of social cohesion and reunification of dispersed kin members.

Despite the stability and continuity of the masquerade society, some rituals can no longer be performed because sacred shrines used for sacrifices can no longer be accessed. They have been taken over by the government under the Land Decree Act of 1978. The fishermen and women in Oloma are also concerned about the constant flare in the creek; they believe it causes great distress to the water spirits. This is an important consideration because the water spirits are an essential aspect to their belief system.

Little is known about the impact of oil on indigenous ritual beliefs. It is not only the physical destruction of oil, but also the metaphysical aspect that equally needs to be acknowledged.

OIL AND HEALTH

One aspect of the impact of oil on the inhabitants of the Niger delta that has received little attention is possible health risks directly associated with oil. Data are scarce and research needs to be done to see whether there is any significant long-term impact. The villagers complain about rashes and other skin ailments, but little is known as to whether this is attributable to oil.

While conducting field research, I observed that women and children suffered from skin problems as a result of oil and chemicals in the water. The women who spend several hours in the water are engaged in the labor-intensive gathering activities of collecting shellfish. Most fisherwomen rub their bodies with palm oil before they fish in order to prevent rashes and other skin ailments. Elderly women mentioned that this is a recent precaution because they did not suffer from these skin conditions in the past. It has been written that a variety of skin conditions may be attributed to contact or exposure to oil. Acne, warts, boils, skin cancer, and photosensitization dermatitis have all been cited (Afiesiama 1985: 169).

It has been reported that those living close to gas flaring sites may be at risk from respiratory illnesses (*Newswatch*, December 18, 1995, 15), and persons living near the flares complain of sterility (Ekoriko 1996: 31).

Contamination of drinking water because of oil spillage or oil production activities is of great concern. It is feared that oil from spillage can seep into the freshwater drinking supplies. Procedures such as canalization or dredging can affect the freshwater drinking supplies by draining the water in the area that can then alter the ecosystem. Some questions need to be considered: What are the health risks to the people who eat fish and shellfish contaminated with oil? Can swimming and bathing in the polluted creeks be dangerous to the health of the people? Can living near a gas flaring area be dangerous? Can the freshwater contaminated by toxic waste be hazardous? Research needs to be done to find out precisely what the dangers are to communities. It is also important that consistent guidelines be established and monitored to examine the impact of oil on the health of the local inhabitants.

CONCLUSION

There is widespread concern with the unfairness of the Nigerian political system toward Rivers State and other states in which the oil wealth of the nation is derived. And the communities in whose home areas oil is mined suffer neglect from federal and state governments, and the oil companies. Their environment is damaged, and their sources of livelihood destroyed through oil pollution. The oil boom which has done so much for and to the Nigerian economy has been little short of a disaster for oil-producing states, and even worse for oil-producing communities (Alagoa and Tamuno 1989: 220–21).

This case study of Oloma shows how one community has been affected by oil; this community is not unique. The problems encountered there are shared by other communities throughout the oil-producing area and are representative for the whole Niger delta. The inhabitants feel that they have not benefited from the oil industry. Although oil is extracted from their areas, causing environmental degradation and disrupting their way of life, they have not been compensated. They are environmental victims.

It is paradoxical that in the past the communities in the Niger delta that wielded great power, authority, and wealth are now labeled as "minorities" struggling to survive in Nigeria. The Nigeria they helped to create, it appears, is currently destroying them. The minority groups in the Niger delta are, as a result, seeking fair representation and compensation from the government as the Ogoni experience has so aptly symbolized. Ken Saro-Wiwa fought for the rights of his people. With the establishment of MOSOP (Movement for the Survival of Ogoni People), he attracted international awareness to the position of those living in the oil-producing communities.

The executions of Ken Saro-Wiwa and eight fellow Ogonis on November 10, 1995, provided a catalyst for nations worldwide to condemn the situation in Nigeria. Alleged human rights abuses by the military government have sparked a fierce debate about the current political and economic climate in Nigeria. Worldwide condemnation of the executions has highlighted the need to understand the underlying issues that ignited the problem. In particular, confusion over the roles and responsibilities of the government and multinational corporations operating in the Niger delta has led many oil-producing communities to speak out. Concern relating to environmental degradation has also been voiced within the country and outside by international organizations. Against this background of political and humanitarian debate it is, however, important not to lose sight of the fact that the environment must be seen in cultural as well as physical terms.

REFERENCES

Afiesiama, S. 1985. "Medical Aspects of the Mangrove Environment." In *The Mangrove Ecosystem of the Niger Delta,* ed. B. Wilcox and C. Powell. Nigeria: University of Port Harcourt.

Alagoa, E. J. 1970. "Long Distance Trade and States in the Niger Delta." *Journal of African History* 11: 319–29.

———. 1971. "The Development of Institutions in the States of the Eastern Niger Delta." *Journal of African History* 12, no. 2: 269–78.

Alagoa, E. J., and T. Tamuno, eds. 1989. *Land and People of Nigeria: Rivers State.* Nigeria: Riverside Communications.

Earl, K. 1962. "Bonny." Nigeria Field.

Ekoriko, M. 1996. "How Safe Are We?" *Newswatch,* January 8.

Green, K. 1982. "Oil and Gas Industries in Bonny: A Critical Appraisal." *Ogolo Magazine* 1.

Horton, R. 1969. "From Fishing Village to City-State: A Social History of New Calabar." In M. Douglas and P. Kaberry, eds., *Man in Africa.* London: Tavistock.

Jewett, A. 1988. "A Contemporary Ethnography: Change and Continuity among the Ibani-Ijo of Coastal Nigeria." Ph.D. diss., University of Cambridge.

Odu, E. A., and A. M. A. Imevbore. 1985. "Environmental Pollution in the Niger Delta." In B. Wilcox and C. Powell, eds., *The Mangrove Ecosystem of the Niger Delta*. Nigeria: University of Port Harcourt.

Onuoba, G. 1985. "Oil Pollution and the Brackish Environment." In B. Wilcox and C. Powell, eds., *The Mangrove Ecosystem of the Niger Delta*. Nigeria: University of Port Harcourt.

Waribor, T. 1976. "Spatial Implications of the Oil Terminal in Bonny." B.A. thesis, University of Nsukka, Nigeria.

Webber, H. 1931. "Intelligence Report on the Bonny Tribe of 1931." Typescript.

Wilcox, B. H. R., and C. B. Powell. 1985. *The Mangrove Ecosystem of the Niger Delta*. Nigeria: University of Port Harcourt.

3

Water

Bono, the lead singer for U2, appeared on *Oprah* in September 2002 to spread awareness of his mission to deal with poverty and health in Africa. When the two came around to the subject of clean and safe water, Oprah noted, "You can't talk about water enough. It's the thing that we in this country take the most for granted." Bono, in his ubiquitous aqua-marine-tinted glasses added, "Women [in Africa] are walking sometimes 10 miles a day to bring water. If everyone gets together, this idea of bringing water to Africa is not far-fetched. It's possible, and we can do it right now. I tell you, it will revolutionize that continent."[1] Perhaps. But Bono seems to have forgotten that there are people getting together to bring water to Africans, but they are not doing it out of the mere goodness of their hearts.

Despite the recent popular claim that all humans have a universal right to clean and safe drinking water, this resource is quickly turning into a hot commodity; multinational companies already provide water for over 7 percent of the globe's population. In this chapter Jon Luoma discusses the current and future consequences of this accelerating trend. While some may benefit from the privatization of water, Luomo shows that the process endangers a sizable population. Nowhere is this more true than in South Africa, where the post-apartheid government struggles to deliver basic services to its poorest population. Jon Jeeter's report—written shortly after the South African cholera outbreak of 2000—puts a human face on the poverty and health problems encountered by a people whose democratically elected government often looks to the market strategies of multinational companies for consulting and contracts.

Jon Luoma, "The Water Thieves" (2004)[2]

Even before the water turned brown, Gordon Certain had plenty to worry about. With his neighborhood in the southern U.S. city of Atlanta in the middle of a growth boom, the president of the North Buckhead Civic Association had been busy fielding complaints about traffic, a sewer tunnel being built near a nature reserve, and developers razing tidy but modest 1950s era houses to make room for new minimansions. But nothing compared to the volume of calls and emails that flooded Certain's home office in May 2002, when the state of Georgia's environmental protection agency issued an alert to North Buckhead residents: their tap water, the agency warned, wasn't safe to drink unless it was boiled first. Some neighbors, Certain recalls, had just given their babies their baby formula when they heard the alert. "I had parents calling me in tears," he says. The things that have happened to the water here have sure scared the hell out of a lot of people." A month later, another boil water alert came; this time when Certain turned on his own tap the liquid that gushed out was the color of rust, with bits of brown debris floating in it.

In fact, complaints about the municipal drinking water from all over the city had been pouring into the office of Atlanta's mayor, Shirley Franklin. Only a couple of years earlier, United Water—a subsidiary of the giant French conglomerate Suez, had taken over the municipal system and promised to turn it into an "international showcase" for public-private partnerships. But instead of ushering in a new era of trouble-free drinking water, Atlanta's experiment with water privatization brought an avalanche of problems—from violations of federal drinking-water standards to major water main leaks that went unrepaired for weeks. (United, meanwhile, was insisting that the city paid it millions of dollars more for its services than had originally been agreed.) By January 2003, after a month-long investigation and threats by the mayor to cancel the contract, United had "voluntarily" withdrawn from what had become more of an international debacle than a showcase.

The debacle in Atlanta might have been a relatively trivial incident if Suez (and a handful of other private water utilities that competed for the contract) hadn't seen the city as a beachhead in their attempts to turn water delivery into a hugely profitable business in both rich northern and poor southern economies. From Bolivia to Ghana to the Philippines, from the United Kingdom to the United States and Canada, a rapidly consolidating for-profit water industry has been attempting to capture a household drinking water "market" that, until recently, had been viewed in most parts of the world not as a cash cow for private corporations but as a public service.

Multinational companies now run water systems for 7 percent of the world's population, and analysts say that figure could grow to 17 percent by 2015. Private water management is estimated to be a $200 billion business, and the World Bank, which has encouraged governments to sell off their utilities to reduce public debt, projects it could be worth $1 trillion by 2021. The potential profits are staggering. In May 2000 *Fortune* magazine predicted that water is about to become "one of the world's great business opportunities" and promises to be to the twenty-first century what oil was to the twentieth.

TAPPED FOR CASH

No one disputes that many of the world's drinking water supply systems are woefully inadequate, and that the situation promises to worsen. In a world with soaring populations and declining supplies, the United Nations has forecast that global per capita water availability could decline by as much as one-third within only two decades. Already, a fifth of the world's population—1 billion people—have no access to safe drinking water and only inadequate stores of water for cooking, bathing, and basic sanitation. In the cities of the developing world, antiquated, often colonial-era water systems are no match for booming populations. Peter Gleick, president of the U.S.-based Pacific Institute for Studies in Development, Environment, and Security, has pointed out that "half the world's people fail to receive the level of water service available to many in the cities of ancient Greece and Rome."

But will going private make things better? Entities such as the World Bank and the IMF appear to think so. They now routinely use their loan-granting power to pressure developing nations to privatize public services, including water delivery, in the hope that forcing government services into the private sector will lead to more faithful repayment of development loans. Companies like Suez and its primary competitors Vivendi and RWE Thames Water promise to use their expertise to build infrastructure and delivery systems in exchange for guaranteed profits on their investment.

In more developed nations where infrastructure is already in place, contracts often take the form of "public-private partnerships" (as in Atlanta), with the local government continuing to own the plumbing, the pumping and filtering stations, and other facilities, and the corporate partner merely managing them.

Advocates of privatization insist that private businesses are inherently more efficient, that for-profit companies can more easily generate financing and that water delivery is just another saleable commodity. To Gerard Payen, the executive who developed Suez's program for worldwide corporate expansion in the water industry, it's a simple free market proposition: "We purify water, and bring this water to your home. We provide a service. It has a cost, and somebody has to pay for it."

There, however, is the rub. Under corporate control, water fees inevitably rise, pushing those least able to pay them to make trade-offs between their water and other basic needs, including food, clothing, medicine, and "extras" like education. Yet whatever privatization's merits or demerits, the trend is already clear: in 1990 private water companies operated in only twelve nations; by the early 2000s, that number had grown to one hundred.

Should water, a basic necessity for human survival, be controlled by for-profit interests? And if it should, can multinational companies actually deliver on what they promise—better service and safe, affordable water?

Already, the two largest players in the industry, Suez and its fellow French corporation Vivendi, manage water for 230 million people—mostly in parts of Europe and, to a smaller extent, the developing world. Now the water corporations are seeking access to the vast and still untapped global markets that remain public entities.

In the United States 85 percent of households get their water from public utilities. In general, water quality is excellent, and the costs of running most municipal water systems remain modest. Yet Atlanta is not the only U.S. city where corporations and their political supporters have been pushing hard for privatization. New and often controversial privatization efforts have been promoted in cities that include New Orleans, Laredo, Texas, and Stockton, California. Water companies have been conducting industry "fly-ins" to Washington to press their legislative agenda with Congress, lobbying for laws that would protect companies from lawsuits over contaminated water and block municipalities from reversing failed privatizations. The U.S. National Association of Water Companies has pushed for a bill that would require cities to consider privatization before they can tap federal funds for upgrading or expanding public utilities and would subsidize any privatization deals.

At the municipal level the lobbying pressure is equally intense, with water companies actively courting local officials and spending hundreds of thousands of dollars supporting privatization in local referendums. "It's hard for local guys to turn these companies away," former Massachusetts water commissioner Douglas MacDonald has said. "They're everywhere, with arms like an octopus."

In the United Kingdom a massive water privatization program was pushed through by the Conservative Party at the end of the 1980s. The ten regional water authorities of England and Wales were turned over to private companies in 1989. Henceforth, the reasoning went, the efficiency of private markets would lead to great improvements to an aging, inefficient water system. The harsh realities of market forces notwithstanding, the government sweetened the deal by absorbing several billion pounds of existing water authority debt, offering tax exemptions on future corporate profits, and selling the businesses at bargain prices.

THE GREATEST ACT OF LICENSED
ROBBERY IN HISTORY

But privatization advocates can hardly point to the U.K. as an example of smooth transition to for-profit water delivery. Prices rose by nearly 50 percent in inflation-adjusted terms in less than a decade, and disconnection rates also soared. The new industry's response to the public outcry over the health perils of disconnecting people's water was to install special prepayment meters at the homes of those at risk of nonpayment. When a household was unable to prepay, the meters automatically shut off its water supply. Meanwhile, water quality steadily deteriorated, and stories began to appear in the press about the lavish bonuses the new water companies were awarding to top management.

As early as 1994 the *Daily Mail* opined that the water companies had become "the biggest rip-off in Britain." "Water bills," the tabloid said, "have soared, and the directors and shareholders of Britain's top 10 water companies have been able to use their position as monopoly suppliers to pull off the greatest act of licensed robbery in our history."

Most observers agree that the situation in the U.K. has improved notably since the Labour government pushed through changes to water legislation in 1999. Prepay meters were eliminated and sharp restrictions on disconnections introduced. A new Office of Water Services now regulates the industry, and it has insisted on new investments in infrastructure along with rate reductions of about 12 percent. Yet the questions remain, how and why can highly regulated monopolies be more economically efficient and whether they do as much public good as properly run and regulated public agencies answerable to democratically elected officials?

Nor is the industry's record any more encouraging in other parts of the world. Developing world cities with private water management companies have been plagued by lapses in service, soaring costs, corruption, and worse. In Manila, where the water system is controlled by Suez, San Francisco-based Bechtel and the prominent Ayala family, water is only reliably available for a few hours a day, and rate increases have been so severe that the poorest families must choose each month between paying for water and two days' worth of food. In 2001 the government of Ghana agreed to privatize local water systems as a condition for an IMF loan. To attract investors, the government doubled water rates, setting off protests in a country where the average annual income is less than $400 a year and the water bill (for those fortunate enough to have running water) can run upward of $110. In Cochabamba, the third-largest city in Bolivia, water rates shot up by 35 percent after a consortium led by Bechtel took over the city's water system in 1999; some residents found themselves paying 20 percent of their income on water. An initial round of peaceful street protests led to riots in which six people were killed. Eventually the Bolivian government voided Bechtel's contract and told the company's officials it could not guarantee their safety if they stayed in town. Privatization has also spawned protests (and in some cases even dominated elections) in Paraguay, where police turned water cannons on antiprivatization protesters.

In the United States the Atlanta debacle appears to have been a major industry setback. "Atlanta was going to be the industry's shining example of how great privatization is," says Hugh Jackson of the Washington-based consumer advocacy group Public Citizen. "And now it's turned into our shining example about how it maybe isn't so great an idea after all."

Peter Gleick is a bit more sanguine, suggesting that, with careful oversight, private operators may be able to provide such otherwise unavailable benefits as access to investment capital, particularly in the developing world. But he cautions: "Water privatisation is not about competition. These are long-term monopoly contracts. This isn't free enterprise, or a competitive market."

Gleick also points out that if governments are so dysfunctional that they cannot run efficient water systems they are also poor candidates for overseeing privatization. They would be ill-equipped to prevent mismanagement or outright corruption. Conversely, he says, "We already know that good governments can run good public water utilities."

"At least when you have public utilities," he adds, "the money they take in stays in the community. With the private companies, the profits are going to go out of your community . . . and probably out of your country, too."

Jon Jeter, "South Africa's Driest Season" (2002)[3]

The postapartheid government has greatly expanded water service, but in many rural villages the resulting water price increases have placed the cost of water beyond the reach of many South Africans.

What the peasants call "the river" is no more than a puddle, really, a shallow accumulation of muddy brown water in Mbabe village on the outskirts of Empangeni in South Africa's KwaZulu-Natal province. The river is maybe a quarter mile from Metolina Mthembu's mud hut, and to get there you walk through a breathlessly gorgeous expanse of green savanna, runaway hills, and sugarcane fields that tumbles along the coast of the Indian Ocean.

Mthembu makes the shoeless trek to the river virtually every day, walking past the tap that was installed just a few feet from her house two years ago. It is bone-dry. With two jobless adult children to feed, and only her pension of roughly $50 a month to support them, the seventy-year-old Mthembu can't always find the money to pay the equivalent of $7 a month for water. And so a well-rehearsed dance has evolved between the old woman and her local utility, a sequence that plays out every few months or so: she falls behind in her payments; they disconnect her tap; she turns to the river until she finds the money to pay her bill. "I know the water is unsafe," she said on a July morning as a young girl in a formless yellow dress crouched in the river behind her, dipping her plastic bucket. "I was a victim of cholera in

February, and then my daughter and my neighbor became sick with cholera as well."

After her new tap was disconnected, Metolina Mthembu was forced to drink river water and contracted cholera. During what Mthembu calls "the old government"—the brutal, white-minority regime that was ousted by South Africa's first all-races election in 1994—she had to walk half a mile to get clean water from a standpipe. She's glad the new government installed a tap outside her home two years ago. But now the water costs money, she notes, and people here are poor. "There are no jobs. We must choose between food and water, so we buy food and pray that the water does not make us ill. It is a bad gamble. Many, many of us have grown sick from the water."

South Africa is only now beginning to emerge from the worst cholera outbreak in its history, a plague of almost epic proportions that began two years ago, just weeks after local authorities began shutting off water service to residents who were late on their bills. Pressured by international lenders such as the World Bank and International Monetary Fund, the government adopted a conservative fiscal measure, known as "cost recovery," which requires public services such as water, electricity, and telecommunications to pay for themselves, often through increased fees; it also encourages turning those utilities over to private companies. Several South African cities have already turned over their water operations to multinational companies like France-based Vivendi Universal and Suez. For the nation's remaining municipal authorities, the first step toward privatization is to try to turn public utilities into profit centers that can attract investors.

Across the globe—from China to Eastern Europe, sub-Saharan Africa to South America—cash-strapped local and national governments are selling off state-owned water operations, making privatization an estimated $200 billion a year business worldwide. Private water companies promise to improve delivery and maximize scarce public resources. But the result has often been far different, according to relief agencies, unions, and nonprofits. They contend that corporations are taking advantage of public resources and subsidies while driving up the price of water and cutting off the poorest users.

At the U.N. World Summit for Sustainable Development in Johannesburg last summer, delegates designated water as one of the key issues facing poor countries. About 1.1 billion people worldwide lack access to clean water, and dwindling supplies could push that number even higher in years to come. "There's a global water crisis, and at the same time water is being increasingly commodified," says Vandana Shiva, founder of the Research Foundation for Science, Technology, and Ecology in India. "We are trusting corporations to be the protectors of our environment and the protectors of our human needs."

"Empangeni" derives its name from the Zulu word *phanga*, which, roughly translated, means "to grab." It is a reference to the uncommonly high number of crocodile attacks that once occurred on the Mlathuze River. Home to South Africa's largest sugar mill, as well as paper factories, aluminum smelters, mines, and upscale game farms, Empangeni is surrounded by Ngwelezana, an all-black township, and the villages of the Madlebe tribe, which during apartheid were autonomous black homelands, or bantustans, that provided white-owned business with cheap labor.

For people living in these communities and others like them, the "cost recovery" policy has meant a dramatic increase in the price of utilities such as electricity and water, even as South Africa's economy has rapidly shed jobs for unskilled workers. To force customers to pay the higher bills, local governments are making use of a tool seldom employed even by the apartheid regime: disconnection of services. Nearly a quarter of South Africa's 44 million people live in households that have had their water cut off at least once since 1996. In Empangeni, local authorities began disconnecting water to nonpaying customers in mid-2000.

As the cutoffs have spread, so too has cholera, with increasing numbers of poor South Africans heading to polluted rivers, streams, even open pits to draw water for bathing, cooking, and drinking. Public health researchers have concluded that the epidemic began in the Empangeni region within weeks of the first water disconnection, and from there the waterborne disease quickly fanned out into seven of South Africa's nine provinces. "No one doubts our government's good intentions," says David Hemson, research director of the government-funded Human Sciences Research Council (HSRC). "But in the name of development, in the name of progress and modernization, we have exposed our most vulnerable populations to this very colonial disease, a disease that is by definition a by-product of backwardness. What does that say about policies like cost recovery?"

In the past two years, KwaZulu-Natal's public hospitals have reported nearly 114,000 cases of cholera, more than five times as many as had been reported in the province over the previous twenty years combined. Nearly 260 South Africans have died from cholera since the epidemic began. Early on, the disease was so rampant that hospitals in and around Empangeni opened fourteen hydration centers, tents where medics worked in twenty-four-hour shifts to provide fluids to patients. When the city ran short of ambulances, the local government appealed to the South African defense forces for help, and for nearly six months soldiers shuttled patients to hospitals and makeshift clinics.

"We were simply running out of capacity and out of space," says Peter Haselau, the manager of Empangeni's main public medical center. "We would get a handle on it in one place and it would break out somewhere else. We got to the point where we thought we might collapse if we got any more cases. The problem was that so many people didn't have money for water, so they were going to traditional sources of water. And that water's no good."

When Nelson Mandela was sworn in as South Africa's first democratically elected president in 1994, a third of the country's population had no electricity or access to clean water, and half had no indoor toilet. In rural areas, it was not uncommon for a single tap to serve whole communities. Since 1994, the African National Congress government has dramatically closed the gap between prosperous whites and poor blacks, building more than 1 million new homes and reducing by almost two-thirds the number of South Africans without running water.

But like the water that flows through Mbabe, the ANC's policies have been both a blessing and curse to poor South Africans, who have overwhelmingly supported the governing party. In its attempt to attract foreign investment, the ANC has all but shed its Marxist roots for a market-driven fiscal plan called Growth, Employment, and Redistribution, or GEAR. So far, GEAR's attempts to privatize state-owned industries, open domestic markets to foreign competition, and keep a lid on public spending have left many South Africans materially worse off than they were in the years before apartheid's collapse. Nearly 500,000 jobs have vanished and more than a third of South Africa's 44 million people survive on less than $2 a day, a figure unchanged since apartheid. Government statistics indicate that a quarter of the workforce is unemployed, and many economists put the number closer to 40 percent.

The coupling of soaring utility costs with higher unemployment has proved especially punishing to poor blacks. As the government prepares to sell the state-owned power company, ESKOM, new pricing policies have caused electricity costs in townships like Soweto to rise by as much as 400 percent. Meanwhile, ESKOM offers lower rates to businesses and municipalities—mostly well-off, white suburbs—that can afford to buy electricity in bulk. According to a study released last year by the Municipal Services Project at the University of the Witwatersrand in Johannesburg (commonly referred to as Wits University), ESKOM cut power to nearly 20,000 households and businesses in Soweto each month last year. "In the hearts and minds of every black South African, nothing will ever compare to apartheid," says Guy Mhone, an economist at Wits University. "But there is a very real frustration now that we have only exchanged the savagery of apartheid for the savagery of an untethered free market."

One South African municipality that has begun to privatize its water operations is Johannesburg, the nation's largest city, which has a utility district that includes dozens of impoverished, all-black suburbs like Soweto and Alexandra. In 2001, the city entered into a partnership with Suez and some of its subsidiaries—despite the fact that Suez tendered the lowest bid. Suez's history of raising prices did not bode well for poor residents, especially since the new utility, Johannesburg Water Management Company, had inherited an apartheid-era white elephant known as the Lesotho Highlands Water Project. This $8 billion scheme to build six new dams in the water-rich country of Lesotho—which is completely surrounded by South Africa—has already caused the cost of water in Johannesburg to nearly triple since the ANC came to power, and many of Alexandra's residents complain that they can no longer afford to pay their bills. Conceived by the apartheid government, the project was supported by the World Bank and other international lenders, who sidestepped international sanctions to finance the deal in 1986. The ANC denounced the arrangement at the time, saying that it strengthened apartheid. But after the ANC took office in 1994, party leaders decided to plow ahead. The first of the six dams, the tallest on the continent, was completed in 1998. Developers expect to build the remaining five over the next eighteen years.

The project is partially financed by international loans that will be repaid by passing the cost on to consumers. A disproportionate share will be paid for by residents of Alexandra. All-white suburbs, home to less than one-tenth of South Africa's population, account for more than half the country's residential water use. But since these communities can take advantage of discounted bulk rates, a household in Johannesburg's white suburbs can fill its swimming pool and water its garden at less than half the cost per liter paid by a family in Alexandra.

Unions, environmentalists, and community groups have appealed to the government to cancel the Lesotho dam project and repair the apartheid era infrastructure instead. "We don't need the water from the dams," says Sam Moiloa, a conservation activist who lives in Alexandra with his wife and two children. "We lose half of our available water through leaks. We should just fix the leaks and our government can use that money they're spending on dams for the rich to improve our standard of living." Advocates also propose charging higher rates to bigger users, allowing well-off households and businesses to subsidize the poor.

Government officials, however, say that making utilities profitable is critical to South Africa's competitiveness at a time when foreign investment is badly needed. "There's a lot of polemics around this issue," says Mike Muller, director general of South Africa's Department of Water and Forestry. "But the truth is that operating costs have to be recaptured, or there is no way to sustain basic services."

Many government officials and business executives also argue that a national habit dating back to the apartheid era—when entire communities boycotted white rule by refusing to pay rent and utilities—is responsible for many of the cutoffs. "You will find in South Africa there exists a culture of nonpayment," says Jacob Maroga, managing director of distribution for ESKOM, the electric utility that the state is preparing to sell. "There are people who have very legitimate reasons for not paying their bills, but there are many more who grew accustomed through our liberation movement to simply not paying a bill. That's not the kind of attitude that's constructive to building a modern, productive economy."

Studies by research organizations such as Wits University's Municipal Services Project, however, suggest that for many families, utility bills have become a major financial burden. Households earning less than 1,000 rand, or $100 a month—about one in two nationally—pay nearly a quarter of their income for utility bills, notes HSRC's Hemson. "This notion of a culture of nonpayment is clearly fantasy," he says.

Historically, Zulus and other African tribes have had little use for dates. Instead, they mark time by great events; so, if you ask a man in what year he was born, he may respond "in the year of the great flood" or in the "time of the great famine." If you ask Josephine Mhiyne about her youngest grandchild, Nomsa, she will tell you that the two-year-old was born in the "time of the great cholera"—in 2000, the year the epidemic began.

"We all had it," she says, sitting on a rug in front of her mud hut while her granddaughter mauls a stalk of sugarcane. "We just thank God that no one died. I got it right after she was born. My stomach was running so bad. It was because we were drinking from the river. I live in fear of the river, but I still return to it for water every day. I have no other option."

Until the recent outbreak, the Empangeni region had not seen a major cholera epidemic since a bad drought in 1982, when some 12,000 cases—less than 10 percent of the number reported in the current epidemic—occurred. In response to that outbreak, town officials built nine communal taps providing clean water to Ngwelezana and the Madlebe villages. It was not uncommon for residents to make several trips a day to fetch water, sometimes walking a mile each way.

In the months before the December 2000 nationwide municipal elections, with unemployment rates soaring and the patience of poor South Africans wearing thin, President Thabo Mbeki and other ANC politicians took to the campaign trail and promised more water and electricity hookups for the poor. Within eight months of the vote, municipal workers in Empangeni had extended water pipes to about seven thousand homes in the outlying villages. There was just one catch: to use the newly installed taps, residents would have to insert a prepaid card into a meter. If someone fell behind in paying the water bill, municipal authorities would cancel the card, leaving residents unable to access their tap.

"We have come to hate those meters," says fifty-nine-year-old Busisiwe Nkwanyana as she and her two daughters fetch water to cook their supper from a muddy pit. "At first we would go to neighbors who still had water and ask to use theirs, but soon no one here could afford the water. No one could use their taps. It was like we had traveled back in time." Nkwanyana came down with cholera late in 2000 after her tap was shut off. Both her daughters soon fell ill, as did two of their grandchildren, a niece, and neighbors on each side of her mud hut.

Part of the problem, says David Sanders, a professor of public health at the University of the Western Cape, is that while the government has expanded delivery of clean water, it has not made much of a dent in providing sewage systems. "The problem is very simple," he says. "People didn't have sanitation and so they shit in the river. People didn't have money to pay for their water and so they went to the river for water."

The government has scored one major success in the epidemic. It has kept cholera from killing most of its victims, a remarkable feat especially given South Africa's high HIV infection rate. Only a quarter of 1 percent of those who contracted the cholera virus since August of 2000 died, notes HSRC's Hemson, one of the lowest fatality rates on record in a major cholera epidemic. But, he adds, "even that came at great expense to the government, and it could have been offset with some adjustments in their policy of cost recovery. The cutoffs cost them more money in the end in dealing with the disease that resulted from it."

In recent months, South Africa's cholera infection rate has finally slowed—in part, experts say, because people have gotten more cautious about the water they use. Still, Metolina Mthembu continues to make her daily trek to the river, navigating the hilly footpaths with an ease that seems impossible for a woman of her age and slight physique. "Sometimes the river gets totally dry," she says, "and you have to walk for two or three kilometers to find water. Or you go without for days at a time." Mthembu cannot imagine any hell worse than apartheid; she makes sure to preface any criticism of the government with that caveat. "But we still live with misery," she says as she climbs the hill separating her home from the copper-colored stream on which she once again depends. "If we could only get water, then we would be really free."

4

Globalizing the Earth's Crust

Humans have always asked a great deal of the ground. On it we have built our shelters; in it we have planted our crops; and under it we have extracted precious metals and minerals that decorate our bodies and fuel industrial growth. According to one historian, by as early as the sixteenth century, silver extracted by Native American slaves for Spain's hoped-for empire "went around the world and made the world go round" (Marks 2007: 8). But over the last two hundred years these processes have accelerated, often leaving a scarred, barren, and poisoned landscape in their wake. In one estimation, by 1994 human beings annually transported more than 42 billion tons of earth, which is not much less than the erosive power of water, which moved 53 tons (McNeill 2000: 30). There are many reasons for scratching the ground; perhaps the most important has to do with the metals, ores, minerals, and fuel that lie hidden under it.

Today's practice of extracting precious metals for global exchange is like an experiment in modern alchemy. Just as we use synthetic chemicals to fertilize our soil and protect our crops from pests, so too must we apply cyanide over large quantities of earth in order to procure precious metals. As Jane Perlezand and Kirk Johnson discuss below, to produce enough gold for a one-ounce wedding band, "miners dig up and haul away 30 tons of rock and sprinkle it with diluted cyanide." The process has environmental and social costs that are passed on to peoples and places around the world. Indeed, the World Bank has encouraged the industry as a means of modernizing developing nations of the world. The peasant villagers of Guatemala and Ghana, however, are less optimistic.

Jane Perlezand and Kirk Johnson, "Behind Gold's Glitter: Torn Lands and Pointed Questions" (2005)[1]

There has always been an element of madness to gold's allure. For thousands of years, something in the eternally lustrous metal has driven people to the

57

outer edges of desire—to have it and hoard it, to kill or conquer for it, to possess it like a lover.

In the early 1500s, King Ferdinand of Spain laid down the priorities as his conquistadors set out for the New World. "Get gold," he told them, "humanely if possible, but at all costs, get gold."

In that long and tortuous history, gold has now arrived at a new moment of opportunity and peril. The price of gold is higher than it has been in seventeen years—pushing $500 an ounce. But much of the gold left to be mined is microscopic and is being wrung from the earth at enormous environmental cost, often in some of the poorest corners of the world.

And unlike past gold manias, from the time of the pharaohs to the forty-niners, this one has little to do with girding empires, economies, or currencies. It is about the soaring demand for jewelry in places like China and India, which consume 80 percent or more of gold mined today.

The extravagance of the moment is provoking a storm among environmental groups and communities near the mines, and forcing even some at Tiffany & Company and the world's largest mining companies to confront uncomfortable questions about the real costs of mining gold.

"The biggest challenge we face is the absence of a set of clearly defined, broadly accepted standards for environmentally and socially responsible mining," said Tiffany's chairman, Michael Kowalski. He took out a full-page advertisement last year urging miners to make "urgently needed" reforms.

Consider a ring. For that one ounce of gold, miners dig up and haul away thirty tons of rock and sprinkle it with diluted cyanide, which culls the rock from the gold. Before they are through, miners at some of the largest mines move a half million tons of earth a day, pile it in mounds that can rival the Great Pyramids, and drizzle the ore with the poisonous solution for years.

The scars of open-pit mining on this scale endure. A months-long examination by the *New York Times*, including tours of gold mines in the American West, Latin America, Africa, and Europe, provided a rare look inside an insular industry with a troubled environmental legacy and an uncertain future.

Some metal mines, including gold mines, have become the near-equivalent of nuclear waste dumps that must be tended in perpetuity. Hard-rock mining generates more toxic waste than any other industry in the United States, according to the Environmental Protection Agency. The agency estimated last year that the cost of cleaning up metal mines could reach $54 billion.

A recent report from the Government Accountability Office chastised the agency and said legal loopholes, corporate shells and weak federal oversight had compounded the costs and increased the chances that mining companies could walk away without paying for cleanups and pass the bill to taxpayers.

"Mining problems weren't considered a very high priority" in past decades, Thomas P. Dunne, the agency's acting assistant administrator for solid waste and emergency response, said in an interview. "But they are a concern now."

With the costs and scrutiny of mining on the rise in rich countries, where the best ores have been depleted, 70 percent of gold is now mined in developing countries like Guatemala and Ghana. It is there, miners and critics agree, that the real battle over gold's future is being waged.

Gold companies say they are bringing good jobs, tighter environmental rules, and time-tested technologies to their new frontiers. With the help of the World Bank, they have opened huge mines promising development. Governments have welcomed the investment.

But environmental groups say companies are mining in ways that would never be tolerated in wealthier nations, such as dumping tons of waste into rivers, bays and oceans. People who live closest to the mines say they see too few of mining's benefits and bear too much of its burden. In Guatemala and Peru, people have mounted protests to push miners out. Other communities are taking companies to court.

In October of 2005 a Philippine province sued the world's fifth-largest gold company, Canada-based Placer Dome, charging that it had ruined a river, a bay, and a coral reef by dumping enough waste to fill a convoy of trucks that would circle the globe three times.

Placer Dome, which also runs three major mines in Nevada, answered by saying that it had "contained the problem" and already spent $70 million in remediation and another $1.5 million in compensation.

Some in the industry have paused to consider whether it is worth the cost—to the environment, their bottom line, or their reputations—to mine gold, which generates more waste per ounce than any other metal and yet has few industrial uses.

The world's biggest mining company, Australia-based BHP Billiton, sold its profitable Ok Tedi mine in Papua New Guinea in 2001 after having destroyed more than 2,400 acres of rainforest. Upon leaving, the company said the mine was "not compatible with our environmental values."

After tough lessons, other companies, like Newmont Mining, the world's largest gold producer, are paying for more schools and housing, trying harder to ease social problems around its mines. "I don't think any of our members want to be associated with a bad operation—notwithstanding it would hurt their ability to open new facilities," said Carol L. Raulston, spokeswoman for the National Mining Association. "News goes around the world quickly now and there is no place to hide."

Critics say corporate miners have been cloistered from scrutiny because of their anonymity to consumers, unlike, say, oil companies, which also extract resources but hang their name over the pump. Last year the mine watchdog group Earthworks began a "No Dirty Gold" campaign, marching protesters in front of fashionable Fifth Avenue storefronts, trying to change gold mining by lobbying gold consumers. "They just said to ask where the gold was coming from and whether it caused social or environmental damage," said Michael E. Conroy, senior lecturer and research scholar at the Yale University School of Forestry and Environmental Studies. "The repercussions in the mining media were huge—some said it was all lies, but retailers began to realize what their vulnerability was."

Tiffany chairman Kolwaski has tried to stay ahead of the controversy. He has broken new ground by buying Tiffany's gold from a mine in Utah that does not use cyanide. But the largest sellers of gold are not luxury outlets like his, but rather Wal-Mart stores, and even Kowalski, a trustee of the Wildlife Conservation Society, hesitated to call any gold entirely "clean."

ASIA'S INSATIABLE APPETITE

Amrita Raj, a twenty-five-year-old bride, was shopping for her wedding trousseau on a recent Saturday in New Delhi, including a wedding set with its requisite gold necklace, matching earrings, and two sets of bangles. For the sake of family honor, the new in-laws would have to receive gifts of gold as well—a "light set" for the mother-in-law, plus a gold ring or a watch for the bridegroom and earrings for a sister-in-law. "Without gold, it's not a wedding—at least not for Indians," Raj said.

For thousands of years, gold has lent itself to ceremony and celebration. But now old ways have met new prosperity. The newly moneyed consumers who line the malls of Shanghai and the bazaars of Mumbai sent jewelry sales shooting to a record $38 billion this year, according to the World Gold Council, the industry trade group.

In 2005 sales surged 11 percent in China and 47 percent in India, a country of a billion people whose seemingly insatiable appetite for gold—for jewelry, temples, and dowries—has traditionally made it gold's largest consumer. That kind of demand leads many in and out of the industry to argue that gold's value is cultural and should not be questioned. The desire to hoard gold is not limited to households in India or the Middle East, either.

The United States, the world's second largest consumer of gold, is also the world's largest holder of gold reserves. The government has 8,134 tons secured in vaults, about $122 billion worth. The Federal Reserve and other major central banks renewed an agreement last year to severely restrict sales from their reserves, offering, in effect, a price support to gold.

That price is not simply a matter of supply and demand, but of market psychology. Gold is bought by anxious investors when the dollar is weak and the economy uncertain. That is a big reason for gold's high price today. For miners that price determines virtually everything—where gold is mined, how much is mined, and how tiny are the flecks worth going after. "You can mine gold ore at a lower grade than any other metal," said Mike Wireman, a mine specialist at the Denver office of the EPA. "That means big open pits. But it must also be easy and cheap to be profitable, and that means cyanide."

That kind of massive operation can be seen at Yanacocha, a sprawling mine in northern Peru run by Newmont. In a region of pastures and peasants, the rolling green hills have been carved into sandy-colored mesas, looking more like the American West than the Andean highlands.

Mountains have been systematically blasted, carted off by groaning trucks the size of houses and restacked into ziggurats of chunky ore. These new man-made mountains are lined with irrigation hoses that silently trickle millions of gallons of cyanide solution over the rock for years. The cyanide dissolves the gold so it can be separated and smelted.

At sites like Yanacocha, one ounce of gold is sprinkled in thirty tons of ore. But to get at that ore, many more tons of earth have to be moved, then left as waste. At some mines in Nevada, one hundred tons or more of earth have to be excavated for a single ounce of gold, said Ann Maest, a geochemist who consults on mining issues. Mining companies say they are meeting a demand and that this kind of gold mining, called cyanide heap leaching, is as good a use of the land as any, or better.

Cyanide is not the only option, but it is considered the most cost-effective way to retrieve microscopic bits of "invisible gold." Profit margins are too thin, miners say, and the gold left in the world too scarce to mine it any other way. "The heap is cheaper," said Shannon W. Dunlap, an environmental manager with Placer Dome. "Our ore wouldn't work without the heap."

But much of those masses of disturbed rock, exposed to the rain and air for the first time, are also the source of mining's multibillion-dollar environmental time bomb. Sulfides in that rock will react with oxygen, making sulfuric acid. That acid pollutes and it also frees heavy metals like cadmium, lead, and mercury, which are harmful to people and fish even at low concentrations. The chain reaction can go on for centuries.

Many industry officials, reluctant to utter the word "pollution," protest that much of what they leave behind is not waste at all but ground-up rock. The best-run mines reclaim land along the way, they say, "capping" the rock piles with soil and using lime to try to forestall acid generation. But stopping pollution forever is difficult. Even rock piles that are capped, in an attempt to keep out air and rain, can release pollutants, particularly in wet climates.

Cyanide can present long-term problems too. Most scientists agree that cyanide decomposes in sunlight and is not dangerous if greatly diluted. But a study by the U.S. Geological Survey in 2000 said that cyanide can convert to other toxic forms and persist, particularly in cold climates. And just as cyanide dissolves gold out of the rock, it releases harmful metals, too.

There have also been significant accidents involving cyanide. From 1985 to 2000, more than a dozen reservoirs containing cyanide-laden mine waste collapsed, the United Nations Environment Program reported. The most severe disaster occurred in Romania in 2000, when mine waste spilled into a tributary of the Danube River, killing more than a thousand tons of fish and issuing a plume of cyanide that reached 1,600 miles to the Black Sea.

That spill led to calls for the gold industry to improve its handling of cyanide. After five years of discussion, the industry unveiled a new code this month. It sets standards for transporting and storing cyanide and calls on companies to submit to inspections by a new industry body.

But the cyanide code is voluntary and not enforced by government. And Glenn Miller, a professor of environmental science at the University of Nevada, says it does not adequately deal with one of mining's most important, unattended questions: What happens when the mine closes?

A ROCKY MOUNTAIN DISASTER

One answer can be found in a rural, rugged area of northeastern Montana called the Little Rocky Mountains. Dale Ployhar often comes to the high bare slopes around the abandoned Zortman-Landusky gold mine to plant pine seedlings on a silent hillside that has been reclaimed by little more than grasses. "I bring lodgepole seeds and scatter them around, hoping they'll come back," he said, looking out over the tiny town of Zortman, population 50.

Zortman-Landusky was the first large-scale, open-pit cyanide operation in the United States when it opened in 1979. The imprint it left on the environment, psyche, and politics of Montana continues today. What happened there—a cacophonous, multilayered disaster involving bankruptcy, bad science, environmental havoc, and regulatory gaps—foreshadowed the risky road that gold has taken in the years since, mining experts, government regulators, and environmentalists say. "There's a lot of bitterness left," said sixty-five-year-old Ployhar, a heavy equipment operator, whose son bought some of the mine lands at a bankruptcy auction four years ago.

Some mining experts say that Zortman-Landusky—a combination of two open pits near Zortman and the neighboring village of Landusky—offered a steep learning curve on how chemical mining worked, and didn't. Others say that overly ambitious production schedules by the mine's owner, Canada-based Pegasus Gold, were to blame. A bonus package of more than $5 million for top executives, announced after the company filed for bankruptcy protection in 1998, did not help.

Mining with cyanide can be tricky even in the best conditions. At Zortman, the company made the mistake of building cyanide heaps atop rock that turned acidic. The cyanide and the acid mixed in a toxic cocktail that seeped from the mounds.

Mining stopped in 1996, and company officials insisted in public comments over the next year that they wanted to be responsible corporate citizens and stay to clean up the property. But the price of gold was falling, then below $280 an ounce, and Pegasus closed its doors. "This became one of the worst cases in Montana," said Wayne E. Jepson, manager of the Zortman project at the Montana Department of Environmental Quality. "But even as late as 1990, one of the last studies for Landusky predicted no acid in any significant amounts."

Environmental risks from hard-rock mines often turn out to be understated and underreported, according to two recent studies. Robert Repetto, an economist at the University of Colorado, examined ten mines in the United States and abroad run by publicly traded companies. All but one, he wrote in a June report, had failed to fully disclose "risks and liabilities" to investors.

The environmental group Earthworks examined twenty-two mines for a report. Almost all of them had water problems, leading it to conclude that "water quality impacts are almost always underestimated" before mining begins. The combination of the regulatory approach and the science is what creates inaccurate predictions," said James R. Kuipers, a consultant and former mining engineer who helped write the study. At Zortman-Landusky, the state wrote the environmental impact study itself, based primarily on information from the company, Kuipers said.

Montana and other big mining states still depend on mining companies for much of the scientific data about environmental impact, or the money to pay for the studies, state and federal regulators say, mainly because government agencies generally lack the resources to do expensive, in-depth research themselves. Some mine regulators defend the practice, saying that having scientific data supplied by companies with a financial interest in the outcome is not necessarily bad if the review is stringent. "What is important to make the system work is that state and federal agencies have the wherewithal and expertise to look at the information," said Wireman of the Denver EPA office.

One lesson of Zortman is that good information is sometimes ignored. In the early 1990s, an EPA consultant and former mining engineer, Orville Kiehn, warned in a memo to his bosses that not enough money was being set aside by the mine for water treatment. Kiehn's opinion, vindicated today, went nowhere. The environmental agency had little legal authority then—and no more today—to protect the public from an operating mine except by filing a lawsuit, as it did in 1995 after Pegasus had already violated federal clean water standards. The company settled the suit in 1996 and agreed to pay $32.3 million mostly to upgrade and expand water treatment. At the time, state officials rejected the idea of squeezing Pegasus to put up more money. Montana's legislature created a special fund for water treatment to make up for it, for the next 120 years, at a cost of more than $19 million.

Washington is also coming to grips with the failure to plan for the cost of mining. The Government Accountability Office, the investigative arm of Congress, sharply criticized the EPA in August for not requiring metal mines to provide assurances that they can pay for cleanups, a failure that it said had exposed taxpayers to potentially billions of dollars in liabilities.

For Montana, the Zortman experience was chilling. In 1998, as the catastrophe was making headlines across the state, voters approved the nation's first statewide ban on cyanide mining, halting any new gold projects. They renewed the ban in 2004.

PROFIT AND POVERTY

Today gold companies are striking out to remote corners of the globe led by a powerful guide: the World Bank. The bank, the preeminent institution for alleviating world poverty, has argued that multinational mining companies would bring investment, as well as roads, schools, and jobs, to countries with little else to offer than their natural resources. For the bank, which tries to draw private investment to underdeveloped lands, the logic was simple. "We invest to help reduce poverty and help improve people's lives," said Rashad-Rudolf Kaldany, head of oil, gas, and mining at the bank's profit-making arm, the International Finance Corporation.

The bank has worked both ends of the equation. At its urging, more than one hundred cash-strapped governments have agreed to cut taxes and royalties to lure big mining companies, said James Otto, an adjunct professor at the University of Denver law school. At the same time, the bank put up money for, or insured more than 30 gold-mining projects, looking for profits.

Though mining was a small part of the bank's portfolio, it was not without controversy as accidents mounted. In one of the worst disasters in 1995 a mine in Guyana insured by the bank spilled more than 790,000 gallons of cyanide-laced mine waste into a tributary of the Essequibo River, the country's main water source.

By 2001, the World Bank president, James D. Wolfensohn, imposed a two-year moratorium on mining investments and ordered a review of its involvement in the industry. Emil Salim, a former minister of environment of Indonesia, led the study. "I said, up to now the International Finance Corporation was only listening to business," he said in an interview in Jakarta. "I said, so now let's give some voice to civil society." Salim recommended reducing the use of cyanide, banning the disposal of waste in rivers and oceans, and giving communities veto power over mining company plans.

But the industry complained. And developing country governments said they liked the bank's loans to gold mines. In the end, the bank settled on more modest goals. It pledged to make environmental impact statements understandable to villagers and to back only projects with broad community support. It also urged governments to spend mining companies' taxes and royalties in the communities near the mines. But critics and environmental groups say the bank demands little from the mining companies in return for its money and its seal of approval.

The bank's guidelines for arsenic in drinking water are less stringent than those of the World Health Organization, and mercury contamination levels are more lenient than those permitted by the EPA, said Andrea Durbin, a consultant to nongovernmental groups pressing for tougher standards. The International Finance Corporation is drafting new guidelines that will clarify what it expects from miners, said Rachel Kyte, its director of environment and social development. But the draft rules give mining companies even more latitude, said Manish Bapna, the executive director of the Bank Information Center, a group that monitors the bank. They will make it easier for companies to evict indigenous people and to mine in some of the globe's most treasured habitats, he said.

Despite the World Bank's two-year review, little has changed, said Robert Goodland, a former director of environment at the bank who was an adviser on the study. "The bank insists on business as usual," he said.

RESISTANCE IN GUATEMALA

The first piece of new mining business the bank invested in after its review can be found today in the humid, green hills of western Guatemala. Bishop Alvaro Ramazzini, a big, burly man who mixes politics and religion with ease, doesn't understand why the World Bank lent $45 million to a rich multinational company for a gold mine in his impoverished region of Mayan farmers. "Why not spend the money directly to help the people?" he asked.

Sprawled across a deep wooded valley, a new mine built by Glamis Gold, a Canadian company, was chosen by the World Bank last year as a new model for how gold mining could help poor people. But the mine has faced protest at every turn. At the June 2004 board meeting of the International Finance Corporation, there was considerable skepticism about its $45 million loan to Glamis.

Members questioned why a $261 million project was creating only 160 long-term jobs and giving money to a "well capitalized" company like Glamis at all, according to minutes of the meeting provided to *The Times* by a nongovernmental group opposed to the project. Others were worried that the IFC was relying too heavily on information from Glamis about the potential for pollution.

The World Bank had pledged to back only mines with broad local support. But on the ground in Guatemala, opposition boiled over in December 2004. Angry farmers set up a roadblock to stop trailers carrying huge grinding machines for the mine. After forty days and battles between police and protesters, the equipment had to be escorted by soldiers.

To persuade villagers of the mine's benefits, Glamis flew nineteen planeloads of farmers to a mine it runs in Honduras. But the villagers of Sipicapa still wanted their voices heard. On a cool Saturday morning in June, more than 2,600 men and women dressed in their weekend best, with children in tow, crowded into the community's yards, churches and verandas to vote in a nonbinding referendum. "We are already regretting that our forefathers allowed the Spaniards to buy our land for trinkets and mirrors," said Fructuoso López Pérez, a local mayor. "So we should vote so our children will thank us for doing right." At that, a church full of local people raised their hands in a unanimous show of opposition to the mine.

Much of the peasants' fury was informed by Robert E. Moran, an American hydrogeologist who was asked by Madre Selva, a Guatemalan nongovernmental organization, to visit the mine and review its environmental impact statement. Moran, who was on the advisory board of the bank's mining study, found it badly lacking. It did not address the "very large quantities of water" the mine would use, or give basic information on the "massive volumes" of waste the mine would produce, he said.

Tim Miller, vice president of Central American operations for Glamis, said the environmental impact statement had been a "working document." In Guatemala City, the vice minister of mining, Jorge Antonio García Chiu, defended approval of the mine, saying it followed four months of consultation.

Kaldany, the IFC official, said the investment and the environmental impact statement were both sound. "We are a bank," he said. "We go on the basis of a business development project. Then, as well, the bank asks, Are we needed? Are we adding any value?" Glamis had already spent $1.3 million on social programs in the villages as part of the bank's requirements, Kaldany said.

At the mine, the grinding and churning of new machinery being tested already echoes across the valley. Production could begin as early as November. Miller, of Glamis, said the mine was a winner for the people, and his company. In fact, he said, Glamis didn't need the bank; the bank came to Glamis. Bank officials "were anxious to make some investments" in the region, he said. The company is expecting to gross $1 billion over the life of the mine, with profits of $200 to $300 million. "That's a return of about 25 to 30 percent," he said.

GHANA: THE SOCIAL COSTS

The men of Binsre on Ghana's ancient Gold Coast carry on their own hunt for gold. Nearly naked, their arms and legs slathered in gray ooze, they sift through the muck in a large pit, using buckets and hard hats, looking for any last scrap.

So far industrial mining has not lived up to its promise for these men and their families. They are illegal miners who find work not inside the highly mechanized mines of Ghana's first-world investors, but on the fringes, scavenging the waste left behind by AngloGold Ashanti, the world's second-largest gold company, based in South Africa.

Six miners have died in the past several years, most overcome by fumes when waste from the mine gushed into the pit, said Hannah Owusu-Koranteng, an advocate for the illegal miners. The mine tried to keep the men out. "We used to use dogs," said AngloGold Ashanti's chief financial officer, Kwaku Akosah-Bempah. "Then they said we were using dogs to bite them." So the mine stopped using the dogs and the men returned.

In the nearby village of Sanso, a few men said they had lost their land to the mine. Now they carve shafts into a mountain of waste rock, where they haul, hammer, chip, and sift. "You wake up one day and you realize your farm is destroyed," said Assemblyman Benjamin Annan, a local politician. "They say they will compensate but it takes one or two years. So people are compelled to go to illegal mining, the way our ancestors did."

Industrial-size shaft mining has existed in Ghana for one hundred years, but with the price of gold soaring, more companies are arriving now, this time bringing open-pit cyanide mines. The investment has been greeted warmly by the government.

Newmont is set to spend a billion dollars on a new mine next year and on a second mine—in one of the badly deforested country's last remaining forest preserves—in 2007. The World Bank is here too, preparing to lend the company $75 million. Together, the bank and Newmont say, they aim to show how social development and gold mining can be married.

Newmont compensated the farmers who were moved off their land. It is offering training for new jobs, like growing edible snails and making soap. It built new concrete and tin-roofed houses to replace homes made of mud. But the mine will create just 450 full-time jobs. More than 8,000 people will be displaced. "The house is okay," said Gyinabu Ali, 35, a divorced mother of five children, who recently moved into her gaily painted two-room house, with a toilet out back, that overlooks several dozen similar units resembling a poor man's Levittown. "I miss my land where I could grow my own food."

Near the mine of Newmont's competitor, AngloGold Ashanti, in Obuasi, only half of the homes have an indoor bathroom, and 20 percent have running water. With the exception of the brick villas of the company executives, Obuasi today looks like a squalid shanty town.

The chief financial officer, Akosah-Bempah, said he was offended by the poor conditions. Most of the company's taxes and royalties had stayed in the capital, he said, leaving the ramshackle town bereft of the benefits of gold mining. "Sometimes we feel embarrassed by going to Obuasi," he said. "Not enough has gone back into the community."

REFERENCES

Marks, Robert B. 2007. *The Origins of the Modern World: A Global and Ecological Narrative from the Fifteenth to the Twenty-first Century*. New York: Rowman & Littlefield.

McNeill, J. R. 2000. *Something New under the Sun: An Environmental History of the Twentieth-Century World*. New York: Norton.

5

The Seas around Us

A seldom noticed but catastrophic disaster is unfolding in the global ocean. There was a time in the middle of the twentieth century when the ocean was viewed by many as inviolable—its size, resources, and diluting power seemed infinite. But since World War II, humanity has put increasing pressures on the ocean. Industrialized nations developed sophisticated technologies for finding and harvesting the ocean's finite fisheries. Some developing countries mechanized their fleets and turned to the ocean to meet their basic protein needs. And many countries continued to use the ocean to dispose of their municipal, industrial, toxic, and even nuclear waste.

But it is equally important to keep in mind that the process of globalization created new and indirect environmental threats. For instance, the green revolution of the 1960s and 1970s caused many Midwestern farmers to vastly increase their use of artificial fertilizers—a technological prerequisite of many high-yield varieties (chapter 8). These chemicals have washed down the Mississippi and are now creating the world's second largest "dead zone" in the previously-fertile waters of the Gulf of Mexico. Julia Whitty's elegant and provocative piece below highlights the many environmental problems our ocean is facing.

Julia Whitty, "The Fate of the Ocean" (2006)[1]

We're in for a wild ride, say the thirteen crew members of the *Oceanus*, salts old and young, most of them Cape Codders with lifelong careers on the water. Consequently, many members of the scientific team—oceanographers, science technicians, and graduate students, along with this observer—scatter across the ship's three decks in the moments before we sail, seeking privacy for our last cell phone calls home, backs turned to the rain, shouting against the wind. At 177 feet and more than 1,000 tons, R/V (research vessel) *Oceanus* is the smallest ship in the long-range fleet of the Woods Hole Oceanographic Institution on Cape Cod, Massachusetts, and I suspect there's not one of us aboard this morning who doesn't wish we were sailing on one of the larger vessels.

Bad weather at sea is exponentially worse than bad weather ashore. The liquid world reacts in a pyrotechnical way to blowing air, exploding into the marine equivalent of a firestorm at winds that onshore might only make you button your coat. We're headed into a force 9 (strong gale) on the 12-point Beaufort scale. Before we make landfall one week hence, we'll have dabbled in force 10 (storm) and skirted force 11 (violent storm) conditions. Force 12 is a hurricane.

Outside of Buzzards Bay, we're slammed with 20-foot seas ripped white by wind and careening unpredictably on the shallow waters of the continental shelf. The swell is abeam of us, and *Oceanus* wallows with the corkscrew motion sailors despise. One by one, those of us not on watch disappear below to set the storm rails on our bunks, wedge our life jackets under the edges of our mattresses, climb in, wait, and hope for intestinal fortitude and good seamanship from Captain Lawrence Bearse's crew on the bridge. The only way to avoid being flung from our bunks by the violent motion is to hold on and hug the wall, which is essentially the outer skin of the vessel. It's a strangely intimate experience below waterline, feeling the ship bowing and flexing against our backs, and absorbing into our bones the deafening thunder of steel as the largest waves drive *Oceanus* nearly to a shuddering stop before her single propeller fights back with the power of 3,000 horses. I'm torn between staying awake and worried in a fascinated kind of way, or falling into oblivious sleep.

A cold front from the north fueled by the remnants of Tropical Storm Tammy, and Subtropical Depression 22 are merging and birthing a midlatitude cyclonic monster destined to grow 1,100 miles in diameter. Twenty inches of rain have already fallen over parts of New England, the region's weightiest rain event since Hurricane Floyd in 1999. A day earlier, en route to Woods Hole and stuck in Chicago by weather so bad it closed down Boston's Logan Airport, I called Ruth Curry, the expedition's chief scientist, to ask what she made of the forecast. "Science doesn't stop for the weather," was her cheery reply.

Concerns about weather are part of what's sending us to sea in the first place. By studying the ocean's chemistry, which affects currents and in turn weather, Curry hopes to better understand how humans may be affecting the critical elements of their life-support system. Data from physical oceanography, marine biology, meteorology, fisheries science, glaciology, and other disciplines reveal that the ocean, for which our planet should be named, is changing in every parameter, in all dimensions, in every way we know how to measure it.

The twenty-five years I've spent at sea filming nature documentaries have provided a brief yet definitive window into these changes. Oceanic problems once encountered on a local scale have gone pandemic, and these pandemics now merge to birth new monsters. Tinkering with the atmosphere, we change the ocean's chemistry radically enough to threaten life on earth as we know it. Making tens of thousands of chemical compounds each year, we poison marine creatures who sponge up plastics and PCBs, becoming toxic waste dumps in the process. Carrying everything from nuclear waste to running shoes across the world ocean, shipping fleets spew as much greenhouse gases into the atmosphere as the entire profligate United States. Protecting strawberry farmers and their pesticide methyl bromide, we guarantee that the ozone hole will persist at least until 2065, threatening the larval life of the sea. Fishing harder, faster, and more ruthlessly than ever before, we drive large predatory fish toward global extinction, even though fish is the primary source of protein for one in six people on earth. Filling, dredging, and polluting the coastal nurseries of the sea, we decimate coral reefs and kelp forests, while fostering dead zones.

I'm alarmed by what I'm seeing. Although we carry the ocean within ourselves, in our blood and in our eyes, so that we essentially see through seawater, we appear blind to its fate. Many scientists speak only to each other and studiously avoid educating the press. The media seems unwilling to report environmental news, and caters to a public stalled by sloth, fear, or greed and generally confused by science. Overall, we seem unable to recognize that the proofs so many politicians demand already exist in the form of hindsight. Written into the long history of our planet, in one form or another, is the record of what is coming our way.

"The root cause of this crisis is a failure of both perspective and governance," concludes the seminal Pew Oceans Commission's 2003 report to the nation. "We have failed to conceive of the oceans as our largest public domain, to be managed holistically for the greater public good in perpetuity." Instead, we have roiled the waters, compromising the equilibrium that allowed our species to flourish in the first place, and providing ourselves with a host of challenges that will test our clever brains and our opposable thumbs as never before. Afloat on arks of dry land, we sail toward a stormy future.

The goal of expedition OC 417 is to sail from Cape Cod two-thirds of the way to Bermuda along a 321-mile-long line known as a transect. We are scheduled to sail outbound nonstop for thirty-six hours until, 385 miles to the southeast, we'll begin to work our way back, sampling waters from the surface to the abyss at twenty-two predetermined stations, identifiable only by their latitude and longitude. In the course of a week, we'll measure temperature, oxygen, salinity, and chlorofluorocarbons in the water column—the equivalent of taking the ocean's pulse, listening to its lungs, looking at its tongue, and making it say "ah."

According to the charts, we are sailing the North Atlantic. But this is a relatively arbitrary marker. In fact, there is only one ocean on earth: a world ocean encompassing 70.78 percent of our planet. The ancient Greeks sensed the ocean was one and portrayed their water god Okeanos (Oceanus) as a river circling the world. Three thousand years later, modern oceanographers confirm the world ocean is connected in riverlike fashion; using a schematic known as the ocean conveyor belt, they portray Okeanos as a Möbius-like ribbon winding through all the ocean basins, rising and falling, and stirring the waters of the world. In this manner, the surface waters we sail in the North Atlantic are destined to flow to the Arctic, to grow colder and sink, and, once at the bottom, to reverse flow southward through the Atlantic, eventually converging with the Antarctic Circumpolar Current, before surfacing in the Northeast Pacific 1,200 years from now. Centuries later, they will arrive back in the North Atlantic, having truly traveled the seven seas.

Or maybe they won't. Things are changing.

In 2005, researchers from the Scripps Institution of Oceanography and the Lawrence Livermore National Laboratory found the first clear evidence that the world ocean is growing warmer. In a novel study combining computer modeling and field observations, and screening for natural weather effects and the impact of volcanic gases, they discovered the top half mile of the ocean has warmed dramatically in the past forty years as a result, clearly and simply, of human-induced, rising greenhouse gases. "The statistical significance of these results is far too strong to be merely dismissed and should wipe out much of the uncertainty about the reality of global warming," reported researcher Tim Barnett of Scripps, who suggests the Bush administration convene a Manhattan-style project to figure out what mitigations may still be possible.

One symptom already manifesting is the melting of the Arctic. Last year set a fourth consecutive record low for ice cover in the Arctic, and scientists now predict the summertime Arctic will be ice-free before the end of this century—a course likely exacerbated by the simultaneous decrease of wintertime Arctic ice. Consequently, the world's 22,000 polar bears, along with their primary prey, the ringed seals who likewise den on sea ice, are likely to suffer localized or even overall decline. Yet the eight nations surrounding the Arctic are rushing to capitalize on the resources emerging from the ice, grabbing for a quarter of the world's undiscovered oil and natural gas; a trove of gold, diamonds, copper, and zinc; the earth's last pristine fishing grounds, which are shifting north as fish follow colder waters; and the fabled Northwest Passage and other Arctic travel routes. Even as some governments deny the existence of global warming, they are racing to map the Arctic seafloor and bolster their territorial claims for exclusive economic zones no one cared about fifteen years ago.

Reinforcing these entrepreneurial dreams is the reality of a feedback loop already in motion. Compact sea ice, with its high albedo (whiteness), reflects 80 percent of the sun's heat back into space, while seawater, with a low albedo, absorbs 80 percent. The reduction in the ratio of ice to water further increases the warming of the ocean, which rises from thermal expansion, creating an even greater surface area of water, which promotes further warming and further melting, nibbling away at even more sea ice. In other words, the melting will be difficult if not impossible to reverse anytime soon.

Along with thermal expansion, melting ice also adds freshwater to the ocean. Until recently, many researchers believed this freshening would have a negligible impact on sea levels or ocean chemistry. But the effects are proving unpredictable. In the Antarctic peninsula, lubricated by summer temperatures registering 3.6 degrees Fahrenheit warmer than forty years ago, ancient ice shelves are disintegrating, enabling the glaciers behind them to surge into the sea with a rapidity startling to scientists. Consequently, fears are growing that if the west Antarctic ice sheet, currently contained by the Ronne and Ross ice shelves, ever surges, it would raise sea levels by as much as twenty-three feet worldwide.

Curry's work aboard *Oceanus* is part of a five-year study monitoring the ocean conveyor belt and its reaction to the freshening ocean. In a 2005 paper published in *Science,* she calculates that 4,558 cubic miles of freshwater from rivers and ice melt have been added to the cold waters between Labrador and northern Europe since 1965. Based on the trends of the past forty years, it would take another hundred years of similar freshening to shut down a critical element of the ocean conveyor belt known as the Atlantic meridional overturning circulation (MOC), the primary heat transport mechanism that awards northern Europe a climate more like that of New England than Alaska—Europe's latitudinal counterpart.

Add enough warming, evaporation, and freshwater, however, and there is potential for enormous change on an accelerated schedule, including the possibility that the Atlantic MOC could shut down faster than expected, which would make Europe colder, possibly cold enough to grow new glaciers. Hollywood sensationalized this scenario in the film *The Day After Tomorrow* and was widely accused of scaremongering. Yet John Schellnhuber, research director of the Tyndall Centre for Climate Change Research in the United Kingdom, calls the Atlantic MOC one of the earth's most critical tipping points, which, if triggered, could initiate rapid changes across the entire planet.

No one knows if we're instigating another ice age. But we do know that the tropical ocean is saltier than it was forty years ago, and the polar ocean fresher. Furthermore, this salinity differential accelerates the earth's freshwater cycle, creating faster rates of evaporation and precipitation, which release more water vapor into the atmosphere, thereby increasing the greenhouse effect and invigorating the global warming that caused the whole problem in the first place.

Curry and I share the two bunks in the chief scientist's cabin, distinct from the other berths aboard by the presence of a private head and shower. She has refreshed our tiny corner of the ship with a cheerful string of white Christmas lights, an antidote to the overhead fluorescents. Curry doesn't spend much time below, however, even though most of the science team members, when not on their twelve-hour watches, are bunked out, hoping for unconsciousness. Curry is usually on station in the dry lab, a space kept water-free to protect sensitive scientific equipment, where she straddles a chair strapped to the counter while working on a laptop secured with a rope tied in half hitches.

She will celebrate her forty-eighth birthday aboard during this trip, though she looks years younger. Fit, with a runner's frame, long blond hair, and steady blue eyes, she is the Hollywood ideal of a female scientist. Yet she possesses the keen mind the movies never capture, and she bears the weight of responsibility of managing a $300,000 research cruise in bad weather. Already she has been forced to reverse the order in which *Oceanus* normally visits each of the twenty-two stations on the transect. And already she's suspended deck operations for one critical night, when huge waves washed aboard in the darkness, swamping her to her waist and knocking her off her feet, nearly sweeping her overboard. When I ask why she doesn't use lifelines on deck, she says the risk of entanglement in the equipment is greater than the benefit of staying tethered to the ship.

"If we can't do deck ops, there's not much else to do out here. I can't write code aboard," she tells me almost apologetically, as she crawls into her bunk. "I'm too brain dead at sea for that." She is asleep within seconds.

In fact, we're all dullards out here, drugged, sleep-deprived, exhausted by the constant bodily compensations of pitch, roll, and yaw. I've combined two powerful seasickness meds, something no doctor would recommend, a strategy that awarded me an hour or two in a strange Quaalude-like realm where I had to remind myself to breathe. But I'm on my feet now, or rather on my backside, wedged into a stuffed chair in the *Oceanus* library and chuckling helplessly at cartoons in *The Prehistory of the Far Side*.

"Do you want to work?" Curry prompts. "I'm short crew." Suddenly

I'm on deck ops, geared up with hard hat, foul-weather gear, life vest, and steel-toed rubber deck boots, crouched on the starboard deck, where unpredictable waves wash over the rail and swamp us to our ankles, knees, or waists.

We are tending the workhorse of oceanography, a 5.5-foot-tall contraption known as a CTD, or conductivity-temperature-depth profiler, a collection of twenty-one four-liter Niskin bottles made from sewer-grade PVC, arranged in a rosette and mounted to a stainless steel circular frame. The package also contains an LADCP, or lowered acoustic Doppler current profiler, which records water velocity. At each of our twenty-two stops, the package is launched overboard and sent to the bottom, transmitting data to onboard computers eleven times a second along its route. On its return, a science tech commands the winch operator to halt the ascent so she can trigger each of the Niskin bottles to open and close their lids, capturing water samples from a variety of predetermined depths.

Dry, the entire CTD rig weighs about 700 pounds; wet and fully loaded, up to 1,800 pounds. To manage it, *Oceanus* carries a hydrographic boom amidships, complete with 30,000 feet of coaxial cable. Launching and retrieving in heavy seas requires phenomenal skill and coordination among crews working on three different decks: the bridge crew up top, the winch operator on the middle deck, and the bosun and whatever science crew are manning the gaffs and lines to steady the CTD as it comes and goes on the main deck. Using only *Oceanus'* single screw and a bow thruster, the bridge must hold the ship steady in twenty-foot seas while ensuring the streaming cable does not contact, and thereby slice through, the steel hull. The work requires finesse and boldness, and Curry, a fearless pro in a seagoing world largely ruled by men, clearly thrives on its rewards.

Adding to these perils is the fact that as the CTD descends, it enters a series of water masses of different density gradients. These are the underwater layers of the ocean conveyor belt, each flowing like a powerful river with its own direction and velocity—a reality made obvious topside when suddenly the cable whips through the water as if hooked to a giant fighting fish.

Curry calls it blue-collar oceanography, and the basics of it—big ships, GPS, depth finders, gyrocompasses, winches, cranes, and miles of cable—are the stuff of modern seafaring, whether for science, transport, harvest, or plunder. Technology drives human effort in the sea the way the wind once did, allowing us to access remote realms for extended periods with such proficiency that in the course of one human lifetime we have learned to pirate every molecule of the sea's supposedly inexhaustible worth.

The technologies we use aboard *Oceanus* are the same employed by at least some of the 4 million commercial fishing vessels plying the ocean at any given moment. Not long ago, the growth of seagoing technologies paralleled the growth in the annual global fish harvest. But 2000 marked a decisive turning point when the global wild fish catch, which grew 500 percent between 1950 and 1997, peaked at 96 million tons despite better technologies and intensified efforts by fishers. Thereafter it has fallen by more than 3 percent per capita a year, declining to thirty-one pounds per capita in 2003, a rate last seen forty years ago. Even more alarming, a 2001 reassessment published in *Nature* suggests the annual catch has actually been falling far longer, about 400,000 tons a year since 1988, a fact concealed by China's misreporting of its annual catch.

Paradoxically, fishing has become so efficient as to be supremely inefficient. One of the biggest culprits is long-lining, in which a single boat sets monofilament line across sixty or more miles of ocean, each bearing vertical gangion lines that dangle at different depths, baited with up to 10,000 hooks designed to catch a variety of pelagic (open ocean) species. Each year, an estimated 2 billion longline hooks are set worldwide primarily for tuna and swordfish—though long-liners inadvertently kill far more other species that take the bait, including some 40,000 sea turtles, 300,000 seabirds, and millions of sharks annually. Thrown dead or dying back into the ocean, these unwanted species (bycatch) make up at least 25 percent of the global catch, perhaps as much as 88 billion pounds of life a year.

All told, pelagic longlines are the most widely used fishing gear on earth, and are deployed in all the oceans except the circum-polar seas. But whereas they once caught ten fish per hundred hooks set, today they are lucky to catch one, evidence the seas are running dry. Abetting their destructiveness are the trawl fisheries, which drag nets across every square inch of the bottom of the continental shelves every two years, trawling some regions many times a season. By razing vital benthic (seafloor) ecosystems, trawlers—the brutal equivalent of fishing the seafloor with bulldozers—level an area 150 times larger than the total area of forests clear-cut on land each year.

Adding to longlines and trawlers is the technology of drift nets, the nearly invisible curtains of monofilament blindsiding the life of the ocean. In the North Atlantic, shark and monkfish nets up to 150 miles long are set 1,600 feet below the surface, then left untended to sail and randomly ensnare life. In the course of operations in stormy seas, many nets are lost or abandoned—though they continue to fill with prey, which attracts predators, which likewise become trapped, die, and decay, attracting more predators. Composed of nonbiodegradable synthetics, deepwater ghost nets fish with nightmarish efficiency for years.

Fishing provides a vivid illustration of the differences in our attitudes toward the land and the sea. Nowadays we refrain from indiscriminately mowing down wildlife for food; imagine slaughtering lions by the hundreds or bears by the hundredweight, along with all the antelope, deer, wolves, raccoons, and wildebeest around them, in government-funded operations, no less. Yet that's what we do at sea, with the world's nations subsidizing 25–40 percent of total global fishing revenues. The National Marine Fisheries Service estimates that $8 billion in revenue and 300,000 jobs could be created simply by better management of U.S. fish stocks, not by continuing subsidies of fishers, their boats, and their gear.

Despite its promise, aquaculture is no better, since three pounds of wild fish are caught to feed every pound of farmed salmon sent to market—creating entirely new fisheries, which deplete hitherto unscathed wild fish populations, including krill, a critical cornerstone of the marine food web and essential to the survival of Antarctic species such as penguins. Furthermore, farmed salmon become severely contaminated by pollutants in their feed chow; some European aquacultured salmon is so badly tainted that people have been advised to consume it only once every five months.

The truth is that the full consequences of modern fishing methods are brutal and far-reaching, and they were not really understood before the release of a seminal study published in 2003, detailing how industrialized fisheries, in a manner akin to virulent pathogens, typically reduce the community of large fish by 80 percent within the first fifteen years of exploitation. Coauthors Boris Worm and Ransom Myers of Dalhousie University in Nova Scotia concluded that in the wake of decades of such onslaughts, only 10 percent of all large fish (tuna, swordfish, marlin) and groundfish (cod, halibut, skate, and flounder) are left anywhere in the ocean. Their study was based on factors modern fisheries managers ignore: historical data; in this case, the catch reports from Japanese long-liners dating from the 1950s, when the global tuna catch was less than 500,000 tons, compared with 3.7 million tons today.

Apparently no one really remembers how many big fish used to inhabit the sea or how big they got. "The few blue marlin left today," says Myers, "reach one-fifth of the weight they once had. In many cases, the fish caught today are under such intense fishing pressure, they never even have the chance to reproduce." The pressure stems from a combination of economics (a single large bluefin tuna can command $100,000 on the Tokyo fish market) and ever-evolving technologies, and this scenario plagues the oceans: The more rare and endangered a species, the more money it generates and the more people who are willing to pursue it. While rich fishers pursue dwindling species with the aid of technology, poor fishers do it through brutal ingenuity, including using poison and explosives, leading to what's known as Malthusian overfishing—when a fishery is overwhelmed yet fishing continues anyway, in ever more destructive and desperate ways, until the complete decimation of species and their ecosystems. Poor fishers do this largely to meet the demand of rich nations—to supply aquarium fish for the United States and live food fish for Hong Kong. Since demand grows in direct relationship to a species' decline, many fish are targeted during their spawning aggregations, thus wiping out entire adult populations along with all their potential progeny. In this way, some coral reef species have been locally extinguished in the course of only one or two spawning events.

The past has much to teach us about what we've forgotten. By analyzing 10,000 historical restaurant menus from Boston to San Francisco, a project called the History of Marine Animal Populations, out of the University of Southern Denmark, finds that lobster was so abundant in the nineteenth century that middle-class Americans snubbed it as food for the poor. Likewise, the day may be near when Hemingway's *The Old Man and the Sea* is seen less as a story of Santiago's plight than of a mighty fish that once roamed the seas and no longer does.

It used to be, in the heyday of wildlife filmmaking, that you could chum off the California coast for a few hours or a day or two and attract dozens of full-size (8 foot) blue sharks, along with a gaggle of youngsters and the occasional, powerful (10 foot) mako or two. But the last time I tried this, only two baby blue sharks, all of four feet long, appeared after days of chumming. In the interval between 1980, when cameramen were forced to work with safety divers to fend off more sharks than they knew what to do with, and 1991, when we were obliged to film the baby sharks close-up with wide-angle lenses to make them look bigger, long-liners, trawlers, and drift netters came to the West Coast.

Sharks are killed incidentally in large numbers by all three forms of industrial fishing, but they are also targeted by their own fishery, primarily for soup. Once a rarefied foodstuff of the elite, today shark fin soup is an affordable luxury for the Chinese nouveau riche who wish to prove their wealth by ordering a $100 bowl of glutinous cartilage flavored with chicken broth. At expensive eateries across Asia, middle-class diners slurp this pricey food, even as the World Conservation Union adds ever more shark species to its red list of threatened species.

Fishing fleets kill an estimated 100 million sharks per year across the globe. In the Gulf of Mexico, the number of oceanic whitetip sharks has plunged 99 percent since the 1950s, driving this once common pelagic species into virtual extinction. A study of the North Atlantic found that overall shark populations have declined more than 50 percent since 1986. Sadly, sharks are slow breeders, with most delivering small litters (some only twins) after reaching a late sexual maturity (some at 25 years old), after which they typically deliver litters at three-year intervals. The results of such slow reproduction make recovery from overfishing notoriously difficult. When porbeagle sharks were overfished by Europeans in the 1960s, the species struggled for the next thirty years, finally achieving some semblance of health in the 1990s, only to become the target of U.S. and Canadian fleets that fished it into commercial extinction in three short years.

The end of big fish in the sea is more than an aesthetic loss. Marine ecologist Mark Hixon of Oregon State University has published widely on coral reef ecosystems, and his work illustrates how biodiversity and community stability thrive in the presence of predators and competitors. The removal of either or both destabilizes the remaining species. Hence big sharks, tuna, swordfish, and halibut are more than picturesque giants; they are keystone species that play greater roles in maintaining ecosystem function than seems obvious based on the size of their population.

Hixon also argues that not all spawners are created equal, and that the most valuable members of fish populations are what he and his colleagues call the big old fat female fish (BOFFFs), who produce eggs of better quality and greater quantity than younger females. Yet fisheries managers continue to target older fish, followed by younger fish, until none can grow old. "This means that BOFFFs are disappearing," says Hixon. "Here on the West Coast, seven out of seventeen well-assessed species of rockfish have been declared overfished since 1999, and we believe that at least part of the explanation for these stock collapses is the result of our failure to appreciate the value of big old fat female fish."

Hixon tells me that we need a Kuhnian paradigm shift in fisheries management. "Current managers learned single-species management, and they're resistant to changing that, even though it seldom works." A scientific consensus signed by him and 218 other scientists and policy experts pleads for an updated approach: "From a scientific perspective, we now know enough to improve dramatically the conservation and management of marine systems through the implementation of ecosystem-based approaches."

As on land, protecting places is the best way to preserve life. In 2003, the World Conservation Union listed 102,102 protected areas on earth. But only 4,116 of these were protected marine areas, preserving less than 0.5 percent of the world ocean, whereas 11.5 percent of the land surface has been granted some form of sanctuary. To reach parity, we need to add twenty-three times as many marine reserves and offshore national parks, or ten times more total area—and perhaps even more, since the liquid medium of the ocean is more interconnected, and the fate of its disparate realms more intertwined than here.

Rachel Carson wrote of the sea that "in its mysterious past it encompasses all the dim origins of life and receives in the end, after, it may be, many transmutations, the dead husks of that same life. For all at last return to the sea—to *Oceanus*, the ocean river." We return to the sea, too, in various husks, including in the form of atmospheric emissions. Sweden, for example, calculates that its populace of 8.9 million carries 2.8 tons of mercury fillings in their mouths, most of which is destined eventually to go airborne in crematoriums.

Crematory emissions are a small but growing percentage of the total global mercury pollution, the vast majority of which enters the food web as a biologically active derivative of the inorganic mercury released by the smokestacks of the coal and chlorine industries. Oxidized in the atmosphere and piggybacking on raindrops, this form of mercury eventually settles to the bottom of oceans and lakes, where it is converted to dangerous methyl mercury by aquatic bacteria, which are eaten by plankton, which are eaten by fish, and bigger fish—with each subsequent meal bioaccumulating in higher levels until apex predators such as tuna and whales carry mercury levels as much as 1 million times higher than the waters around them.

As do we. Epidemiological studies show that mercury levels among Arctic peoples are high enough to cause neurobehavioral effects, while a Hong Kong study revealed that 10 percent of the region's high school students suffer mercury poisoning from eating tuna and swordfish. The European Union warns pregnant women to limit their consumption of both tuna and swordfish because of brain damage to their unborn children, and the U.S. Food and Drug Administration warns pregnant women, lactating women, and young children not to eat swordfish, shark, tilefish, or king mackerel, though the powerful tuna lobby succeeded in keeping tuna off that list. The EPA now estimates at least one in eight American women of childbearing age has unsafe levels of mercury in her blood, and as many as 600,000 of the 4 million babies born in the United States in 2000 were exposed to unacceptable levels because their mothers ate a diet rich in fish (in a continuation of bioaccumulation, the level of mercury in a fetus' blood can be 70 percent higher than its mother's). Yet the Bush administration, circumventing the Clean Air Act, has enabled coal-fired power plants to delay curtailing significant mercury emissions until 2018.

It's midnight over the Gulf of Mexico, the skies stripped of clouds and glittering with stars as 25-knot winds blow down from the north. For most of the residents of the bayou country of southern Louisiana, these are welcome winds; only a month has passed since Hurricane Katrina made landfall, and eleven days since Hurricane Rita, and these northerlies are cold and dry enough to dismantle any additional tropical storms from the top down. It's also blowing sufficiently hard that Captain Craig LeBoeuf decides to sail *R/V Pelican* through the Intracoastal Waterway and out into the Gulf at Morgan City, so that dawn will light our way along the shallow shelf where more than 100 hurricane-broken oil rigs and drilling structures foul the waters.

This once was one of the most prolific bodies of water on earth, a place where the outflow from the Mississippi River introduced freshwater nutrients into a deepwater environment. But long before Katrina, the Gulf had become one of the world's most polluted marine ecosystems, with mercury loads among the highest ever recorded, including levels in blue marlin thirty times above what the EPA deems safe for human consumption. An average of ten tons of mercury comes down the Mississippi every year, with close to another ton added by the offshore drilling industry. Equally alarming, a sizable portion of the Gulf is so biologically dysfunctional on a seasonal basis that it's known as a dead zone—the largest such area in the United States and the second largest on the planet, measuring nearly 8,000 square miles in 2001, an area larger than New Jersey.

Dead zones occur wherever oceanic oxygen is depleted below the level necessary to sustain marine life, a result of eutrophication, or the release of excess nutrients into the sea, usually from agricultural fertilizers. Fifty years ago no one imagined that the green revolution would prove so lethal to the world ocean. But now we know that chemical fertilizers cause plants to bloom in the sea as miraculously as they do on land, with deadly consequence. It's no coincidence that almost all of the nearly 150 (and counting) dead zones on earth lie at the mouths of rivers.

The Gulf of Mexico suffers the downstream effects of the mighty Mississippi, which drains 41 percent of the contiguous United States, including all the intensively farmed breadbasket. This outflow delivers enough nitrogen to stimulate explosions of plankton and microalgae, some of which form the red tides that produce major fish kills and dolphin or manatee die-offs. At even higher densities, as these plankton die en masse and settle to the bottom, they fuel a bloom of bacterial decomposers, which consume all the available oxygen in the water. The resulting condition, known as hypoxia, strikes the Gulf whenever oxygen levels fall below two milligrams per liter—an annual summertime event in the warming waters of the Gulf since the 1970s. For sea life, it's as if all the air were suddenly sucked out of the world. Those creatures that can swim or walk away fast enough may survive. Those that can't, die.

Nancy Rabalais shows me around *Pelican*'s home in Cocodrie, in far southern Louisiana. Three months ago, as the newly appointed executive director of Louisiana Universities Marine Consortium (LUMCON), she took the helm of this 75,000-square-foot complex of laboratories, teaching facilities, apartments, offices, and seagoing vessels. So far her tenure has been largely spent digging out of the mud, repairing the wind damage, and casting an eye to the weather. "This used to be a beautiful place," she says of the striking waterfront facility built on stilts. Now it's boarded up with storm shutters and surrounded by bulldozers, piles of garbage, stacks of dismantled roofing, stripped palm trees, and muck. Only the estuarine wetlands all around seem untouched, lovely, given that hurricanes are a familiar part of their evolutionary world.

Rabalais is weary. It's late. She still has a two-hour drive ahead of her to Baton Rouge, where she teaches at Louisiana State University—though I suspect she would rather board *Pelican* for a couple of days and leave her worries behind. Instead, she's relying on her research associates and graduate students to conduct the scientific cruise she normally looks forward to each month. A Texan by birth and schooling, she has been diving these waters since it was a fun thing to do; nowadays it requires a certain courage. A week earlier, while diving in zero visibility on a research station twenty-six miles offshore, Rabalais encountered an alligator at the surface blown out to sea by one or both of the hurricanes. Diving to the bottom, she "felt something bump against my ankle. But I figured a gator wasn't diving sixty-five feet deep, so it must have been something else."

Rabalais calls the Gulf of Mexico hypoxic zone the poster child of dead zones because it's been so well documented by herself and others over the past twenty years. Oddly, it acts like a living thing: growing in spring, thriving in summer, decaying in fall, gaining in size almost every year. Core sediment samples and computer hindcasting pinpoint its birth date to the aftermath of World War II, when a surplus of nitrogen destined for TNT was redeployed as agricultural fertilizer.

By one o'clock the next afternoon, we've already visited four of the seven stations on the day's transect, launching and retrieving the CTD in quick time because water depths here are rarely more than 180 feet. Along with collecting conductivity, temperature, and depth data, Rabalais' crew aboard the *Pelican* is also conducting HPLC (high performance liquid chromatography) analysis: quantifying and separating pigments, which indicate chlorophyll and hence phytoplankton abundance. The six young men and women work efficiently, hurrying back to the mess deck between workstations, where the satellite TV plays back-to-back college football games.

But for a first-time visitor to the northern Gulf of Mexico, this is far too fascinating a world, in a futuristic kind of way, to ignore. The horizon in all directions is dotted with what from a distance look like small mangrove islands. Only these are oil and liquid natural gas rigs, with all their attendant satellites. At any given time, at least fifty structures punctuate the horizon, and often more than one hundred. When we draw close, they prove enormous. Servicing them are countless powerful and speedy crew boats, most bigger and faster than *Pelican*, along with a constant fleet of helicopters in flight between rigs. Although we're out of sight of land, there is no silence and no hint of wilderness anywhere. This is an urban ocean, the first I've ever seen.

Even more strange is the lack of visible sea life. Generally, in waters this far from shore yet still atop the productive continental shelf, we'd be seeing feeding aggregations of seabirds, fish, billfish, sharks, and marine mammals. But here there is only emptiness and the occasional bobbing flight of a laughing gull. It's the same underwater, apparently, only there's not enough visibility to actually see it; sometimes, according to Rabalais, when the water is clear and the hypoxia is in full swing, the bottom is full of decaying sea life.

And this is only one of many dead zones. Robert Diaz, a hypoxia expert from the Virginia Institute of Marine Science, calculates the global number is doubling every decade. Furthermore, he suggests that at least in some areas hypoxia is rapidly becoming a greater threat to fish stocks than overfishing, since it disperses them off their feeding, spawning, and maturation grounds. And he predicts that hypoxic zones will only increase as the ocean warms further, citing a modeling study predicting that a doubling of atmospheric carbon dioxide will double rainfall across the Mississippi River basin, increasing runoff by 20 percent and decreasing dissolved oxygen in the northern Gulf by up to 60 percent.

Close to fifty hypoxic zones fester on the coasts of the continental United States, affecting half of all our estuaries. The situation is worse in Europe, with fourteen persistent dead zones that never go away, and almost forty others occurring annually, the biggest and worst being the 27,000-square-mile persistent dead zone in the Baltic Sea, which is nearly the size of South Carolina. Not all of these are caused by river-borne nitrogen. Fossil fuel-burning plants along the Ohio River loft airborne emissions that help create hypoxic conditions in the Chesapeake Bay and Long Island Sound. Excess phosphorus from human sewage, as well as nitrogen emissions from automobile exhaust, impact Tampa Bay. Other dead zones suffer from the nitrogen fixation produced by leguminous crops.

Interestingly, we know how to solve these problems. Rabalais and others have engineered an action plan that calls for the reduction of the Gulf hypoxic zone to just under 2,000 square miles by 2015. "There are modeling studies that show if you reduce nitrogen fertilizer applications by 12 to 14 percent, you can reach the target without losing crop production. And there are lots of ways to reduce," she says, listing best management practices such as a reduction in fossil fuel use, cleaner municipal wastewater discharge, restoring wetlands, regulating pen-feed operations, and banning wintertime fertilizer applications.

The problem is, most of these changes need to take place six hundred or more miles upstream and be agreed on by dozens of headstrong states. "We're moving slowly," Rabalais admits. "Five years into the process, we're finding that we haven't really done a whole lot, and there's a lot of resistance from the large agricultural and fertilizer corporations." At best, it will take years to revitalize the dead zone. Meanwhile, as we dither, the target drifts farther away; European studies of fallow fields show that leaching of nitrogen continues decades after cropping and fertilizing have ceased.

In the liquid realm offshore, change is more fluid than here on the land. I got a sense of this years ago, while diving the pristine reefs along the edge of the Gulf Stream in the Bahamas, where I began to notice the corals strangling under the spread of gauzy marine plants. With each passing year, the reefs became more populated with filamentous algae and contained fewer live corals, fish, and invertebrates. Today I can date the film footage in my library by the obvious decline of biodiversity on those reefs.

These changes coincided with the unprecedented die-off of the once populous sea urchin *Diadema antillarum*. Beginning in 1983 in Panama, these pincushion-like creatures began to succumb to an unidentified pathogen, dying within days of exposure. Over the next thirteen months, following surface currents, the mortality spread eastward and northward, encompassing the entire Gulf of Mexico, the Caribbean, and the tropical Atlantic to Bermuda, 2,500 miles from onset. No known New World population was left intact, and up to 99 percent of these sea urchins died in the worst marine invertebrate epidemic ever seen—possibly due to infection by spore-bearing bacteria traveling through the Panama Canal from the Pacific.

In the wake of the epidemic, filamentous algae, which the sea urchins ate, exploded across the reefs. St. Croix saw a 27 percent increase in algal biomass within five days of the sea urchin die-off. In the course of two years, Jamaica's reefs increased in algal cover from 1 percent up to 95 percent. More algae left less room for new coral colonies to recruit; twenty-three years later, the reefs of the region still echo with the effects, appearing so radically redesigned that many no longer exist as coral-dominated systems at all but as seaweed-dominant systems akin to farms of undersea lettuce. Even more significant, these changes appear to be permanent, since the primary surviving predators of the filamentous algae—herbivorous fishes—have been, and continue to be, extensively overfished by humans in the region. *Diadema antillarum* has not recovered either, a victim apparently of too few animals scattered over too wide an area to effectively spawn.

Across the world ocean, marine diseases are on the rise, fueled by, among other things, the desertification of Africa, which raises huge volumes of dust that off-loads bacterial and fungal spores into the weakened seas. Many coral diseases have appeared more frequently in the past ten years, including white-band disease, black-band disease, dark-spots disease, red-band disease, white plague, white pox, yellow blotch disease, and so on. Photographs of reefs from the 1930s show little or none of these infestations.

With or without pestilences, coral reefs are under assault, and the exhaustive 2004 *Status of Coral Reefs of the World* warns that global warming is the single greatest threat to corals, with 20 percent of the world's reefs so badly damaged they are unlikely to recover and another 50 percent teetering on the edge. Within the next fifty years, massive coral bleaching events on the order of the 1998 El Niño, which damaged or destroyed 16 percent of the world's reefs, will become regular, possibly annual occurrences. Sadly, most of the so-called nurseries of the sea face similar prognoses. Fifteen percent of the world's seagrass beds have disappeared in the past ten years alone, depriving marine species—from juvenile fish and invertebrates to dugongs, manatees, and sea turtles—of critical habitats. Likewise, kelp beds are dying at alarming rates; 75 percent are gone from Southern California alone—victims of, among other things, the demise of sea otters that regulate populations of kelp-eating sea urchins.

Among the most frightening news for coral reefs is the increasing acidity of the ocean as a result of rising levels of carbon dioxide. Scientists at the National Oceanic and Atmospheric Administration recently estimated the ocean has absorbed 118 billion metric tons of CO_2 since the onset of the industrial revolution—about half of the total we've released into the atmosphere—with 20 to 25 million more tons being added daily. This mitigation of CO_2 is good for our atmosphere but bad for our ocean, since it changes the pH. Studies indicate that the shells and skeletons possessed by everything from reef-building corals to mollusks to plankton begin to dissolve within forty-eight hours of exposure to the acidity expected in the ocean by 2050.

Coral reefs, buffeted by so many stressors, will almost certainly disappear. But the loss of plankton is even more worrisome. Collectively, marine phytoplankton have influenced life on earth more than any other organism, since they are significant alleviators of greenhouse gases, major manufacturers of oxygen, and the primary producers of the marine food web. Yet because many phytoplankton produce minute aragonite shells, these pastures of the sea may not survive changing pH levels. Zooplankton, meanwhile, are largely composed of the larval forms of all the ocean's other life forms—from fish to squid to shellfish—whose calcium carbonate constructions are also unlikely to survive changed pH levels. By facilitating radical changes in these, the immense populations of the very small, we might as well erase the world as we know it, one bone, one seashell at a time.

Years ago, while I was filming aboard a small sailboat in the Turks and Caicos Islands, someone on the crew found a message in a bottle floating miles from any land. Since we did not readily have the means to open the barnacle-encrusted cap, the skipper took it to the stern of the boat, steadied his aim against the rocking of the waves, and with one blow from a hammer knocked the glass neck off. Four of us crowded close, yet none could catch the paper as it accidentally slipped overboard. Four of us dove in, but none could find the note in the currents swirling underwater.

As matters stand, we miss many messages, even those that wash ashore. Walk any beach these days and you'll likely find miniature SOS signals littering the tide line: seabirds drowned in fishing nets, plastic flotsam, globules of oil, castaway cargo from containers lost overboard. Seek in the waters just offshore and you may well find male fish bearing eggs or ovary tissue, the unfortunate results of living near sewage outflows, where chemicals, including the copious quantities of pharmaceuticals inhabiting our bodies, flow to the sea. Despite the ocean's fetch, there is no place on it where our impact is not seen, felt, or heard.

Noise is our newest assault, including the low-frequency active (LFA) sonar used by the military to detect submarines and by the oil and gas industry to search for fossil fuels. The loudest sound ever put into the seas, LFA sonar could soon be deployed across 80 percent of the world ocean, at an amplitude of 230 decibels, strident enough to kill whales and dolphins and already causing mass strandings and deaths in areas where navies conduct exercises. A few people misfortunate enough to be in the water near LFA sonar tests have suffered lung vibrations, seizures, disorientation, and nausea. No one knows what effects these extreme noises have on the majority of marine life that "see" underwater with their acoustical senses.

Meanwhile, plastic pollutants masquerade as familiar marine objects. David Barnes of the British Antarctic Survey finds that invertebrates which normally hitch rides on floating wood or pumice are increasingly grabbing lifts on floating plastics; the presence of so many new "boats" has doubled the spread of exotic species in the subtropics and more than tripled it at high latitudes, threatening biodiversity worldwide. Furthermore, fish and invertebrates commonly mistake the ubiquitous pellets of partially degraded plastic, "nurdles," for zooplankton and ingest them, poisoning themselves and all who eat them, while sea turtles and marine mammals perish from consuming plastic bags, which resemble jellyfish.

Increasingly, persistent organic pollutants (POPs) such as DDT and PCBs are being found in such high levels in marine animals that some living creatures meet our definitions of toxic waste, including many whales, dolphins, and seals. Female mammals off-load POPs in their breast milk, lessening their own toxic load while poisoning their children. Perhaps consequently, killer whale calves from Puget Sound and the Canadian southwest are dying in the first year; adult male orca, which have no off-loading capabilities, are also dying off. In 2005, the National Marine Fisheries Service listed this population as endangered. Currently there is no such listing for the people who rely on marine mammal meat, even though the accumulation of POPs in the tissues of Greenland Inuits has nearly reached levels known to suppress the immune system.

The problems facing the world ocean are virtually all human-induced, and many are beginning to cross-pollinate. Jellyfish populations expand in response to red tides and hypoxia, as well as to the depletion of their competitors, such as menhaden. This, combined with the virtual extinction of jellyfish-eating sea turtles (leatherbacks have declined 97 percent in 22 years), leaves more food for those jellies that prey mostly on other jellyfish. Thus the nearly independent jelly web is expanding—and increasing its impact on human fishers, including forcing the closure of the Gulf of Mexico shrimp fishery in 2000, when twenty-five-pound jellyfish native to Australia swarmed so heavily that shrimpers were unable to retrieve their nets.

In a similar vortex of cause and effect, researchers from NASA and the

U.S. Geological Survey forecast that Alaskan earthquakes will increase in the wake of retreating glaciers, triggering more tsunamis, as happened dramatically in similar warmer epochs of the past. Freed of the immense weight of these rivers of ice, tectonic stresses are released, sometimes for the first time in millennia. Many scientists also believe that a warmer ocean is making hurricanes bigger, faster growing, and stronger; in 2005 Hurricane Wilma prompted a call for a new Category 6 on the Saffir-Simpson scale, or a new scale altogether. And because bigger storms destroy more coastal wetlands and mangrove forests, they also incidentally reduce the land's natural buffering against storms and earthquake-generated tsunamis.

Even as we spend millions looking to space for dangerous asteroids that might threaten all life on earth, we are the asteroid that has already landed. A modeling study from the National Center for Atmospheric Research in Colorado suggests that global warming, not an asteroid strike, triggered the earth's most severe extinction event 251 million years ago during the Permian-Triassic era, long before the dinosaur die-off. Atmospheric CO_2, fueled by massive earth-building volcanic eruptions in Siberia, warmed the ocean to depths of 10,000 feet, increasing salinity, shutting down the ocean conveyor belt, and trapping oxygen and nutrients so deep that most of the world ocean became a hypoxic dead zone. With hardly any sea life left to scrub the atmosphere of carbon dioxide, global warming accelerated. In the end, the Great Dying came close to destroying all life on earth, precipitating the demise of 95 percent of all marine species and 70 percent of all terrestrial vertebrates, leaving fungi to rule the world for many an eon.

At no time in human history has so much scientific inquiry been focused so intensively in one direction: on the anthropogenic changes in our world. As a result, we are learning more, and more quickly than ever before, about how the life-support systems of earth work. Science now recognizes that the ocean is not just a pretty vista or a distant horizon but the vital circulatory, respiratory, and reproductive organs of our planet, and that these biological systems are suffering. Much effective treatment is suggested by computer-modeling studies, which the Bush administration, with its fear of science, negates—even though computer models are the same powerful tools that enable us to put men into space, to run wars, and to forecast financial trends.

Back aboard *Oceanus* in the stormy North Atlantic, we've reached the Gulf Stream at last, where the seas have stretched out with the increased depth, easing our ride a little. Surrounded on every horizon by menacing black skies, complete with downpours and bolts of lightning, we bask for an hour or two in a spotlight of sunshine that illuminates the endless cobalt of the deep, the platinum spray of the surface. Three of us—Ruth Curry, Guy Mathieu, and I—are out on deck tending the CTD, which has just returned from its four-hour journey to the bottom of the ocean. Mathieu, a retired scientist with the Lamont-Doherty Earth Observatory, is collecting samples from the Niskin bottles for analysis of their chlorofluorocarbons—those synthetic chemicals in refrigerants and aerosols so damaging to the earth's ozone layer, yet so useful as tracers for measuring the timescale of movements within the ocean conveyor belt.

Curry taps the bottles for oxygen analysis, and I follow up collecting salinity samples. Although conditions are wet, rough, and slippery, we smile, enjoying our time on deck. Five hundred miles from land, we are deep inside the embrace of the ocean, and as we work, we are touching water that an hour or two ago rode the Deep Western Boundary Current 17,000 feet deep, headed for Antarctica. The sea, always a place of awe, is made even more awe inspiring by the feel of its cold, buried tides.

In late 2005 a British oceanographic team, conducting research similar to Curry's, announced findings that the Atlantic MOC—the critical factor keeping the North Atlantic warm—has slowed by 30 percent. Although the surface Gulf Stream apparently still flows as usual, the deeper waters are undergoing massive, silent changes, with virtually all of these shifts rapidly taking place since 1998.

But aboard *Oceanus*, this news is still six weeks in the future, and we are happy, at least in this moment, to be at sea in bad conditions collecting good data that may well lead to bad news. The tempest around us is beautiful yet seemingly manageable—until the winds, whistling steadily at forty knots, increase sharply, ripping off the whole surface of the sea, not just the tops of the swells. The whistling grows ominously louder and splits into harmonics of deeper- and higher-pitched voices. Literally over our heads, the low pressure storm systems have merged, and within the hour we're running south as fast as *Oceanus* will go.

No one who survives time at sea is ever less than humbled by its power over life.

II

CONSUMING CULTURE

Chris Jordan, Radio

6

Consuming the Culture of SUVs

Through careful marketing design, the automobile has become inextricably bound into the American identity. One of the most successful advertising campaigns in recent history, for instance, promises American consumers a kind of frontier experience, the potential to tame a wilderness through the purchase of a sport utility vehicle. As such commercials pull on our heartstrings, they obscure the human and environmental resources that went into producing the vehicle as well as the environmental catastrophe that piles up as the vehicle is used.

Through an analysis of magazine and newspaper advertisements since the 1990s, Paterson and Dalby demonstrate the "biopolitics of empire." The militarized politics of the "new global order" are reproduced and, to an extent, legitimized in the advertisements for SUVs that promise a similar control over terrain while providing a false sense of security, luxury, and comfort. And to bring it around full circle, the global political order, reinforced by the advertisements, is busy at the work of oil politics that materially provides for the massive energy required to keep the SUVs moving. Paterson and Dalby's study implies that the SUV, truck, or car—considered the twentieth century's most environmentally destructive technologies—is part and parcel of the imperial practices of global politics. This drama becomes comfortable and familiar to us through the popular press. In this manner the massive ecological footprint of the increasingly globalized automobile industry becomes invisible.

Matthew Paterson and Simon Dalby, "Empire's Ecological Tyreprints" (2006)[1]

> We will strike at a time and place of our choosing.
>
> —"No Boundaries," Ford Corporation

91

ADVERTISING IMPERIAL

Contemporary geopolitics provides a setting in which contemporary consumer cultures work.[2] Specifically, what many term an emerging "imperial geopolitical structure" operates as a political condition of possibility for the marketing of vehicles in particular ways. Connected to Empire's complex formation, the themes invoked in this marketing vary across its differing elements. These thematic differences can be understood through a number of distinctions: North American or European; SUV or other cars; imperial or nonimperial.

At the same time, such vehicles are themselves central to the (re)production of both the material conditions of Empire and its geopolitical identities. Contemporary consumer cultures provide a site where we can make claims about the nature of contemporary geopolitical formations. As ads invoke symbols to sell cars, the nature of such symbols can tell us something about what sort of imperial formation is in process.

Of course, cars, or perhaps more precisely automobility (Böhm et al. forthcoming) are widely recognized as important, producing a range of ecological changes and degradations (Freund and Martin 1993; Paterson 2000). Thus to interrogate car advertising in this way is to ask fundamental questions about how environmental degradation is legitimized.

Broadly, we want to read advertising for cars since the early 1990s through two distinct patterns of themes distinguishing different marketing strategies. This follows loosely the distinction in Hardt and Negri's (2000) highly contested account of Empire between its monarchical element, operating via military force, and its aristocratic element, operating via law and the regulation of capitalist reproduction (Hardt nd Negri 2000: 314–19). Loosely, the themes corresponding to the monarchical element appear predominantly in North America while its aristocratic elements are more prevalent in Europe.

Hardt and Negri are useful for us in this context not because their account is beyond reproach or critique, but for three arguments that are useful for heuristic purposes. First, they refuse to identify Empire as a geopolitical formation with a narrow account of American imperialism. Second, they argue that Empire is reproduced not only through brute force but through biopolitics, "a form of power that regulates social life from its interior. . . . Power can achieve an effective command over the entire life of the population only when it becomes an integral, vital function that every individual embraces and reactivates of his or her own accord" (Hardt and Negri 2000: 23–24). Third, they emphasize the flexible nature of imperial rule: it operates not in a uniform manner but through adaptations to local conditions. There are many critiques of Hardt and Negri, including some from explicitly green perspectives (Chaloupka 2004). But what is useful for us in this context is that a consideration of car ads shows that, despite their clear shortcomings in terms of their explicit theorization of environmental politics, their consideration of subjectivity or biopolitics enables a consideration of how Empire's politics is played out at the level of individual lives and thus the practices through which individuals are enmeshed in producing environmental degradation.

In one marketing strategy, then, advertising imagery emphasizes themes of conquest, mobility, power. Such themes routinely operate via the conquest of nature (always with North America's own imperial past and present underpinning this logic) and frequently utilize military imagery and connections between the cars and their military precursors. This is exemplified in the emergence of the SUV and associated advertising.[3]

By contrast, the marketing of many cars operates via a wider range of themes, which nevertheless we want to read as invoking elements in the formation of Empire. One dominant theme here is the intertext between the automobile and other forms of technology. These figure the car as an accomplishment of cultural sophistication (as opposed to crude force), and interpellate the reader as a subject within a relational network rather than an autonomous being in opposition to the external world.

At one level, then, these ads are designed to sell specific brands of cars. At another, they reproduce a broader consumer culture. While this is important, what we are primarily interested in here are the cultural intertexts that are drawn on in order to sell cars, not whether or not these ads actually make people behave in particular ways (buying SUVs) and with particular socio-ecological consequences (causing oil wars). Consumers of cars are nevertheless symbolically connected to, and serve to legitimate, a dominant form of geopolitics and a range of ecological consequences, which at the same time their consumption materially renders necessary.

What follows is an attempt to flesh out the above claims through a reading of magazine and newspaper ads for cars from the early 1990s through to the present time. We do not claim that this is an objective account of all car advertising in this period, but we do suggest that these ads are representative of certain genres that have been important in selling cars in this period. We do not address the intentionality of the advertisers with regard to the images we claim they portray; rather, our concern is with reading the ads themselves.[4] At least regarding the SUV ads, we do have fairly good reason to believe that the advertisers were very clear about the images they intended to portray. Clotaire Rapaille, for example, marketing adviser for Chrysler in relation to its SUV ads during the 1990s, explicitly invoked images in SUV ads suggesting that "if there's a crash, I want the other guy to die" (Bradsher 2002: 100; Gunster 2004: 15–16). First, then, the SUV ads.

CONQUERING NATURE

The big print suggests a "detailed look at the new Jeep Cherokee." Perched on a ledge overlooking a grand vista the new Jeep Grand Cherokee proudly boasts its pedigree as the latest in automotive experience. "All you have to do is drive one," according to the slogan beneath the announcement of the imminent arrival of the vehicle. The iconography is not subtle; here is a proud beast proclaiming its capabilities to all residents of the surrounding landscape. The capabilities are obvious simply from the positioning of the machine in silhouette on the side of the cliff. A visual play on the term "detail," the Jeep is the small but significant detail on the landscape that it so obviously masters. The small print of course matters less than the simplicity of the imagery; that the animal/vehicle is obviously very capable simply by its position on the landscape. But the small print focuses not only on the technicalities of how the vehicle controls and dominates its surroundings while securing the bodies inside: the temperature controls, Quadra drive, antilock brakes, and other attributes. It also emphasizes the novelty and uniqueness of these features: "the first and only" driver's side airbag in an SUV, the "revolutionary all-the-time four-wheel drive." Of course this buys into the long history of the Jeep itself, the original American SUV with an overt military origin and militarist identity. But it is also reinforced visually by the photograph which is taken at dawn, suggesting new beginnings. This imagery and the association of new beginnings are irredeemably in American discourse, Christian and millenarian; the Jeep is the bearer here of Manifest Destiny, doing God's work finding and dominating new lands in the American West. That the name Cherokee is an appropriation of a Native American name only reflects a more general pattern of such appropriation of what European colonization destroyed.

But the domination of nature is not enough; it has to be civilized. This is made unambiguously clear in the slogan that accompanies an ad for the Nissan Pathfinder: "Suddenly, even nature is more civilized."[5] The styling in the ad is aggressive and broad shouldered, but despite its retention of its rugged characteristics, the interior is unquestionably comfortable, luxurious. Thus the urban conquest of external nature is emphasized as the vehicle is pictured driving on a rural track. Ergonomic seats and sound systems, heated leather seats and automatic climate control accompany one into the wilderness ensuring the Pathfinder never leaves the luxuries of town behind.

Rugged individuals and colonial power, unrestrained freedom to go anywhere and the technical capability to accomplish all this are rolled into one package, simultaneously suggesting the necessity of escape but the importance of bringing what one is escaping with one too. Luxury and landscape combine in the perfect consumer experience powered by big engines and all-wheel drive systems. The consequences of such regal existence are never considered. The driver consumer is sovereign over the external disconnected landscapes that are there for no other purpose than to be subdued as a clear illustration of the prowess of the driver. But this is a driver unconstrained by any connection to the rest of the world, master, or possibly mistress, of all they survey. This is the quintessential imperial subject of North American aspiration, the rugged frontiersman overcoming all obstacles and becoming fulfilled in his destiny to conquer all.

A similar juxtaposition of vehicle and nature structures the advertisement for the Ford Explorer Sport Trac. Here, a moose standing beside a rural track is designated a hitchhiker. It is so far from regular roads that no human could possibly be there in search of a ride, but also you (the consumer of the Explorer) are clearly so far from regular roads that even a moose is in need of a lift. "No boundaries," the slogan of Ford's advertising campaign for its SUVs, emphasizes the capabilities of the vehicle to go anywhere and conquer any terrain because of its technical capabilities.[6] The slogan itself is produced as literally breaking through onto the page through something attempting to cover it up. Unrestrained mobility is the principal virtue exemplified by this rugged vehicle. Subsequent versions of the theme included skiers being towed up a snowy slope, and then in a marvellous piece of hubris, proud Ford Escape drivers roving the lunar surface. Once again the ability to drive unrestrained by nature suggests the acumen and accomplishment of both vehicle and driver. No boundaries suggests that there is nothing in the way of Ford SUV drivers; nowhere they cannot go. But the intertext with global politics is immediate and obvious. No boundaries invokes a globalized world where the transgression of previously impervious borders is now the norm.

The all-new Cadillac Escalade removes any doubts about the identity of this huge SUV, or about the imperial connotations of SUV advertising, when it is simply designated as "conqueror of the world." But in this case its royal pedigree is emphasized by the juxtapositions of photographs of the vehicles on a street with playing card representations of king and queen (global domination being a game, but a game of cards, rather than dominoes, which has different geopolitical imagery), and by deploying suitably royal blues, reds, and yellows. "Conqueror of the world. Kinda just rolls off the tongue." One can apparently get carried away while driving this vehicle with its huge 345 horsepower engine and the eleven speaker sound system. But domination has its downsides, or perhaps responsibilities. As it is "easy to feel invincible," "modesty" is advised "when out in public." The ad is certainly hubristic, the royal prerogatives likewise; the tropes of conquest and superiority are celebrated in this luxury SUV. Conquest imagery is written into the name of the car, which means "scaling the walls with ladders."[7]

Empire's geographical reach is emphasized in Land Rover's new Discovery, which, as well as operating in both urban and rural settings, operates throughout Europe, Africa, South Asia, and the Middle East. Indeed the

2003 version is apparently a "whole new way to see the world." The vehicle is presented in a collage of landscape settings which overlap with the vehicle itself, suggesting with considerably less bravado than Ford that no boundaries apply to a discoverer. Rather, the image presents the Discovery as the integrator of the world; it brings all its regions together as it enables the driver to discover the world. The driver here is clearly American (the ad appears in the *New York Times Magazine*); at the same time as it invokes empire through global domination, it invokes American cultural sensibilities about superior European culture and the lack of an authentic American history; the images are distinctly either European cultural (the Bilbao Guggenheim), historical (a German/Loire valley castle, a medieval fort in the Middle East), or distinctly colonial (an Indian elephant, African deserts, and savannahs). They are the most well traveled vehicles on earth, available with no less than 368 improvements and a whole planet to test them on. Its redefined appointments include once again a V8 and new interior color themes, satellite navigation, and DVD-playing capabilities to entertain the driver in all four corners of the world.

This Land Rover ad follows a series of ads for vehicles in the Land Rover fleet which at times invoke extraordinary colonialist imagery. In one TV ad for the Freelander, the vehicle is "released" from the back of a truck into the wild somewhere in southern/eastern Africa, watched warily by African game reserve wardens as it escapes in the manner of a newly released rhinoceros. With the immediate connections back to game hunting in the colonial era (in which Land Rovers were used as the vehicles to hunting) to the colonial politics of game reserves across sub-Saharan Africa, the Freelander ads recall a colonial past (in which nature conservation was closely implicated) which the reader (as upper-middle-class consumer able to afford a Freelander) is enjoined, if ironically, to valorize. The later series of ads, for the Discovery, figure the vehicle's owner back in "civilization," but having brought back odd artifacts from similarly colonized spaces.

The discourse of conquest, implicit and frequently explicit, in these advertisements draws on a familiar repertoire of American historical tropes. Most obviously the conquest of the wild west and the subjection of the wilderness encapsulate themes of American expansion and success in the eradication of what were repeatedly represented as savage threats to the orderly expansion of agricultural settlement. Wilderness itself is a formulation that eradicates the native human presence from the landscape reflecting the doctrines of *terra nullius* that facilitated the expropriation and subsequent occupation of native territory. The conquest of nature was also the conquest of the wild, both animal and human, and entailed the construction of Americans as rugged individuals.

Rugged individuals are men mostly, who can tackle the harsh physical reality of the frontier, subdue wild animals, and clear land. But men also respect the capabilities of the animals they kill and respect the awesome scale of the continent they subdue. Their purpose is to provide for wife and children, to protect and direct the matters of the nuclear family with its profound divisions of labor and its distinction between interior domestic safety and prosperity and external challenges and dangers. Technology, machines, and the skills that go with these things relate to weapons as well as transportation. Consumption is a domestic matter, a sphere of feminine competence subordinate to the male's geopolitical ordering.

America is not, however, according to the conventional national mythology, an empire. European states conquered other places, sent troops overseas, and got into conflicts. But Americans supposedly stayed at home and looked to internal matters. But the assumption of the nonimperial sources of American conduct requires both a considerable amount of historical amnesia, and a geographical sleight of hand where recent borders are taken as historically fixed boundaries. America manages to subdue nature and conquer territory without being an imperial power. Its Manifest Destiny to dominate the Americas is understood in the Monroe Doctrine as an anti-imperial strategy for keeping Europeans out. Conquest becomes destiny, violence and displacement become security and liberty. Thus freedom and the universal aspirations of modernity are incorporated within a powerful self-referential American set of universal categories widely and implicitly understood by readers of SUV advertisements.

The SUV is perhaps too easy a target. Its tropes of domination, off-road exploration in wilderness, and power and aggression are familiar and usually unsubtle. The SUV has also widely been the site of particular critique during the 1990s and beyond. Such criticisms concern questions of safety, fuel efficiency, pollution, but also have often implicated the rise of the SUV with the enhancement of U.S. oil dependence and thus the "need" to engage in military adventures to secure access to oil resources (Bradsher 2002; Luke 2001; Vanderheiden 2004). But the explicitly colonizing, dominating tropes of SUV ads do not exhaust the imagination of car advertisers; neither, however, does the presentation of cars in relation to other forms of imagery mean that their material practices are not bound up with Empire. And while one of the elements of SUV advertising is the civilization of nature, cars and their drivers themselves inhabit a predominantly urban universe. While still attempting to sell cars, then, many ads operate differently in terms of their relations to geopolitics.

NETWORK DRIVING

An ad for the BMW 5 series in the U.K. has a rather different take on the car's symbolisms which nevertheless invoke highly militarized imagery.

Advertising the car via its use of heads-up display, the ad suggests that "you receive vital information without having to look down."[8] The technology itself is of military origin, having been developed primarily to enable fighter pilots to navigate without having to look away from what is directly in front of them. The images reflect this military heritage, with one distinct image in the left hand of the ad containing a screen with a military plane circled as in a target, and another directly below that of contour lines, a rectangle and cross, again suggesting targets for delivery of weapons systems. Alongside three different images of the car itself, and one showing the top of the dash-board with the heads-up display above it saying the middle-ring road is 500 meters away and the car is traveling at 38km/h (a screen image then repro-duced at a larger scale subliminally across the whole ad), the image is marked by four strips of male eyes running across it.

These eyes are intended to emphasize the importance of vision and con-centration in driving activity (and by extension how a heads-up display helps this), but also serve to connect the car symbolically to a set of technologies of surveillance which the heads-up display exemplifies. The overall image presented is one where such technologies enable an orientation both to the car itself and the outside world predicated on control and mastery. But while this is closely related to the images of rugged outdoor heroism in most SUV ads, the crucial difference is the way in which a range of technologies—GPS, heads-up display, onboard computers—are the condition of possibility of this control. The masculinist subject here is therefore not the warrior but the technocrat. Or perhaps more precisely, it is the hybrid subjectivity of the two, in which the civilian consumer is figured as inhabiting a quasi-militarized world in daily life—quotidian driving being analogous to air-borne targeting.

BMW presents the car as engendering a network subjectivity in another ad for the 5 Series, but this time without express military imagery. The ad consists of a collage of images of roads, with the car at the bottom left con-nected in multiple ways to possible destinations via the roads in the collage. This time the connections to the notion of networks rather than surveillance are given more prominence in the way these technologies are figured, both in the images and in the slogan "Active steering. You don't need it like you didn't need a mobile phone." The slogan has a number of possible readings. At its most basic, it renders the car (and its active steering) as progressive by virtue of the connection to the mobile phone, now understood as a more advanced technology but one which is made to appear older than active steering. This reflects a range of ads which present cars as progressive by connection with computer or communications technologies. Wernick (1990), for example, begins his account of car advertising with an ad for IBM in 1980, which features a horse rider encountering his first car in the early twentieth century. The ad suggests that as people were initially scared of cars, now they may be afraid of computers, but over time they will be accommodated to them. Wernick shows how the computer was being sold by reference to the car as a symbol of progress. Now the reverse is often true. For example, in 2001, an ad for the Ford F150 ran (in Canada) which contrasted the car as symbol of rugged masculinist independence (the truck owner is putting up a fence on his Midwestern land, establishing his dominion) with those of the feminized communications technologies (the voiceover discusses the romantic comedy film *You've Got Mail* with Tom Hanks and Meg Ryan; the gendered point of the ad is precisely that the male truck owner has not seen this movie). But the slogan in the BMW ad also refers to the way that novel consumer items first appear as fripperies but after a time become understood as indispensable. It also, in conjunction with the image, connects the two as both enable successful navigation through the complex network space of the road, with one enabling successful cornering, the other enabling contact to be restored and directions found once one is lost.

The imagery of the collage itself constructs striking associations. The car is figured in terms of its position in a network of roads—or perhaps more appropriately and suggestively, in a collage of representations of such a road. This representation mirrors the spatiality of mobile phone networks, with each image as a cell. The representation takes the car through the standard set of images—from airport car park through cloverleaf intersections and highways, through forests, mountains, deserts, fields, ending in a city. Once again, the subject attains his (despite the absence of a visible driver in the car, the overall coding of the ad as masculine is clear enough) mobility, control, autonomy, through his participation in the network. Indeed, the contrast with the dominant SUV images is striking—the subject's freedom here is only to be attained through participation within the road network, not through his rejection of it. But it is nevertheless a narrative of control: "this intelligent system augments what is already a highly responsive set up, by seamlessly adapting the steering response from agile to ultra-agile and back again according to driving conditions." Not only therefore is the subject conditioned by its relationality with other subjects and the network in which it operates and which constitute its subjectivity, the conditions of control are about responsiveness and agility, not toughness and domination.

A further extension of this logic of network or relational subjectivity can be seen in a series of Honda ads for the Jazz.[9] With touchy-feely cartoon images (resonant of the Yellow Submarine cartoon style) and music (in the TV versions) the ad suggests two possible forms of sociality engendered by the driver's participation in the road network. Recognizing that a dominant form is one where cars don't "get on," where cars do "cut each other up," and so on, it exhorts the reader/driver to create a more hospitable/friendly form of driving, and interpellates the reader as Jazz driver and thus as sociable participant in the network. The name Jazz, supported by the random, free form of the cartoon road, combines with the ads message to create an image of the car's freedom as flexibility, adaptability, accommodation with others. Here a more explicit rejection of the car as domination/conquest is adopted in favor of a subjectivity based on a recognition of others and our interdependence with each other and dependence on the successful functioning of networks. It also has rather different cyborg images than those of the BMW, suggesting that it is cars which don't get on and which cut each other up, and humans which have the potential agency to turn the other cheek or let others pull away first.

The "technology at the service of sociality" image is given a different twist by ads for the Nissan Micra.[10] A series of Micra ads involve various neologisms—simpology, modtro, funamic, and the like—which combine two words for effect, but more importantly project the Micra as new, innovative, progressive, precisely because one needs new words to encapsulate its essence. This is not only, however, about figuring the car (the ad suggests "it takes a whole new language to describe it"), but gives the sense that the Micra requires a new subjectivity on the part of its driver ("do you speak Micra?"). These neologisms are each given dictionary-like phonetic spellings and definitions after, and alongside the "do you speak Micra?" slogan, are accompanied by the phrase "SHIFT_expectations," emphasizing the progressive character, principally by the artifact of the underscore, which suggests an email or Internet address.

In some ads these tactics are overlaid with a relatively crude form of imagery. Underneath the word "simpology," defined as the "perfect balance between *simp*licity and tech*nology*," is the car, simply facing the viewer, in front of a row of wind turbines. The imagery is obvious: to present the car as benign in ecological terms, through its (misleading) association with renewable energy, through the analogous combination of the two components of the neologism. The effect is then given a social twist as the headlights are on (although the car is empty), and the text at the bottom reveals them as "friendly headlights" that "stay on long enough to see you to your front door." Combined with the image of wind turbines, there is a presentation here of a discourse of security predicated on subtle shaping of the world around—lighting a space to render it safe, working with the forces of nature—rather than on the images of sheer power and domination in the SUV ads.

This theme is picked up in our final example, the Ford Mondeo. The protection imagery, this time explicitly family oriented, is clear through the slogan for "tigers with cubs to protect." The car is figured this time in front of a futuristic building with the word "Zoo" on the outside. Beyond the buildings are woodland and stone walls, producing a sense of an English country park scene. The connection made is with the zoo as protector of wild animals. The text supports the protection imagery, and concludes "because it can be a jungle out there." This takes us back to SUV imagery, where the same urban jungle metaphor is at times invoked (here it is underscored with a stormy sky), but the mechanisms of protection are again strikingly different. Here, an understated emphasis on technical performance, design (emphasized through the steel and glass architecture of the zoo, in brushed steel like the car), technology, as opposed to brute force, is the chosen means for producing security.

READING IMPERIAL ADS

In a colloquial sense, contemporary geopolitics can be read through these ads as the emergence (or consolidation) of a specifically American empire. This consists of the rapid expansion of military reach by U.S. forces over larger and larger areas of the globe, since the end of the cold war, combined with a set of discourses within the United States with its origins in Manifest Destiny and extra-territoriality but emphasizing recently its right to intervene globally more or less at will, and the correspondingly limited nature of other states' sovereignty ("no boundaries") (Ferguson 2004). Overlaid with this general narrative is a discourse among critics of U.S. imperialism (and some of its supporters) about the oil-specific nature of U.S. imperialism (Harvey 2003; Klare 2004). Made most forcefully and obviously in relation to the invasions of Kuwait in 1990–1991 and the invasion of Iraq in 2003, but more generally in relation to the war in Afghanistan and the establishment of U.S. bases in Central Asia (to secure U.S. control of oil pipelines from Central Asian oilfields) to the war in Kosovo (again, to control the other end of one of these pipeline routes), the specific sites where the United States extends its global imperial reach can be seen to be often determined by the U.S. needs to secure control of oil supplies. Furthermore, in many of these critiques, the development of the SUV market is seen as underpinning the increasing dependence on Middle Eastern oil and the search for control over its alternatives (Klare 2004).

In this context, the differences in the ads are read as a distinction between those invoking imperial themes and nonimperialist ads. These ads predominately operate in North America as opposed to Europe. But where they operate outside the United States, they interpellate their consumers into a specifically American mode of understanding space, nature, power, territory, and so forth, which makes up the imperial constellation. The SUV ads reflect the U.S. imperial reach, and operate to recode the SUV as producing security rather than the geopolitical insecurity involved in the American imperial moment/project, as well as by the extraction and consumption of the oil itself. At the same time, this reading makes sense of the distinctions between militarist and non-militarist ads, where either the latter are coded feminine

(Jazz, Micra, in particular) or non-militarist masculinities are rendered deviant (as in the F150 ad noted above). By contrast, the car ads can either be read as simply responding to something other than geopolitics, or as in some way playing on car users' implicit anti-imperial (or more simply anti-excess, but we read the two as related) sensibilities through a strategy of differentiation from SUVs: "wouldn't it be nice if cars got on?"

This then leads to another more general way of reading the ads in terms of different accumulation strategies. Here, the SUV ads represent the discursive underpinnings of "carboniferous capitalism" (Dalby 2002; Mumford 1934)—the strategy of accumulation premised on cheap access to fossil energy sources. This mode of development has long been dominant in North America, with abundant resources, a stronger discourse concerning such abundance, and the legacy of U.S. continental expansionism. By contrast, the other car ads can be read as embodying elements in an alternative accumulation strategy which is usually called ecological modernization. The focus on advanced technology (from GPS to windpower) at the service of controlling or mitigating the downsides of automobility, combined with the emphasis on sociability as opposed to hostility, can be seen as elements in this discourse. This discourse is increasingly dominant in continental Europe as a strategy of promoting accumulation while reducing a range of ecological impacts traditionally produced by growth. In relation to cars, it can be specifically seen in the way that the integration of networking technologies into cars is understood in Europe (Urry and Sheller 2000), as illustrated discursively in the ads above. In its dominant form, then, it can be read in terms of global politics as a competitive strategy by states (Barry and Paterson 2004; Mol 2001), and thus as a means by which environmentalism can be accommodated to the evolving global economic order.

The ecological modernization/carboniferous capitalism distinction can be read easily enough alongside the U.S. oil imperialism one. Carboniferous capitalism generates geopolitical necessities for widespread interventions to secure access to oil resources, while ecological modernization entails a strategy of development without such geopolitical implications. This certainly enables the specificity of the SUV images to be captured (whereas Hardt and Negri's account misses this specificity). But this misses the tensions within the ads which suggest a more complex set of relations. At one end of the spectrum, the version of ecological modernization entailed in the ads is extremely weak at best (Christoff 1996), entailing a focus on technical fixes as solutions to ecological problems, a mode of automobility which is less ecologically destructive than would otherwise be the case. But even here it contains its tensions, in that the focus on sociability suggests stronger versions of ecological modernization emphasizing discursive democracy and reflexivity (Beck, Lash, and Giddens 1994) and operates as a site around which critiques of weak ecological modernization within readers of the ads might operate. If cars might be enabled to get on, then why would one want to *own* one, since private ownership is precisely the source of hostility or otherness in relation to the commodity/technology.

But it is also necessary to be more critical of the oil imperialism–SUV equation. Although symbolically SUVs figure as domination and empire, both within the ads themselves and for critics of the rise of the SUV, materially, other cars and their users cannot be so neatly disentangled from the webs of oil dependence and its geopolitics.[11] Many of the arguments for the specific ecological ills of SUVs, and particularly to their culpability in relation to the increases in oil imports and thus generation of geopolitical instability, relate to their poor fuel efficiency. But what this misses is that the fuel economy of individual cars is relatively unimportant as a component of the overall fuel consumption by economies as a whole. Far more important is increases in the kilometers traveled by drivers and most importantly in the numbers of car drivers per se (Newman and Kenworthy 1999). Thus since the ads at some point are all engaged in a project of attempting to increase the consumption of (particular) cars, they are all therefore constructing the subject in relation to the empire which it helps to produce. At the same time, some of the car ads contain within themselves the militaristic imagery which suggests their complicity with or consistency with an imperial form. The BMW ad discussed is the most obvious example here.

Thus a neat reading of the two sets of ads as imperial/nonimperial breaks down fairly quickly. All of the ads should therefore be read as part of the legitimation of an imperial mode of geopolitics, and the differentiation of elements in imperial power as emphasised by Hardt and Negri helps then to explain their variations. Hardt and Negri's (2000) account of Empire suggests a constitution of Empire consisting of three moments or elements of power: monarchical, aristocratic, and democratic (2000: 314–19). "Monarchy . . . is presented as a global police force and thus as a form of tyranny" (315). "The aristocratic . . . deploy(s) its hierarchical command and its ordering functions over the transnational articulation of production and circulation, not only through traditional monetary instruments, but also to an ever greater degree through the instruments and dynamics of the cooperation of social actors themselves" (316). Finally, "the democratic forces that in this framework ought to constitute the active and open elements of the imperial machine appear rather as corporative forces, as a set of superstitions and fundamentalisms, betraying a spirit that is conservative when not downright reactionary" (316).

But broadly, the ads can be read through these elements. The dominant SUV images of rugged masculinity, domination of nature, and conquerors of the world reflect the monarchical moment, while the more technocratic masculinism in for example the BMW ads make sense in the context of the aristocratic moment which focuses on regularizing, standardizing, law, but also the biopolitics of producing new network subjectivities ("the dynamics of the cooperation of social actors themselves"). Both encompass the democratic element in that they consist of the mechanism by which the potentially "active and open elements" are coopted and produced as either conservative (BMW) or reactionary (SUV).

The element of Empire which emphasizes that the power in/of Empire operates biopolitically is essential to understanding how these ads thus interpellate all their readers as colonizing subjects; that is, they illustrate to their readers the interrelation between their daily lives and their continually performed automobile subjectivities and global political dynamics. But it is also highly suggestive of (even though Hardt and Negri fail to make this connection, and indeed the occasional mentions of environmental politics they make suggest they might resist it), is that biopolitics can be read not only as about the management of human subjectivities but the production of and management of nature as a whole. While this reading is intuitively and broadly consistent with many elements in green theory which emphasize the intertwining of human systems of rule and the domination of nature, it insists that such nature is now inextricably produced by the specific ways that capital (operating often through the daily practices of the multitude) operates, and cannot be understood at any level as outside society.

BRINGING IT ALL HOME

All these themes come together in what appears to be an advertisement for the Hummer printed in the *National Geographic* magazine of June 2004. The cover story concerns "The End of Cheap Oil." One of the vignettes in the article on how oil is an essential part of practical life in many parts of the world is structured as though it were an advertisement for a Hummer. The double page image shows a small boy in the foreground. He is being chased on a driveway by a small, radio-controlled yellow model Hummer. This vehicle is being controlled by the boy's brother who is pictured sitting on the tailgate of a yellow truck version of a Hummer. In the background is a lawn with shrubs suggesting suburban affluence. The caption in the margin under the little boy states "The New Station Wagon, 7263 pounds, 10mpg, $400 monthly diesel bill." On the facing page in smaller print the scene of suburban life is explained thus: "The family car is tons of fun for two young fans, who turn it into a grandstand as they test-drive a pint-size Hummer near Atlanta, Georgia. 'They even camp in it,' says their mother. She bought the H1 for business but now drives it everywhere. 'I know it's not fuel efficient, but I love knowing that anything I bump into, I win.' "

The Hummer is a derivation of the American military transport, the Humvee, first brought to public attention by its widespread use in the 1991

Gulf War. Its huge size makes it one of the largest SUVs on the road. Its replication as a toy for the entertainment of children, underscored by the yellow color, raises the question of its status as an adult vehicle, and implies that it is a plaything as much as a practical mode of transportation. The theme of networked and remote-controlled vehicles is there too, suggesting technical acumen even among children. But overarching all this is the admission by the mother that even if it isn't fuel efficient that doesn't matter given the feeling of superiority implied in winning when she bumps something. The sports metaphor, drawing on the theme of the vehicle as grandstand for the boys, suggests that driving too is a game, one in which big toys give you a better chance of winning. Presumably her two sons are not what get bumped.

The dismissal of the consequences of one's actions, or at least their dismissal in the face of the more highly valued victory in the game of driving, encapsulates both the theme of the individualist and the overarching right to go anywhere; the vehicle is literally driven everywhere, regardless of the consequences to either environment or others. The derivation of the Hummer from a military vehicle used in the Gulf War for oil connects directly to the theme of empire as the military conquest of resources in the periphery. It also suggests an enmeshment in complicated matters of political economy where the vehicle is needed for business but driven for pleasure. Sports and utility in one vehicle. The military relations of empire have been domesticated into the new station wagon; its violent origins repackaged in the language of games, the consequences denied in the celebration of consumption. The infantilization of consumption culture is now complete. Fun is all and the consequences of one's actions unconsidered. The sociopathology of empire has been completely domesticated; nature civilized, and the history of violence justified by the representation of vehicles in tropes of harmless childhood entertainment.

All of this suggests both the importance of understanding such social productions as an integral part of the material practices of empire, and also as part of the biopolitical production of the subjects of Empire. These subjects are however not all alike, nor are they interpellated in similar ways in the advertisements we read here. Within Empire modes of living are diversified, but the common theme of the car as the quintessential commodity of private consumption, also entails the production of imperial subjects.

While therefore it may be useful to claim as Hardt and Negri do, that the current period of Empire is marked by a dominant social relation of war, premised on the "double exception" of emergency measures required to deal with terror and the operation of an American exceptionalism which implies that the rules of normal politics do not apply, clearly the specific operations of imperial forces require further explanation. This reading of automobile advertising suggests that the material flows of petroleum are an important part of these practices, and that the biopolitics of carboniferous capitalism specifically require military control of the oilfields. American forces literally police the flows of resources, justified in terms of the production of the kind of consumption epitomized by the tropes of imperial freedom in SUV advertisements. But the crucial additional point, ironically captured in the BMW advertisement celebrating the adoption of military instrumentation, is that these vehicles too reproduce the imperial subject even when portrayed as urban (European) sophisticates far from the tropes of rural domination.

REFERENCES

Barry, John, and Matthew Paterson. 2004. "Globalisation, Ecological Modernization, and New Labour." *Political Studies* 52, no. 4: 767–84.

Beck, Ulrich, Scott Lash, and Anthony Giddens. 1994. *Reflexive Modernization.* Cambridge: Polity.

Böhm, Steffen, Campbell Jones, Chris Land, and Matthew Paterson, eds. Forthcoming. *Against Automobility.*

Bradsher, Keith. 2002. *High and Mighty: The Dangerous Rise of the SUV.* New York: Public Affairs.

Chaloupka, William. 2004. "The Irrepressible Lightness and Joy of Being Green: *Empire* and Environmentalism." In Paul Passavant and Jodi Dean. eds., *Empire's New Clothes: Reading Hardt & Negri,* 199–216. London: Routledge.

Christoff, Peter. 1996. "Ecological Modernisation, Ecological Modernities." *Environmental Politics* 5, no. 3: 476–500.

Dalby, Simon. 2002. *Environmental Security.* Minneapolis: University of Minnesota Press.

Ferguson, Niall. 2004. *Colossus: The Rise and Fall of the American Empire.* New York: Penguin.

Ford Motor Company. 2000. *Connecting with Customers: 2000 Annual Report.* Dearborn, Mich.: Ford Motor Company.

Freund, Peter, and George Martin. 1993. *The Ecology of the Automobile.* Montreal: Black Rose Books.

Gunster, Shane. 2004. "You Belong Outside: Advertising, Nature, and the SUV." *Ethics and the Environment* 9, no. 2: 4–32.

Hardt, Michael, and Antonio Negri. 2000. *Empire.* Cambridge: Harvard University Press.

Harvey, David. 2003. *The New Imperialism.* Oxford: Oxford University Press.

Klare, Michael. 2004. *Blood and Oil: The Dangers and Consequences of America's Growing Dependency on Imported Petroleum.* New York: Metropolitan.

Luke, Timothy. 2001. "SUVs and the Greening of Ford: Reimagining Industrial Ecology as an Environmental Corporate Strategy in Action." *Organization & Environment* 14, no. 3: 313–35.

Martin-Jones, David. Forthcoming. No Literal Connection: Images of Mass Commodification, U.S. Militarism, and the Oil Industry." In Böhm et al. eds., *The Big Lebowski.*

Mol, Arthur. 2001. *Globalization and Environmental Reform: The Ecological Modernisation of the Global Economy.* Cambridge: MIT Press.

Mumford, Lewis. 1934. *Technics and Civilization.* New York: Harcourt.

Newman, Peter, and Jeffrey Kenworthy. 1999. *Sustainability and Cities: Overcoming Automobile Dependence.* Washington, D.C.: Island Press.

Paterson, Matthew. 2000. "Car Culture and Global Environmental Politics." *Review of International Studies* 26, no. 2: 253–70.

Shah, Saubhagya. 2002. "From Evil State to Civil Society." *South Asian Himal,* November 10–17.

Shukin, Nicole. Forthcoming. "The Mimetics of Mobile Capital." In Böhm et al. eds., *The Big Lebowski.*

Urry, John, and Mimi Sheller. 2000. "The City and the Car." *International Journal of Urban and Regional Research* 24, no. 4: 737–57.

Vanderheiden, Steven. 2004. "The Case against the SUV." Presented at the 2004 meeting of the Western Political Science Association, Portland, OR, March 2004.

Wackernagel, Mathias, and William Rees. 1996. *Our Ecological Footprint: Reducing Human Impact on the Earth.* Gabriola Island, B.C.: New Society.

Wernick, Andrew. 1991. *Promotional Culture: Advertising, Ideology and Symbolic Expression.* London: Sage.

Williamson, Judith. 1981. *Decoding Advertisements: Ideology and Meaning in Advertising.* London: Marion Boyars.

Worldwide Fund For Nature. 2004. *Living Planet Report 2004.* London: WWF.

7

Ecotourism

On the face of it, ecotourism seems to be a win-win for everybody—the usually white, privileged people from developed countries get to tour the rare, fragile regions of the world, and the people and the environments of lesser developed countries benefit economically from the tourists. But this is really just an assumption. The recent popularity of ecotourism represents the logic of globalization enthusiasts, but the rarely heard criticisms by the people of those rare and fragile environments similarly represent the erased social and environmental costs of globalization.

Ecotourists and the people whose lands they tour have vastly different worldviews. Anthropologist Andrew Walsh gives us a rare glimpse of the thoughts of people living in a Madagascar village that sits next to an ecotourist preserve that is off-limits to the local population. Ecotourists, Walsh finds, engaged in a kind of fantasy disguised as an authentic search for an engagement with nature. But the local villagers have a difficult time distinguishing the difference between ecotourists and their previous history with colonialism. Reflecting on one of his informant's thoughts on ecotourists, Walsh powerfully states the obvious: "Foreigners never just look; they are always looking for a reason."

Andrew Walsh, "The Obvious Aspects of Ecological Underprivilege in Ankarana, Northern Madagascar" (2005)[1]

> How is information concerning the troubles of a system to be introduced into that system in ways that will help to avoid, ameliorate, or correct those troubles rather than exacerbate them?
>
> —Rappaport 1993

> For one thing, it is necessary to state the obvious.
>
> —Rappaport 1979

About one hundred kilometers south of the northern Malagasy city of Antsiranana, travelers on Madagascar's National Route 6 encounter a pair of roadside signs standing no more than four meters apart. The larger of the two signs—a billboard set back from the road—welcomes French speakers to the northern boundary of the Ankarana Special Reserve, a protected conservation area that has been drawing increasing numbers of foreign ecotourists over the past decade. This sign asks only that visitors to the reserve obey the credo of ecotourism worldwide by "taking nothing but photographs and leaving nothing but footprints" during their brief stay in the region. The second, much smaller sign is intended for people likely to be on foot and reads simply and economically "Ala Fady," warning Malagasy speakers to keep out of what has been labeled the "taboo forest."

It would be hard to find an image more suggestive than this one of the disparities that affect and inspire many of the people with whom I have been doing research over the past five years. Malagasy residents of Ambondromifehy, a sapphire-mining and sapphire-trading town located on the highway just south of these signs, are well aware that the Ankarana reserve is a place in which foreigners are welcome and they are not. Indeed, this well-publicized fact is the source of much speculation around town, as locals wonder why they are restricted from a place to which already more privileged others have easy access. As the reserve happens to be an important local source of sapphires, a commodity destined ultimately for foreign consumers, one popular theory around town suggests that the foreigners who come here are taking more than just photographs with them when they leave. Or maybe, some imagine, there is some commodity other than sapphires that foreigners are finding in the reserve, something Malagasy people do not yet know about. What is certain to many in Ambondromifehy is that foreigners must be doing something more in Ankarana than just looking at what the local environment has to offer; anyone who suggests otherwise, visiting anthropologists included, is either deluded or complicit.

Before proceeding with any further discussion of my informants' speculations about foreigners, I should note that they are mistaken in at least one sense. From what I have observed over the years, the bulk of foreigners who visit the Ankarana reserve do so for the reasons that recent commentators on the world's growing ecotourism industry might expect (see, e.g., Carrier and Macleod 2005; Duffy 2002; West and Carrier 2004). Foreigners come to this place for more than just its spectacular landscape; they come in search of authentic ecologies, adventure, learning, communion with nature, and so forth, spurred by desires well rooted in Western traditions of tourism and environmentalism, which are themselves phenomena with their own unique cultural and historical foundations. Ecotourists come, in other words, for reasons that people with worldviews rooted in other traditions cannot possibly be expected to fully appreciate. No wonder, then, that people in Ambondromifehy misinterpret the interests of these foreigners. Lacking an appreciation of the profoundly historical and cultural motivations and values on which ecotourism is based, Ambondromifehy's observers lack the means for understanding what brings ecotourists into their midst. Or so some might assume.

To anthropologists trained in the tradition of relativism, there is something appealing about the line of argument suggested above, not least because it offers such a familiar role for us, as anthropologists, to fill: expert relativist mediator. Just as there is much about the unique ethnoecologies of people living in places like Ankarana that we might make familiar to foreign observers, there is much exotic in ecotourism that we might usefully explain to people living in places like Ankarana. Indeed, in undertaking the latter task, we might well ally ourselves with some conservationists in hoping that by helping people living in and around endangered environments to understand the values and motivations underlying ecotourism, we might encourage them to emulate this ethos for the sake of sustainability. Unfortunately for the expert mediator, however, relativist approaches such as that suggested here tend not to go over very well in Ambondromifehy—and for good reason. The people here understand perfectly well that what most significantly differentiates them from the foreigners they observe speeding through town in baggage-laden four-wheel drive vehicles has little to do with motivations or values. Indeed, when conversation in Ambondromifehy turns to foreigners, residents are at least as likely to speak of shared desires as of different ones. Many of my informants too would like to travel in the comfort of air-conditioned four wheelers, drink only chilled drinks, and buy cigarettes by the pack instead of the piece. More importantly, they too would like to be able to cross the boundaries of the Ankarana reserve whenever they want, without threat of reprisals, and benefit from whatever it is that foreigners are finding. As Ambondromifehy's speculators see it, what is most obviously lacking and needed in Ankarana is not a lesson in relativism but justice.

This perspective in mind, I find myself faced with a dilemma that has been of late the focus of much discussion and debate among "new ecological" anthropologists (Kottak 1999) and political ecologists. How does one go about writing effective accounts of what, in their introduction to *Ethnographies of Conservation* (2003), David Anderson and Eeva Berglund call "ecological underprivilege": accounts that might actually influence public and political debate over the fate of people living near, or exiled from, protected areas around the world? Two well developed possibilities seem appropriate to the case at hand. The first, found in Anderson and Berglund's book, suggests that we undertake projects of what might be called "ethnographic exposition." As Anderson and Berglund write, "Generat[ing] a robust anthropological contribution to ecopolitics" requires that we devote ourselves to "making visible" a number of things: not only "the people marginalized by the 'anti-political' nature of many conservationist accounts" (2003: 3) or "the effects of environmentalism on [such] marginal peoples in a context of economic polarization, but [also] the lifeworlds of environmentalists themselves" (2003: 4). Another related possibility, found in contributions to Charles Zerner's recent edited collection *Culture and the Question of Rights* (2002), is that we might usefully serve as "boundary crossing translators" (2002: 4), communicating moving accounts of distinctive resource claims to the powerful players who police the access of marginalized people to contested environments.

Although I admire both approaches and have applied them in my work, they assume, as plans of action, that the expositions and translations we come up with will receive the consideration they deserve. This may not be a safe assumption. For reasons well analyzed in both of the sources just mentioned, many of the processes and policies that have precipitated and continue to foster situations of ecological underprivilege around the world owe more to "generic" (Gewertz and Errington 2001), "antipolitical" (Ferguson 1990), or merely "legible" (Scott 1998) understandings of human ecologies than to anthropological ones. And although I recognize the importance of continuing to confront such overly simple understandings with more complex renderings, I wonder if there is not something else we may do as well— something that would convey a sense of ecological underprivilege that is both sufficiently legible and sufficiently complex to do justice to the predicaments of the people with whom we work.

In this chapter, I pursue this admittedly ambitious goal by setting myself a very modest task: communicating a few obvious points about the current situation in Ankarana. As my epigraphs and the phrasing in the chapter title suggest, my approach is inspired in large part by the work of Roy Rappaport. With Rappaport, I share a concern that in our "eagerness" to display our ethnographic virtuosity by searching out and finding "more than meets the eye" in what we study, "anthropologists have . . . tended to overlook," or at least downplay, the obvious: "that which does meet the eye" (1979: 173). The obvious points I have in mind here are quite simply those things that my informants and, hopefully, my audiences do not need an expert relativist mediator like me to explain to them; things like the message communicated by the pairing of the two signs with which I began. My debt to Rappaport does not end with the "obvious," however. The fact that I approach the task at hand by privileging the perspectives of my informants is also inspired by his work, specifically by his argument for an engaged "Anthropology of Trouble" (Rappaport 1993). However skilled we might be at making the unseen visible, I expect that Rappaport would encourage us to make the unheard "audible" (1993: 301). The most important thing of all, perhaps, in a "world in which the domination of privileged discourse . . . threatens to make other discourses inaudible or unintelligible" (Rappaport

1993: 301), is that we not allow our finely honed ethnographic discourse, however critical, to drown out the things, however obvious, that our informants have to say about the conditions afflicting them.

Mindful (as Rappaport was) of the fact that "an expedition into the obvious calls for justification" (1979: 174), I should note that the approach suggested here has often been called for, but rarely undertaken, in studies of tourism and conservation (Stronza 2001). Much important work has been done on how influential conservationist and tourist discourses have so often miscast the people living in or near protected areas as ecologically noble savages, infantile dependents, or victims of the tragedy of the commons (Gezon 2004; Harper 2002; Theodossopoulos 2003; West 2001). In contrast, however, relatively little has been made of how these same people return such gazes, fitting their observations of and experiences with conservationists and tourists into their own influential and historically rooted worldviews. My informants in Ankarana subscribe to influential ethnoecologies—unique culturally grounded perspectives on the environment that do not necessarily jibe with those of foreign conservationists and ecotourists. But they also subscribe to unique and influential political ecologies—understandings of the complex workings of power that ensure that most in Ankarana are, as people there say, "left behind" (*tavela*), in spite of living and working in a resource-rich region. To my mind, unique political ecologies such as these—political ecologies of the poor (Martinez-Alier 2002), we might say, emerging under specific political, economic, historical, and ecological circumstances—are worthy of greater attention, especially by those of us accustomed to thinking of political ecology as a singular field of academic debate. If, as Arturo Escobar has noted, "an important goal of political ecology is to understand and participate in the ensemble of forces linking social change, environment and development" (1999: 15), it seems only reasonable that we carefully consider the insights of those inhabitants of the places in which we work who have been striving to achieve this goal in their own distinctive ways. Local inhabitants of such regions are likely to understand firsthand what Nancy Lee Peluso and Michael Watts have argued is the case worldwide: that "specific resource environments . . . and environmental processes . . . are constituted by, and in part constitute, the political economy of access to and control over resources" (2001: 5). Such people are also keen observers of how "entitlements" (2001: 5) to these resources are distributed, reproduced, and disputed on local, national, and global scales, adopting unique views of the complex workings of global political economy that could only come from their direction. In taking the perspectives and observations of such people seriously, we may even discover that what they find obvious about their predicament is not quite as obvious to us as we might have previously imagined. Inclined as we are toward methodologies and modes of analysis suited to exposing and translating, anthropologists may be more prone than anyone to downplaying, ignoring, or even forgetting those aspects of ecological underprivilege that can so easily go without saying.

The remainder of this chapter is divided into five sections. First, I offer a brief overview of ecotourism in Ankarana, focusing in particular on how the diverse interests of people living in this region are variously served and thwarted by the local ecotourist trade and the conservation efforts under which it has developed. Second, I discuss just what it is that many in Ambondromifehy take to be obvious about the increasing numbers of foreigners in Ankarana. Third, I illustrate some of the deeper insights that come from these same observers' reflections on the obvious. Fourth, I discuss other, less suspicious perspectives on ecotourism and conservation in the region. And finally, I reflect on the sort of research that led to this article and its connection to the points found herein.

ECOTOURISM IN ANKARANA

That Madagascar is today among the world's hottest ecotourist destinations owes a great deal to its well-publicized reputation as a "naturalist's paradise." The U.S. travel agency through which I sometimes book my flights describes the island as "untouched," "unspoiled," and "undiscovered," an "Eden-like garden of riches, filled with a diversity of life and geography unequaled anywhere else on earth" (Cortez Travel 2005). Rivaling this Edenic reputation, however, is Madagascar's renown as what one *National Geographic* reporter called an "environmental hell" (Bellows 2001). It is a place that Conservation International lists among the most "threatened conservation priority areas on the planet" (2005). Interestingly, and contrary to what some might expect, this latter reputation has likely done as much for the island's ecotourism industry as the former. Following a strategy applied around the world, ecotourism has been promoted as an important component of conservation efforts in Madagascar. Thus it is largely thanks to the efforts of a variety of international conservation organizations working in cooperation with the Malagasy State that visitors to the island have such a wide array of easily accessed and well-serviced ecotourist destinations from which to choose. However, it is not only foreign tourists and local environments that are meant to benefit from such efforts. Ecotourism is said to be of greatest benefit to people living near areas of conservationist concern, as it provides them with employment opportunities and other immediate benefits while at the same time teaches them to evaluate local resources and ecosystems in new and more sustainable ways.

However promising the emergence of international ecotourism might seem to some, there is considerable evidence to suggest that its promotion in conservation hot spots around the world has not served to accomplish conservation and development goals—or link the two as its proponents had hoped. As Joe Bandy noted more than a decade ago, "the flourishing ecotourism industry [worldwide] . . . [has] benefited travel agencies and tour operators of overdeveloped countries significantly more than the local governments and peoples of the South" (1996: 553). In addition, there is little evidence that it has—and much concern that it has not—done much to stop the destruction of biodiversity in conservation priority areas. More recent assessments are similarly critical, questioning the faulty assumptions that seem to underlie many ecotourism projects and exposing the rarely acknowledged interests behind this global industry's rapid growth (Duffy 2002; Mowforth and Munt 1998; West and Carrier 2004). The only points about the international ecotourism industry that everyone seems to agree on are (1) that it is growing rapidly and (2) that its effects are being felt more than ever in some of the world's most marginal locales.

The Ankarana reserve's recent rise as a popular ecotourist destination can be attributed to a number of factors. Of primary importance is its favorable location, not far from a national highway on a well-traveled tourist route running between the city of Antsiranana and the island of Nosy Be, both popular destinations in their own rights. Ankarana has the distinct advantage of being both easily accessible and sufficiently remote, offering different sorts of ecotourists the different sorts of experiences they are after. Also important, of course, is what the reserve has to offer in the way of attractions. In Ankarana, ecotourists can find the lemurs, chameleons, butterflies, birds, insects, crocodiles, and bats for which Madagascar is known, as well as the unique terrain and spectacular caves of the Ankarana massif, the immense limestone (karst) formation from which the region takes its name. Finally, there is the reserve's well-developed infrastructure. Thanks to the efforts of the Malagasy State, the World Wide Fund for Nature, and a variety of other organizations dedicated to promoting ecotourism in the region, visitors to the reserve have access to amenities including campsites, latrines, four wheeler trails, walking paths, sturdy viewing platforms, and informative plaques, as well as well-trained guides who can lead them on standardized circuits.

As Bandy might have predicted, the Ankarana reserve's increasing popularity as an ecotourist destination has not brought benefits to all, or even many, living in its vicinity. What local benefits have come have been concentrated mostly around the reserve's few entry points, including the highway side town of Mahamasina in which a fee office, interpretive center, and reserve entrance were established in the mid-1990s. Here, a neighborhood of reserve administrators, guides, and hoteliers has emerged where there were once only a few houses. From the perspective of these people, to whom I return later in this chapter, ecotourism has been a very good thing. To residents of the larger community just south of the reserve entrance, however—

many of whom do not have the skills, inclinations, or connections necessary to profit from the ecotourist trade—all of this local development and foreign interest has been inconsequential at best.

Thirty kilometers north of Mahamasina sits Ambondromifehy, another roadside community on the fringes of the Ankarana reserve that has seen great changes over the past decade because of increasing foreign demand for Malagasy resources. Around the time of the construction of the reserve entrance in Mahamasina in the mid-1990s, Ambondromifehy was a village of about four hundred agriculturalists. A few years later, following the discovery of sapphires in the region, it had exploded into a densely packed boomtown of some 15,000 people, the majority of them young male migrants drawn from throughout Madagascar by the promise of easy fortunes. As is to be expected, this influx of prospectors had profound effects on local ecosystems. Given that the region's most prized unprotected mining sites were snapped up early and then carefully guarded by well connected and equipped Malagasy and foreign enterprises, Ambondromifehy's thousands of independent prospectors found themselves with little choice but to take their shovels and flashlights into the Ankarana reserve in search of their fortunes (Walsh 2003). Unsurprisingly, such artisanal mining became a matter of immediate concern to the organizations charged with protecting the Ankarana reserve. Not only was this mining seen to be unsustainable and destructive to local ecosystems, it also posed a serious threat to the region's burgeoning ecotourism. Early efforts at educating prospectors regarding the potentially disastrous effects of their work failed, however, and in 1998 the national police were called in to lend a hand in enforcing reserve boundaries. Still, so long as a market for illegally mined sapphires remained, even the threat of violence, imprisonment, and hefty fines did not keep miners out of what both they and conservationists took to calling the "taboo forest" (*ala fady*).

To this day, miners continue to work illegally within the Ankarana reserve and continue to find markets for what they find. They also continue to resist and be suspicious of efforts at convincing them to keep out of the "taboo forest." Understanding why this is the case requires an appreciation of what these people take to be obvious about the reserve and the foreigners it attracts. I discuss this in the following section. Before proceeding, however, it should be noted that the perspective outlined below is not one that is shared by all in Ankarana. This perspective has emerged within the distinctive context of Ankarana's sapphire trade (Walsh 2002, 2003, 2004). Lisa Gezon's research in long-standing communities on the western side of the Ankarana reserve concerning local people's involvement with and attitudes toward conservation efforts offers an interesting counterpoint to what is presented here (Gezon 1997, 2004, in press).

CONFRONTING THE OBVIOUS

The man who convinced me of the need for paying closer attention to the obvious aspects of ecological underprivilege in Ankarana was Nivo, a seventy-year-old longtime resident of Mahamasina. Knowing that he had spent much of his forty years in the region working in the service of foreign explorers, film crews, researchers, and tourists, I first interviewed Nivo with the hope that he might have a great deal to say about why it is that foreigners come to Ankarana. I was right. Nivo told me in our first conversation that foreigners come to Ankarana because of the thick forest and the opportunities that the local environment provides them for walking, looking at animals, and "taking in the breeze" (*mangala tsitsiko*). I pressed him for more, however, asking him why it is that foreigners would want to come to Ankarana to do these things when they could just as easily walk in forests, see animals in a zoo, or "take in the breeze" at home. I was surprised by the simplicity and forcefulness of his answer. "They have enough money to do it!" he exclaimed. He explained further,

> Dollars and French francs and Malagasy francs aren't the same. 50 French francs becomes what, 50,000 Malagasy francs? How could they not have enough money to fulfill all of their *plaisirs* [desires]? They exchange 100 of their francs and they get enough to do whatever they want . . . they get a rice sack full of money. They have enough money, I said! We are different. Our money is *boozaka* . . . [the grass used] to make the roof of your hut. (Conversation with author, June 2, 2004.)

What sort of an explanation of ecotourist behavior was this? Certainly not the sort that I was expecting when I asked the question that inspired it. Instead of reflections on foreign values and motivations, what I got was the obvious: foreigners come to Ankarana because they can.

The perspective from which an obvious point as this is particularly meaningful is one that is shared by most, if not all, of my informants in Ambondromifehy. It is also a perspective that some others might find hard to fully appreciate. To get a sense of what I mean by it—and of how easily it can be overlooked or dismissed in the course of ethnographic investigation—consider the following brief thought experiment. Suppose that you were an ethnographer asked to explain why foreigners go to places like Ankarana. How would you respond? You might well begin, as many have, by reflecting on the unique historically and culturally rooted motivations behind such travel, and then proceed, again as others have, by suggesting that places like Ankarana offer foreigners the opportunity to pursue and maybe even consume some of things that they most value. Now suppose that you were asked a slight variation of that question: Why is it that people from Ankarana do not travel to the places from which the foreign tourists they observe come? If you knew anything about Ankarana, Madagascar, and the world, you would most likely answer without much thought to matters of motivations or values. Overseas travel is simply not an option for the vast majority of people from Ankarana. Not only do most lack the disposable income for airfare but also they are constrained by bureaucracies and exclusionary immigration policies that make getting passports and international visas extremely difficult. In the following paragraphs, I suggest that this latter approach—one that privileges the relevance of the easily observed capacity for action over that of the hard-to-discern values and motivations underlying action—is the one that my informants tend to take when making sense of the foreigners in their midst. As they see it, what is most significant about the foreigners who come to Ankarana is not the fact that they want to do the sorts of things that they do, but that they can. And they take this perspective for the same reason that you or I might when explaining why it is that more people from Ankarana cannot be found vacationing in Europe or North America: because to do otherwise would be to ignore the obvious.

In suggesting that all of my informants in Ankarana share and privilege an appreciation of the obvious political and economic disparities that separate them from foreigners, I do not mean to suggest that they share one critical voice. Reflections on the obvious come in many guises—including the speculating that many do about what it is that foreigners might really be up to in the Ankarana reserve. To illustrate what I mean by this, I here return to my informants' suspicions.

As mentioned earlier, many sapphire miners and traders in Ambondromifehy speculate that it is sapphires that have been drawing increasing numbers of foreigners to the Ankarana reserve over the past decade. After all, it is well-known that all locally mined sapphires are destined for foreign markets, and that only foreigners know what to do with these stones (Walsh 2004). Why would foreigners not come to Ankarana to prospect for sapphires themselves? Many of them stop in Ambondromifehy on their way to or from the reserve to look at what is available locally. Another theory I heard frequently is that there is some other commodity of great value that foreigners are after within the reserve—one that, as was the case with sapphires only ten years ago, remains unknown to Malagasy people. One common suggestion in this vein is that foreigners come to Ankarana in search of mercury, a commodity that I was assured is easily collected in the large jerry cans that they often bring with them on their trips into the reserve.

Stories circulating in Ambondromifehy about the behavior of foreigners within the reserve only reinforced the notion that there is much more than just picture taking going on there. One miner told of seeing a group of well-provisioned foreigners entering a cave and not emerging until several hours later, exhausted. If they were going to "take nothing but pictures," he wondered, why would they have so much equipment with them and why would it take them so long? And what is so exhausting about taking pictures? Another miner reported having once been hired to act as a porter for a group of foreigners touring the reserve. He carried their packs to the entrance of a cave that they wanted to see and was then told to wait for them. They took their packs with them. When they came out of the cave, they returned their packs to him. Now, however, the packs were much heavier. What was inside? he wondered. Why, for that matter, would they make him wait outside of the cave during their visit if they were not up to something that they meant to keep secret? Still another miner spoke of seeing a four wheeler being unloaded of so much baggage and equipment that it could only have belonged to a team of foreign sapphire prospectors. Why else would these people need so much stuff?

Ambondromifehy's speculators backed up their theories about foreigners' interests and activities in Ankarana with reference to more than just anecdotes, however. The most compelling evidence for the cases they made lay in the fact that the Ankarana reserve was so obviously reserved by and for foreigners. Although the reserve is now overseen by a Malagasy agency, almost everyone I spoke with understood that it was first established by the French during colonial times and was long managed by the World Wild Fund for Nature, itself misidentified by most as American. Many also noted the suspicious coincidence of the amelioration of the reserve's infrastructure—its roads, paths, campsites, and so forth—and the discovery of sapphires in the region. Why now? they asked. More importantly: Why here? Of all the places that could have been chosen for protection and visiting, foreigners chose this one, a place that happens to contain a windfall of little blue stones for which Malagasy people have no use and of which foreigners cannot seem to get enough.

In speculations like these, there was no doubting the role played by the foreign and national conservation organizations that oversee the reserve. Working in cooperation with foreign and Malagasy governments, what these organizations really conserve, many assumed, is the exclusive access of foreigners to the resources they desire. Some even guessed that these organizations help to regulate the differing claims of differing foreign nationalities. In one discussion, for example, a miner disagreed with my assurance that the reserve's well-known campsites, the Campement des Anglais and Campement des Americains, were named for the nationalities of the first research and film crews to use these clearings as home bases. Instead, he argued that these sites marked competing foreign claims to the reserve's resources. The fact that these campsite names were recently changed to Malagasy names was to him more a sign of a cover-up of previously transparent English and U.S. interests in the region than, as I suggested, of efforts at symbolically reinforcing the Malagasy State's claims to guardianship of the reserve. Other

observers highlighted the likely connections between today's foreign prospectors and those of the past, stressing the obvious importance of the fact
that Ankarana was first established as a protected area at the end of French
rule in Madagascar. Some argued that the French have always known about
the value of what could be found in this place, and this is why they set it
aside while they could. One trader even described the caves at the center of
the reserve as one of France's "safes" (*coffres*), something into which the former colonial ruler could dip occasionally if in need of a little extra cash.

Despite these rumors of foreign involvement, however, the most significant high-level culprits to many in Ambondromifehy were corrupt Malagasy
politicians and state officials, compatriots who were suspected of having
ceded control of this place and its resources to foreign interests in return for
personal gains. One trader even suggested that Malagasy officials had used
the reserve's untapped mineral wealth as collateral for international loans,
only to go on and "eat" (*mihinana*) this money themselves with little
thought to the debts they incurred. This last speculation might seem ludi-
crous were it not, in part, so close to reality. As it happens, Ankarana is
among the many protected areas around the world to have benefited from
what has been called "debt for nature swapping," a strategy whereby
conservation-friendly international organizations (like USAID, in the case
of Madagascar) relieve a small portion of an underdeveloped nation's debt in
return for a commitment of national resources to conservation projects.

As this last point suggests, there is more truth to some of these seemingly
far-out speculations than might first meet the eye. Most generally, it should
be acknowledged that in a context like Ankarana, where ecotourism is being
promoted as a significant component of a sustainable development strategy,
what conservation efforts actually conserve is, among other things, the
access of foreigners to the resources they desire. It is certainly obvious to
people in Ambondromifehy that the protected area from which they are
meant to be restricted is not actually protected from or for all people, but
only from those who would like to use its resources in the pursuit of short-
term benefits and for those who can afford to explore it at great length and
with unclear goals in mind. This last point concerning the connectedness of
conservation, affluence, and foresight is both obvious to many in Ambondromifehy and especially relevant to efforts at understanding the perspectives of these people. I now elaborate on this with some deeper reflections
on the obvious.

DEEP PLAY IN THE TABOO FOREST

One morning in June 2004, I instigated and recorded a revealing conversation
with a group of sapphire miners and traders in Ambondromifehy. The topic

was a familiar one: foreigners and what makes foreigners and Malagasy people different. In the following paragraphs, I cite this conversation extensively, both for the insights it offers on matters touched on above and to illustrate how my informants' reflections on the obvious lead them to unique and profound understandings of the global political economy in which they find themselves enmeshed.

Bera, a trader, spoke first. As he saw it, what makes the foreigners who come to Ankarana so different from the Malagasy people who live here is their "way of looking at things" (*fomba fizahana*). Bera noted that

When foreigners look at something, . . . they look at it deeply (*latiny*).They ask themselves whether [a] thing is "true/real" (*marigny*) or not. Does it have any meaning, or no meaning? Only when they've done this do they leave it. A Malagasy person looks at something and says [looking only at the surface], "Yes, this is black," even though there might be something important inside of it, they don't concern themselves with that. (Conversation with author, June 15, 2004.)

According to Bera, looking "deeply" in the way that foreigners do means taking time to consider things extensively and with an eye to all of their possible unseen meanings and uses, commercial or otherwise. Malagasy people are different, he claimed. With reference to the Ankarana reserve in particular, Bera continued with self-deprecating exaggeration:

We Malagasy who go there, we just use our slingshots on birds . . . we go after lemurs, we go after birds, we go after fish in the lakes there. We don't know anything about these things. If we see a chameleon, we might poke it with a stick and then keep going. None of us ask, "What kind of a tree is this here?" "What might this be medicine for?" We don't care about this. "Can this plant cure people, or not cure people? Will it kill them?" We don't care about this. We see all of these fruits on the trees, if we try them and they're not sweet, if they're bitter, we throw them away and that's it! (Conversation with author, June 15, 2004.)

The particular way in which foreigners look at things, another trader added, is the product of a particular way of life that they have and Malagasy do not. "So it has to do with what people learn to like and dislike?" I asked, still interested in local perspectives on foreigners' distinctive motivations. "No," came the answer, "it has nothing to do with what people like and dislike, but with how children are raised" (conversation with author, June I5, 2004). He explained that children raised amidst affluence—*agnatiny valera* (literally, "surrounded by value")—know what things are worth. If people see things that have great value in a place far from home—as was the case with the foreigners who first came in search of sapphires—they will take these things away with them. "There are few Malagasy people who have been raised surrounded by value," he noted, "so there is nothing in our upbringing to lead us to recognize that such and such a thing has value" (conversation with author, June 15, 2004).

It is more than just affluence, however, that accounts for foreigners' inclinations to look at things in the way that they do; affluence enables foreigners to be prospective. Where Malagasy people only look "one meter ahead," one miner noted, "foreigners look one thousand meters ahead" (conversation with author, June 15, 2004). Picking up on this point and that of different child-rearing practices, Bera added:

> When Malagasy children play, they don't pay attention to what they are doing. When foreigners played in the past, their play led to the production of something important. Like the foreigners who invented airplanes. At the start it was a kind of a game that they played on the tops of mountains . . . they tried [building airplanes out of] bicycles first. But with Malagasy, if kids play with something they get yelled at. . . . I think the way in which foreigners raise children is to let them play and break things in the house because you never know what the child will be good at doing. Parents let children do this because they are wealthy enough. If something breaks, they can just buy another one. (Conversation with author, June 15, 2004.)

Bera illustrated this last point with the hypothetical example of a Malagasy child who wants to learn how to fix watches. He explained that no Malagasy parent could afford to give his or her child a watch to tinker with knowing that there is a good chance that the child might break it. For wealthier foreigners, however, what is another watch? Getting back to his main point, Bera speculated that the children of foreigners are encouraged to engage in what we might call, with apologies to Clifford Geertz (1973), *deep play*. In other words, foreigners' children are encouraged to take apart watches and other things, to play with and look at them deeply, to examine their inner workings to get at and understand what makes them tick. Fixing the watch is not the point. It is the deep play itself that is important, ensuring unknowable future dividends to those who can afford to engage in it now. Bera then linked this example to the situation in Ankarana. Who knows why foreigners come here, and whether they are conservationists, tourists, explorers, prospectors, or something else? The obvious fact remains that, even if it might seem that they are only playing, foreigners' interest in this place is telling in and of itself. Foreigners never just look; they are always looking for a reason.

This last point should be the most obvious of all. By suggesting that all foreigners, regardless of their motivations, approach Ankarana as affluent prospectors enabled by political and economic privilege, Bera offers a rubric under which virtually all foreign visitors to Madagascar, past and present, may be grouped. What were the precolonial explorations of merchants, and the colonial-era projects of administrators, entrepreneurs, missionaries, and explorers, if not both borne of affluence and essentially prospective? For that matter, what is Western environmentalism if not founded in the deep play of forward-thinking activists, scientists, and environmental nongovernmental organizations? The very facts that Malagasy environments have been classified as "endangered" at all and that efforts are being made to conserve them might be taken as both products and indications of the prospective perspective that Bera had in mind. At best, international conservation efforts in places like Ankarana suggest the developed world's legitimate but irresolvable anxiety over the planet's future; at worst, they may be taken as serving the interests of international bioprospectors (Shiva 1997). Either way, the message of conservation projects in places like Ankarana remains the same: sustainability at best for some, but prospecting, however well-intentioned, as usual for others. The notion of sustainability itself may be usefully questioned with Bera's political ecology in mind. Although *sustainable development* has been famously defined in the Brundtland report as "development that meets the needs of the present without compromising the ability of future generations to meet their own needs" (Brundtland 1987: 43), it should not be forgotten that those who advocate the need for others to embrace sustainability have never pursued such modest ends for themselves. Deep players that they are, promoters of sustainability aim to "meet the needs" of individual, national, and global futures without compromising the status quo that enables such pursuits. Indeed, Bera might well have predicted what has evidently come to pass in these days following the Kyoto Protocol—specifically, that much of the developed world's taste for the chase of global conservation goals wanes whenever calls to think about the future of the planet are set against more powerful concerns over what such foresight is likely to cost at home. It is only when "can we afford to?" is refigured, often by environmentalists, as "can we afford not to, given the potential consequences of our inaction?" that prospective interest returns, and newly acceptable sacrifices are likely to be made. A key point here, of course, and one that must be kept in mind whenever considering situations of ecological underprivilege around the world, is that acceptable sacrifices are only ever acceptable to those who can afford them.

So what, then, of the inhabitants of Ankarana who can afford to sacrifice certain sorts of access to the resources of the Ankarana reserve and actually choose to do so and would have others do the same? I turn to them next.

OTHER PERSPECTIVES

Some residents of the Ankarana region can afford to make certain sacrifices for the sake of conservation, and some have livelihoods that depend on such sacrifices being made. Unsurprisingly, then, not everyone living around the reserve supports the activities of Ambondromifehy's miners and traders; neither do all agree with their speculations about foreigners. Nivo, the man with I whom I began my discussion of the obvious, was among the many I spoke with who took a dim view of stories circulating about the possible secret contents of the Ankarana reserve. "If there was something [of great value] here," he once told me,

> wouldn't I know about it? Would I be living in a shack like this? Wouldn't I have a cement house by now? . . . would I be asking God for food? Wouldn't my courtyard be full of cars? . . . I'm here living in this bamboo hut with cockroaches all over the place . . . Go and look if you think you're going to find [sapphires or mercury], go and look so that you can become rich! (Conversation with author, June 2, 2004.)

Those involved in the region's ecotourist trade were also dismissive of Ambondromifehy's speculators. Knowing just how incompetent most foreigners are when it comes to negotiating the bush, reserve guides were especially amused at stories portraying their clients as savvy explorers. They know perfectly well that foreigners look exhausted all the time because they generally cannot stand the heat, that the jerry cans they bring with them are for bathing and cooking water, that they do not leave their packs with unattended porters because they are untrusting, and that all of the baggage they lug around with them is nothing more than the result of overpacking. Not that these observers buy into the International Ecotourism Society's simple depiction of ecotourism as "responsible travel to natural areas that conserves the environment and preserves the well-being of local people" (Russell and Wallace 2004: 1). Leading up to eight different visitors a day on tours through the reserve, guides know better than anyone what a diverse lot ecotourists can be. As Jean-Paul, a six-year veteran of guiding, noted

> There are some [tourists] who aren't even interested in animals. Some who are only interested in trees. They don't know the kinds of trees, but they ask all about them. There are some others who are only interested in insects . . . they don't care about anything else. It's important to know what they want to see, so that you know where to take them. (Conversation with author, June 6, 2004.)

Some want to hike; others would rather ride in a four wheeler as far as they possibly can. Some want to talk; others demand silence. Some stop at length to look at or photograph the plants, animals, and rock formations that their guides point out; others cannot be bothered. Some ask questions about what they are seeing; others appear bored by the whole thing. Some know a great deal about the environment; others will believe anything you tell them. Shockingly, some never even make it far out of their campsite, preferring to spend their days soaking up the forest and waiting for the animals they are in search of to come to them. When asked to obey the rules of the reserve, most are very good about it. Others are *maditry,* or "badly behaved," insisting on feeding lemurs, shining lights on sleeping bats, and walking off trails even though they know they are not supposed to. And although most guides are strict with their charges, reporting infractions to reserve officials, I have heard of others who are wary of doing anything that might lose them several days' wages and tips.

Reserve administrators living and working in Mahamasina also understand what a diverse group of foreigners the Ankarana reserve attracts. Still, several I spoke with felt that ecotourism remains an important component of the conservationist project to which they are dedicated. Almost all of the foreigners who come to Ankarana, one reserve employee told me, share in what he called an *esprit conservateur,* a "conservationist spirit," that distinguishes them from many of the region's inhabitants. Another referred to this same quality as a *goult,* or "taste," for nature that local people must rediscover before it is too late. From this perspective, foreign visitors set an important example for local people by living in harmony with the environment: taking nothing but pictures and leaving nothing but footprints, just as the sign directs. However, neither reserve employees nor the guides cited earlier ever lost sight of the obvious. It was obvious to these observers—as it was to Bera and others in Ambondromifehy—that foreigners approach the Malagasy environment because they can afford to do so. The conservationist spirit or taste for nature that foreigners have may be the product of enculturation at home, but the fact that they can service this spirit and taste in Ankarana is not. The latter is quite simply a product of their greater political and economic capacities.

Perhaps the best lesson that can be gleaned from the obvious points raised in this chapter is that ecopolitical tensions in Ankarana are not well understood as a result of people with different tastes, motivations, and values misunderstanding one another. Neither are they likely to be anything but exacerbated by efforts at sensitizing people, such as those in Ambondromifehy, to more sustainable ways of thinking about the environment. These tensions are the result of the conflicting perspectives of members of two differently positioned groups in the region: (1) people who do what they do because they can afford to and (2) people who do what they do because they cannot afford not to. This final point is so obvious that even people whose livelihoods depend on the existence of ecotourism and the Ankarana reserve acknowledge it. In the course of another conversation in the spring of 2004, this time with a group of reserve guides and administrators, one reserve employee provocatively posed a rhetorical question to the others: "Why do people living around the reserve continue to exploit it illegally in the way that they do?" (conversation with author, May 28, 2004). He told the group that they do so, because they "would rather die tomorrow than die today" (conversation with author, May 28, 2004)—using a phrase I have often heard used to refer to Ankarana's most marginal residents. When this is the sort of choice that people face—dying tomorrow or dying today—the reasons for the seemingly unsustainable behavior of some should be obvious to all.

CONCLUSION

Although some may take this discussion as just another critical jab at ecotourism, conservation, or their mixture in what one Malagasy friend calls "ecolonialism," it is not intended as such. I agree with Anderson and Berglund (2003), Joe Bandy (1996), and others cited earlier that the organizations, ideologies, policies, and procedures that play such important parts, at different scales, in creating and fueling ecopolitical tensions in places like Ankarana should be subjected to the same sort of scrutiny as are any other manifestations of human endeavor. However, I am also aware of the danger of mistaking easy targets for good ones. Take ecotourists, for example. Is there any group of foreigners in Ankarana more likely to be ridiculed by means of an ethnographic account of the obvious? Stumbling into the forest with too much luggage, untrusting of porters, and believing just about anything their guides tell them, the prototypical ecotourist pictured in the previous pages might well seem the perfect foil or fool for an expert relativist mediator like me. Savvy explorers? Hardly.

According to the people who work with them, many ecotourists cannot even figure out how to bathe from a bucket. Deep players? Please. How much can they possibly learn over their standard three days in the region? Anyone who claims to know more than an ecotourist must be careful, however. After all, the reputation of these foreigners as deep players and savvy explorers must come from somewhere. Ecotourists are certainly not the first or only foreigners to take an interest in Madagascar's unique ecologies and natural resources, nor is the island's reputation as "undiscovered" or "untouched" an invention of the ecotourist industry. Northern Malagasy environments have long figured among the world's resource frontiers, supplying foreign demand for everything from hardwoods to gold to tortoise shell. Less obvious to some, these same environments have also long served foreign demand for the training and discoveries of amateur and professional researchers. Over the years, the Ankarana reserve has seen its fair share of scholarly deep players, people whose essentially prospective research concerning the region's unique flora, fauna, and geology (to name but a few possibilities) has resulted in studies that may or may not have had lasting impact in specialized fields of mostly foreign concern. As I have made clear in the preceding pages, and as is obvious to all of the people to whom I owe this chapter's contents, I am as much a deep player in Ankarana as anyone.

The conversation cited extensively above ended as many of my conversations in Ankarana have—with one informant or another deciding that they had given me enough of their time. The first person to bail out was a miner named François. Up to the moment he left, his contribution to the conversation was comprised almost entirely of questions. "I want to ask you something," he always began, politely and usually out of the blue. He would then continue, "Are there crazy people where you are from?" or "Are there Malagasy people where you are from?" or "How long does it take to get here from where you are from?" (conversation with author, June 15, 2004). Others in the group admonished François for asking things that took us far from the topics I had proposed, but I assured them all that I was always happy for opportunities to exchange knowledge with people who had been helpful to me. And so, as the conversation proceeded, I was occasionally called to discuss the treatment of the mentally ill in North America or list the occupations and regions of origin of the Malagasy people I had met in Canada, or reflect on what one does for twelve hours on the flight from Paris to Antananarivo. About an hour into our discussion when, at my instigation, talk turned to the possible uses that foreigners may have for sapphires, François announced his leave by slinging his mining bar across his shoulder and remarking that he did not particularly care what foreigners did with sapphires, so long as they kept buying them. It was time, in other words, for him to leave my work and get back to his own. I thanked him for his participation, and he thanked me in return.

> This has been a good talk that we have had here . . . we have spoken about many things. When I think back on it, there will be some things [from this conversation] that I will take and apply in my daily life. The things that I don't like, I have heard them but I won't use them. It is like what you do. The things that are significant to you, you will write down in your book. The things that aren't [important] get taken away by the wind. (Conversation with author, June 15, 2004.)

As François understood perfectly well, my interest in the conversation we shared was essentially prospective. He rightly assumed that I would take their recorded words away with me so that I could later sift through them, picking out the bits that I found relevant and useful for whatever projects I had in mind. After all, I am a foreigner, and I travel to Ankarana for a reason. True, I speak Malagasy, do not spend much time in the Ankarana reserve, and tend to associate more with Malagasy people than with other foreigners, but this does not make my deep play any less obvious. It is there in my running tape recorder, and in the fact that I conduct interviews in Malagasy but scribble notes in English. It is there in my asking different people the same questions over and over again, in my stories of travel to and from Madagascar, and in my promises to return again in the near future. It is also there, of course, in my training.

The sort of deep play that Bera attributed to foreign affluent prospectors is essential to the production of good ethnography. As Jeremy MacClancy recently noted, what makes ethnographers so good at "disentangling" complexities, especially when investigating matters as complex as tourism, is that they have learned to "listen to . . . competing voices of members from different interest groups . . . [and to] compare their words with their deeds in order to disentangle the overlapping realities, and . . . clarify . . . various misconceptions and consequent confusions" (2002b: 421). We consider as much as we can in preparing to write ethnography because we can never be sure what will and will not be important from the start. The same uncertainty prevails when contemplating the end results of all of this work. "The boundaries of what is 'socially relevant' research," MacClancy writes, "are constantly shifting, in tune with changing circumstances. What may appear to be abstruse scholarship one day may become material of great political import the next day" (2002a: 14).

This essentially prospective perspective is one that I have learned to take in my work, and one that I share with many others in the discipline. It is also, of course, precisely the perspective that François, Bera, and others in Ambondromifehy would expect of a deep player like me. Although they are uncertain and often ask about how I am able to make a living from what I do, they understand perfectly well that I am able to take the prospective perspective that I so obviously do because I can afford to. There is little doubt in my mind as to what Nivo would say about why I do what I do in Ankarana. Regardless of my motivations, I do what I do, he would say, because I can. And he would be right. This final nod to the obvious is intended as nothing more than a caution to anyone tempted to use the privilege of ethnographic discourse to explicitly or implicitly position themselves in contrast to, or outside of, the forces that precipitate situations of ecological underprivilege around the world. This point is not intended to cause paralysis, however, leaving those to whom it rings true stuck obsessing over questions of why we approach the things that people say and do in the way that we do, or whether we have anything more to offer the world than any other frequent fliers. After all, as my informants in Ambondromifehy made quite clear to me, it is only people who overlook the obvious possibilities for action enabled by privilege who are likely to dwell on motivations at the expense of all else.

REFERENCES

Anderson, David G., and Eeva Berglund, eds. 2003. *Ethnographies of Conservation: Environmentalism and the Distribution of Privilege.* New York: Berghahn.

Bandy, Joe. 1996. "Managing the Other of Nature: Sustainability, Spectacle, and Global Regimes of Capital in Ecotourism." *Public Culture* 8: 539–66.

Bellows, Keith. 2001. "Madagascar Tourism." news.nationalgeographic.com/news/2001/07/ 0724_TvTravMad.html (accessed July 19, 2005).

Brundtland, Gro Harlem. 1987. *Our Common Future: The World Commission on Environment and Development.* Oxford: Oxford University Press.

Carrier, James G., and Donald V. L. Macleod. 2005. "Bursting the Bubble: The Socio-Cultural Context of Ecotourism." *Journal of the Royal Anthropological Institute* 11, no. 2: 315–34.

Conservation International. 2005. "Madagascar and the Indian Ocean Islands." http://www.biodiversityhotspots.org/xp/Hotspots/madagascar/Pages/default.aspx (accessed August 19, 2008)

Cortez Travel. 2005. "Madagascar. Untouched. Unspoiled. Undiscovered." www.airmad.com (accessed July 19, 2005).

Duffy, Rosaleen. 2002. *A Trip Too Far: Ecotourism, Politics and Exploitation.* London: Earthscan.

Escobar, Arturo. 1999. "After Nature: Steps to an Antiessentialist Political Ecology." *Current Anthropology* 40, no. 1: 1–30.

Ferguson, James. 1990. *The Anti-Politics Machine: "Development," Depoliticization, and Bureaucratic Power in Lesotho.* Cambridge: Cambridge University Press.

Geertz, Clifford. 1973. "Deep Play: Notes on the Balinese Cockfight." In *The Interpretation of Cultures,* 412–53. New York: Basic.

Gewertz, Deborah B., and Frederick K. Errington. 2001. "On the Generification of Culture: From Blowfish to Melanesian." *Journal of the Royal Anthropological Institute* 7, no. 3: 505–25.

Gezon, Lisa. 1997. "Political Ecology and Conflict in Ankarana, Madagascar." *Ethnology* 36, no. 2: 85–100.

Gezron, Lisa. 2004. "Finding the Global in the Local: Environmental Struggles in Northern Madagascar." In Susan Paulson and Lisa L. Gezon, eds., *Political Ecology across Spaces, Scales, and Social Groups,* 135–53. New Brunswick, N.J.: Rutgers University Press.

———. In press. *Global Visions, Local Landscapes: A Political Ecology of Conservation, Conflict, and Control in Northern Madagascar.* Walnut Creek, Calif.: AltaMira.

Harper, Janice. 2002. *Endangered Species: Health, Illness and Death among Madagascar's People of the Forest.* Durham, N.C.: Carolina Academic Press.

Kottak, Conrad. 1999. "The New Ecological Anthropology." *American Anthropologist* 101, no. 1: 23–35.

MacClancy, Jeremy. 2002a. "Introduction: Taking People Seriously." In *Exotic No More: Anthropology on the Front Lines.* Jeremy MacClancy, ed. Pp. 1–14. Chicago: University of Chicago Press.

———. 2002b. "Paradise Postponed: The Predicaments of Tourism." In *Exotic No More: Anthropology on the Front Lines,* 418–29. Chicago: University of Chicago Press.

Martinez-Alier, Joan. 2002. *The Environmentalism of the Poor: A Study of Ecological Conflicts and Valuation.* Cheltenham, U.K.: Edward Elgar.

Mowforth, Martin, and Ian Munt. 1998. *Tourism and Sustainability: New Tourism in the Third World.* New York: Routledge.

Peluso, Nancy Lee, and Michael Watts. 2001. "Violent Environments." In *Violent Environments*, 3–39. Ithaca, N.Y.: Cornell University Press.

Rappaport, Roy. 1979. "The Obvious Aspects of Ritual." In *Ecology, Meaning, and Religion*, 174–222. Richmond, CA: North Atlantic Books.

———. 1993. "The Anthropology of Trouble." *American Anthropologist* 95, no. 2: 295–303.

Russell, Andrew, and Gillian Wallace. 2004. "Irresponsible Ecotourism." *Anthropology Today* 20, no. 3: 1–2.

Scott, James. 1998. *Seeing Like a State: How Certain Schemes to Improve the Human Condition Have Failed*. New Haven: Yale University Press.

Shiva, Vandana. 1979. *Biopiracy: The Plunder of Nature and Knowledge*. Boston: South End.

Stronza, Amanda. 2001. "Anthropology of Tourism: Forging New Ground for Ecotourism and Other Alternatives." *Annual Review of Anthropology* 30: 261–83.

Theodossopoulos, Dimitrios. 2003. *Troubles with Turtles: Cultural Understandings of the Environment on a Greek Island*. New York: Berghahn.

Walsh, Andrew. 2002. "Saving Souls, Preserving Bodies: Religious Incongruity in a Northern Malagasy Mining Town." *Journal of Religion in Africa* 32, no. 3: 366–92.

———. 2003. "Hot Money and Daring Consumption in a Northern Malagasy Mining Town." *American Ethnologist* 30, no. 2: 290–305.

———. 2004. "In the Wake of Things: Speculating in and about Sapphires in Northern Madagascar." *American Anthropologist* 106, no. 2: 225–37.

West, Paige. 2001. "Environmental Non-Governmental Organizations and the Nature of Ethnographic Inquiry." *Social Analysis* 45, no. 2: 55–77.

West, Paige, and James G. Carrier. 2004. "Ecotourism and Authenticity; Getting Away from It All?" *Current Anthropology* 45, no. 4: 483–98.

Zerner, Charles. 2002. *Culture and the Question of Rights; Forests, Coasts, and Seas in Southeast Asia*. Durham, N.C.: Duke University Press.

8

Technology and the Green Revolutions

One of the most widely held beliefs of those living in industrialized countries is that a key component—perhaps *the* key component—of modernity is technological progress. So fervent is our belief in the technological good that we seldom pause to consider the possibility that embracing technology comes with often hidden and usually unanticipated social and ecological costs. Rarer still is the knowledge that these costs are not spread evenly around our increasingly globalized world. Clearly, technology girds the entire globalization process. Not one article in this volume fails to consider, in part, a multiplicity of technologies that play some role in global exchange. Therefore it may seem strange that we decided to devote an entire chapter to the subject on its own merits. In our classes we ask students to examine some of their most axiomatic beliefs, and we have found that their faith in technological progress is usually the hardest to shake. Because our lives promise to become even further enmeshed in technological apparatus, and because technological advances lie at the heart of the consumption, production, and the waste cycle, we believe it is essential for students to have a well-rounded view of technology in our modern society.

Our sense of technological optimism goes back some two hundred years and achieved its climax in the postwar period. Perhaps the most representative example of this euphoria was the attempt by First World scientists to create new hybrid varieties of staple grains capable of unprecedented high yields. These high-yield varieties (HYVs) were to be a blessing for the impoverished billions of the Third World—a dynamic of agricultural globalization known today as the "green revolution." Despite the high yields, embracing the technology of HYVs came with a seldom mentioned suite of social and environmental costs that were more typical than revolutionary. There has been no more ardent critic of the green revolution than ecologist Vandana Shiva, who juxtaposes it to the globalized world of genetically modified organisms

(GMOs). Indeed, as Shiva demonstrates, the fruits of both modern biotechnology and the green revolution may have been borne of the same tree.

Vandana Shiva, "Pepsico for Peace? The Ecological and Political Risks of the Biotechnology Revolution" (1991).[1]

The Punjab crisis, characterized by violence and discontent, is in large measure linked to the unanticipated effects of the technological fix of the green revolution that was ironically aimed at preventing violence and containing discontent through the technological transformation of Indian agriculture. The main elements of the technological fix of the first green revolution were:

1. The replacement of diverse mixed crops and rotational cropping patterns of cereals, pulses, and oilseeds produced primarily for self-consumption, with monocultures of introduced wheat and rice varieties produced primarily for the market
2. The substitution of internal resources of the farm with purchased inputs of seeds, fertilizers, pesticides, energy, and so on
3. The enclavization of food production for the entire country in a small region

The green revolution has been projected as having increased agricultural productivity in an absolute sense. At the level of resource utilization, the new seed fertilizer technology was clearly counter productive, both with respect to natural resource inputs like water, as well as industrial inputs such as fertilizer use. This is clear in the case of rice where some indigenous high-yielding varieties compared with the yields of the green revolution varieties, but used substantially less water and fertilizer inputs. Richaria reported yields of 4,000 kg and more in rice cultivation in Baster, and Yegna Iyengar recorded rice yields above 5,000 kg/ha in South India (Richaria 1986; Iyengar 1944: 30). Even in the case of wheat, and particularly true in Punjab, increase in yields was achieved; the increase in cost of inputs did not affect the gain in yields. Productivity with respect to water use and fertilizer use thus actually declined, as summarized in table 8.1.

In terms of energy, the green revolution technology is far more inefficient than the technologies it displaced. When food energy output from rice-growing systems is compared with the total energy input, the energy use in agriculture is found to have declined. The pre–green revolution systems have energy ratios of around ten, but with the introduction of the green revolution this level is more than halved. With industrial agriculture, the ratio is further reduced to one, and as much energy is being expended in these systems as is being obtained from them in the form of food (Bayliss-Smith 1984).

Table 8.1. Comparison of Productivity of Native Varieties and Borlaug Varieties of Wheat

	Native Variety	Borlaug Variety
Yield kg/ha	3,291	4690 (Gill 1978: 193)
Water demand	12″ 5.3 cm	36″ (Kang 1982: 204) 16 cm
Fertilizer demand	47.3	88.5 (Desai 1979:390)
Productivity with respect to water use (kg/ha/cm)	620.94	293.1
Productivity with respect to fertilizer use (kg/ha/kg)	69.5	52.99

While the increase in productivity was the primary objective of the green revolution, in terms of resources and energy, the productivity actually declined. The increase that was achieved in the early phases was at the level of financial returns. In fact, the motive force for the green revolution technology package came from profits for agribusiness and profits for farmers. However, the ecology of the green revolution demanded increasing costs of inputs and resulted in decreasing profits for the farmers of Punjab. Agricultural income stagnated or began to decline. In less than two decades, the green revolution had become financially and ecologically unviable, though it succeeded in the production of surpluses of specialized crops in a specialized region for a short period, based on high inputs, high subsidies, and high support prices.

There are two options available for getting out of the crisis of food production in Punjab and making agriculture economically viable again. The first is to move away from resource and capital intensive agricultural technology to low-cost agriculture by making food production economically and ecologically more viable again, through the reduction of input costs. The second option is to move away from staple foods for domestic markets to luxury foods and nonfood crops for export markets, with a new dependence on imports of high technology inputs like seeds and chemicals. It is the latter option that has been officially adopted as the strategy for the second agricultural revolution in Punjab.

The main elements of the technological fix of the second green revolution are:

1. The substitution of wheat and rice produced for domestic markets with fruits and vegetables produced for the export of processed foods
2. The substitution of green revolution technologies with new biotech-

nologies, integrated more deeply with farm chemicals on the one hand and food processing on the other
3. The total neglect of staple food production as a primary objective of public policy

PEPSICO FOR PEACE?

The Pepsico project to be located in Punjab is at the center of the new agriculture policy. It has been viewed by commentators as a catalyst for the next agricultural revolution, and a program for peace. The first agricultural revolution was also to have been a strategy for peace and prosperity. It delivered violence and discontent. Will the second agricultural revolution in Punjab succeed where the first failed?

The Pepsico project, now called Pepsi Foods, was first proposed in 1986 as a collaboration between Punjab Agro-Industries Corporation, Voltas, a subsidiary of the Tata's, and Pepsico, the U.S. multinational. The project consists of (1) an agro-research center to develop improved varieties of seeds using biotechnology, (2) a potato- and grain-based processing plant to produce high-quality food products, (3) a fruit and vegetable processing plant for processing fruits, (4) and a soft drink concentrate unit to make soft drink and juice concentrates. The cost of the project was initially Rs21 crore, of which Pepsico's share was about Rs3.59 crore. The project envisaged an export of Rs20 crore in the first year alone. The total value of exports over ten years was expected to be Rs194 crores. About 74 percent of the total outlay of Rs22 crores on the project was in the processed food sector. The plan was to utilize one lakh tons of fruit and vegetables, which will be grown on land that now grows cereals. The import component of the project was estimated at Rs37 crores over a period of ten years. In March 1989, the partners in the Pepsico project announced a doubling of their investment. They now plan to invest more than Rs50 crores in the project (Kumar 1984).

In spite of two years of controversy and debate, the central government cleared the Pepsi project on September 19, 1988, and the minister of the newly formed Food Processing Industry Ministry justified it on the grounds of diversification of agriculture, increase in agricultural income and employment, and restoration of peace and stability in Punjab. The project has been criticized for creating a new dependency, sacrificing self-reliance and going against the national interest (Sidhu). Like the green revolution in Punjab, the Pepsico program for peace claims to offer a technological fix for a political crisis. Like the green revolution before it, it holds the potential to aggravate the crisis by introducing new vulnerability in agriculture.

SEEDS OF ECOLOGICAL VULNERABILITY

The miracle seeds of the green revolution were meant to free the Indian farmer from constraints imposed by nature. Instead, large scale monocultures of exotic varieties generated a new ecological vulnerability by reducing genetic diversity and destabilizing soil and water systems.

Punjab was chosen to be India's bread-basket through the Green Revolution, with high response seeds, misleadingly called high-yielding varieties (HYVs). The green revolution led to a shift from earlier rotations of cereals, oilseeds, and pulses to a paddy wheat rotation with intensive inputs of irrigation and chemicals. The paddy wheat rotation has created an ecological backlash with serious problems of waterlogging in canal-irrigated regions and groundwater mining in tubewell irrigated regions. Further, the HYVs have led to large-scale micronutrient deficiencies in soils, particularly iron in paddy cultivated areas and manganese in wheat cultivated areas.

Table 8.2.   The Green Revolution in Punjab: Indicative Costs and Benefits

Costs	Benefits
Decline in pulses production from 370 to 150 thousands metric tons between 1965 and 1980 (Johl 1985).	Increase in rice production from 292 to 3,228 thousand metric tons between 1965 and 1980 ("Punjab Floods" 1988).
Decline in oilseeds production from 214 to 176 thousand metric tons between 1965 and 1980 (Johl 1985).	Increase in wheat production from 1916 to 7694 thousand metric tons between 1965 and 1980 ("Punjab Floods" 1988).
Destruction of genetic diversity with introduction of rice and wheat monocultures.	
Forty new insect pests and twelve new diseases in rice monocultures (Sidhu).	
Soils degraded by salinity, soil toxicity, micronutrient deficiency.	
2.6 lakh hectares waterlogged.	
Punjab floods in 1986 linked to Bhakra dam. 65% of 12,000 people killed. Loss to state, Rs1,000 crore (Bhattacharjee 1988). 50,000 hectares of land destroyed through sand deposits exceeding 60 cms in some places ("Floods Reduce" 1989).	

These problems were built into the ecology of the HYVs even though they were anticipated. The high water demands of these seeds necessitated high water inputs, and hence the hazards of desertification—through water logging in some regions and desiccation and aridization in others. The high nutrient demands caused micronutrient deficiencies on the one hand but were also unsustainable because increased applications of chemical fertilizers were needed to maintain yields, thus increasing costs without increasing returns. The demand of the HYV seeds for intensive and uniform inputs of water and chemicals also made large-scale monocultures an imperative. And monocultures being highly vulnerable to pests and diseases, a new cost was created for pesticide applications. The ecological instability inherent in HYV seeds was thus translated into economic nonviability. The miracle seeds were not such a miracle after all. It is in the background of this ecological destruction caused by monocultures that the call for the diversification of Punjab agriculture was made by the Johl Committee in 1985 (Johl 1985). A policy for diversification involves an increase in the genetic diversity in cropping systems. However, the Pepsico project and the associated new seed policy that was announced in September 1988 threaten to further erode the genetic diversity in agriculture by narrowing the crop base, and increasing its ecological vulnerabilities through the introduction of exotic varieties of fruit and vegetable monocultures.

An integral part of the Pepsico project is the introduction of new varieties of fruits and vegetable seeds to be developed at the agro research centre being set up at Ludhiana. The claimed objective is to develop improved varieties of potato, tomato, and selected crops using biotechnologies like clonal propagation and tissue culture.

However, the experience of the green revolution shows that "improved seeds" is a contextual term, and genetic improvement for one objective can be a loss in terms of other parameters in another context. Thus for Pepsi, improving the potato implies making it more appropriate to its processing plant. The processing of potatoes and grain will be with imported machinery, which is supposed to handle about 30,000 tons of potatoes and 1,600 tons of grains per annum. The processing plant will determine the potato varieties to be planted, which will displace the native table varieties of potatoes. It is not that India does not grow tomatoes and potatoes. These are, however, table varieties to be consumed directly. There is no production of processed varieties; Pepsi will introduce these. From the point of view of the processing industry, the shift from table varieties to processed varieties is an improvement. For the consumer, it is a loss because the shift transforms food into raw material, to be consumed only through processing, not directly.

Potatoes for processing are being introduced in the name of diversification. But given the experience of potato cultivation in the United States, from which Pepsico technology is being transferred, it will lead to genetic uniformity and high vulnerability. Today in the United States only twelve varieties of the 2,000 species of potato are cultivated. Forty percent of all potato cultivation is of a single variety—the Russet Burbank. In 1970, only 28 percent of America's total potato acreage was planted with this variety. Growing acres and acres of the same kind of potato is ecologically very vulnerable. With Pepsico's biotechnology research center, the potatoes planted will be genetically identical since they will be reproduced vegetatively from a single plant variety. It matters little that the company's research farms develop 50,000 potential new potato varieties every year because the imperatives of seed and food processing demand uniformity in cultivation, and it is cultivated diversity or uniformity which is linked to vulnerability to disease and pestilence.

The Pepsico project will encourage genetic uniformity because it integrates seeds with processing, the farm with the factory. It is precisely such a push that led to the spread of the Russet Burbank. The McDonald's corporation needed the Russet Burbank because of its size. For example, 40 percent of all McDonald's fries must be two to three inches long. Another 40 percent must be over three inches, and the remaining 20 percent can be under two inches; the Russet Burbank fits perfectly (Bhattacharjee 1988: 2089). The economic forces of food processing push cultivation to a single crop yielding uniformity in spite of the known dangers of genetic uniformity, threatening the ecological stability of agriculture more than it has been in the past.

The introduction of uniformity is justified as a tradeoff for raising yields of horticultural crops miraculously. Pepsi's promotion literature states that "yields of horticultural produce in India are substantially lower than international standards." The project proposal for Pepsi Food argues that "in Mexico, Pepsi's subsidiary, Sabritas, launched a seed program that increased potato yields by 58 percent—from 19 to 30 tons per hectare in three years" (Doyle 1985: 205). In India, comparable yields have been achieved by farmers and agricultural scientists. As Usha Menon reported, potato yields of more than 40 tons per hectare have been realized during field trials in Jalandhar by the Central Potato Research Institute (Menon 1989). Yields averaging about 50–60 tons per hectare are also achieved by Gujarat farmers, who grow their potatoes on river beds in Banaskantha district. Just as in the first green revolution, the existence of indigenous high-yielding varieties of rice was denied to justify the introduction of high-response varieties. The Pepsi project denies the achievement of Indian farmers and scientists in order to make Pepsico's role indispensable. And just as the destruction of genetic diversity in the first green revolution cannot be ecologically or economically justified, the introduction of new ecological risks through projects like Pepsico are also unjustified.

Horticultural crops, especially when cultivated as monocultures, require high doses of pesticides. The genetic uniformity of processed varieties will thus increase the ecological hazards of pesticide use. The biotechnological revolution in agriculture is presented with the promise of miraculous fertilizers and pest-free crops. The dominant assumption of the liberalized seed policy is that it would ensure the supply of the best available seeds from anywhere in the world, and this would give a fresh spurt to our agricultural production.

As the experience of the green revolution in Punjab amply demonstrates, seeds based on exotic strains and dependent on high energy and chemical inputs make for ecological instability and high vulnerability. The new seed policy of 1988, which has brought the import of seeds and seed-processing under the purview of open general license (OGL), is closely associated with shifts in agricultural policy as symbolized by the Pepsico project. These shifts aggravate the vulnerabilities created by the green revolution while dispensing with some of the earlier safeguards. Green revolution seeds like wheat and rice were seeds of staple food crops, even though they contributed to genetic erosion and the decline of crops like pulses and oil seeds. The focus of the new seed policy is on seeds of flowers, vegetables, and fruits, not food staples. While the seed policy mentions import of seeds for crops like pulses, oilseeds, coarse grains, vegetables, and fruits, the international seed market is exclusively oriented toward the development of crop varieties that are widely traded on global markets. The new seed policy will thus imply the erosion of indigenous crops and crop varieties, while introducing heavier use of toxic agro-chemicals.

Biotechnology will increase the use of farm chemicals since breeding for pesticide and herbicide resistance is the dominant focus of biotechnology research in agricultural crops. For the seed-chemical multinationals, this makes commercial sense especially in the short run, since it is cheaper to adapt the plant to the chemical than adapt the chemical to the plant. The cost of developing a new crop variety rarely reaches US$2 million whereas the cost of a new herbicide exceeds US$40 million (Fowler 1988). Herbicide and pesticide resistance will also increase the integration of seeds, chemicals, and the control of multinational corporations (MNCs) in agriculture. A number of major agrochemical companies are developing plants with resistance to their brand of herbicides. Soybeans have been made resistant to Ciba-Geigy's Atrazine herbicides, and this has increased annual sales of the herbicide by US$120 million. Research is also being done to develop crop plants' resistant to other herbicides such as Dupont's Gist and Glean, and Monsanto's Roundup, which are lethal to most herbaceous plants and thus cannot be applied directly to crops. The successful development and sale of crop plants resistant to brand-name herbicides will result in further economic concentration of the agro-industry market increasing the market power of transnational companies.

For the Indian farmer this strategy for employing more toxic chemicals on pesticide- and herbicide-resistant varieties is suicidal. In India, thousands of people die annually as a result of pesticide poisoning. In 1987, more than sixty farmers in India's prime cotton growing area of Prakasam district in Andhra Pradesh committed suicide by consuming pesticides because of debts incurred for pesticide purchase (Ramprasad 1988). The introduction of hybrid cotton created pest problems. Pesticide resistance resulted in epidemics of white-fly and boll worm, for which the peasants used more toxic and expensive pesticides, incurring heavy debts and being driven to suicide. Even when pesticides and herbicides do not kill people, they kill people's sources of livelihood. The most extreme example of this destruction is bathua, a green leafy vegetable rich in vitamin A that grows as an associate of wheat. However, with intensive chemical fertilizer use, bathua becomes a major competitor of wheat and has been declared a weed that is killed with herbicides. In India 40,000 children go blind each year for lack of vitamin A (Mira Shiva, personal communication to author), and herbicides contribute to this tragedy by destroying the freely available sources of vitamin A. Thousands of rural women who make a living weaving baskets from wild reeds and grasses are losing their livelihood because the increased use of herbicides is killing the reeds and grasses. The introduction of herbicide-resistant crops will increase herbicide use and thus increase the damage to economically and ecologically useful plant species. Herbicide resistance also excludes the possibility of rotational and mixed cropping, which are essential for a sustainable and ecologically balanced agriculture, since the other crops would be destroyed by the herbicide. U.S. estimates now show a loss of US$4 billion per annum due to crop loss as a result of herbicide spraying. The destruction in India will be far greater because of higher plant diversity, and the prevalence of diverse occupations based on plants and biomass.

Strategies for genetic engineering for herbicide resistance which are destroying useful species of plants can also end up creating superweeds. There is an intimate relationship between weeds and crops, especially in the tropics where weedy and cultivated varieties have genetically interacted over centuries and hybridize freely to produce new varieties. Genes for herbicide tolerance, pest resistance, and stress tolerance that genetic engineers are striving to introduce into crop plants may be transferred to neighboring weeds as a result of naturally occurring gene transfer (Wheale 1988: 172).

The outcome of the free import of genetically engineered seeds and crop varieties will drastically increase the requirements for chemical herbicides for use on herbicide-resistant crops developed by agrochemical companies. The consumption of agro-chemicals to overcome the superweeds associated with the green revolution has been ecologically and economically a disaster for peasants. The increased use of pesticides and herbicides with the introduction of crops engineered for herbicide tolerance will spell total doom.

The alternative strategy of genetic engineering of pest-resistant crops is not commercially desirable for agrichemical concerns in the short run. It is also not ecologically infallible in the long run, since genes for disease resistance can mutate, or they can be overcome by other environmental pressures, leaving the crop vulnerable. Introduced crops are more prone to pest and disease attacks than native varieties, and they often introduce new pests and diseases in ecosystems.

The release of bioengineered seeds needs to be viewed in the context of the historical experience with the green revolution varieties which brought with them new diseases and pests, even while it was claimed that new varieties were bred for resistance to pests. Since 1966, when new rice varieties were released in Punjab, forty new insects and twelve new diseases have appeared. TN(I), the first semidwarf variety released in 1966, was susceptible to bacterial blight. In 1968, IRB, which was considered resistant to stem rot and brown spot was released, but proved to be susceptible to both diseases. PR 106, PR 108, PR 109 were especially bred for disease and insect resistance. Since 1976, PR 106 has become susceptible to white-backed plant hopper, stem rot disease, rice leaf folder, hispa, stem border, and several other insect pests (Sidhu). There is clearly no invulnerability in breeding for disease resistance. The more the technological claim to invulnerability, the greater is the ecological creation of vulnerability.

The liberalized seed policy has reduced the checks, controls, and safeguards for the release of new seeds while it opens the door for the introduction of new ecological hazards through the new varieties. The procedures laid down under the new policy for testing and trial of the imported seeds are weaker than those prevalent during the green revolution phase, when breeding technologies were less hazardous, and seeds used to be imported from the international agricultural research centers, not from MNCs and private breeders.

Introduction of diseases with introduced plant varieties is the norm, not the exception. For ten years McDonald's has been trying to move the Russet Burbank to Europe, in spite of hundreds of European varieties being cultivated. When McDonald's tried to introduce the Russet variety in Holland in 1981, the potatoes had to sit in quarantine for eight months before they could be given trial plantings. But the potato proved vulnerable to the European potato virus and was not accepted in Europe (Doyle 1985: 207). Such safeguards for rejection are being diluted in India. The usual norm for commercial release of seeds produced under alien agro-climatic conditions is three successive years of trial for occurrence of pests and diseases. The new seed policy has reduced this to a one-season trial, which increases the risk of introduction of disease and pests. Further, all requirements for postentry quarantine have been removed. Thus if crop diseases escape the quarantine check at entry, they can create havoc in the country's ecosystems.

Finally, in the case of genetically engineered seeds and planting material, conventional quarantine methodologies are inadequate since the transgenic material itself is a source of ecological hazards.

Our risk assessment frameworks are highly inadequate for the task of assessing the impact of the deliberate release of new plant varieties on ecosystems. Instead of developing methodologies for assessing risk and strengthening regulations and structures for the protection of people's health and safety, the government has diluted quarantine procedures and removed import controls. Liberalization has meant freedom for corporate giants to test, experiment, and sell their products without constraint, without controls. This necessarily means destroying for citizens the right to freedom from hazards posed by the new technologies and products.

SEEDS AND DEPENDENCY

The biotechnology revolution, which spurs the shifts in India's seed policy, differs from the green revolution in terms of corporate control and the control of bioregions. The biotechnology revolution is predominantly private in character. The green revolution was spearheaded by the international agricultural research centers like CIMMYT and IRRI organized by the Consultative Group or International Agricultural Research which is controlled by governments, private foundations, agribusiness corporations, and multinational development banks. The private corporate interests such as agrochemical and agribusiness transnationals thus functioned through the program set by public or quasi-public institutions, which they could influence and from whose agricultural strategies they stood to gain.

With the biotechnology revolution, the private corporate multinational interest has become the spearheading sector of agricultural policy. The Pepsico project and the new seed policy signals this new trend in which the technologies are not transferred from CIMMYT or IRRI to ICAR or PAU and on to the farm. This time, transnational corporate capital will go directly with the latest technology to the remotest farm. Private interests or profits will thus be the dominant driving force in the biorevolution, increasing the control of multinationals, decreasing the role of governments and citizens of the Third World (table 8.3) (Fowler 1988).

The new seed policy seems to repeat the old mistakes of the green revolution of selling false miracles and threatens to render totally uneconomic the cultivation of staple food grains for local consumption by small farmers, thus threatening our food security as a nation. The dependence on import of seeds on the one hand and export of processed foods on the other has the very real danger of creating new forms of poverty and deprivation within the country, and making us totally dependent on a handful of multinational interests for the supply of inputs and the purchase of our agricultural com-

Table 8.3. Comparing the Revolutions

Green Revolution	*Gene Revolution*
Summary	
Based in public sector	Based in private sector
Humanitarian intent	Profit motive
Centralized R&D	Centralized R&D
Focus of yield	Focus on inputs/processing
Relatively gradual	Relatively immediate
Emphasis on major cereals	Affects all species
Objective	
To feed the hungry and ease Third World political tension by increasing food yields with fertilizers and seeds	To contribute to profit by increasing input and/or processor efficiencies
For Whom	
The poor	The shareholder and management
By Whom	
CGIAR has 830 scientists working in 8 institutes reporting to U.S. foundations	In the USA alone, 1,127 scientists working for 30 agbiotech companies
Industrialized countries	
Quasi-UN bodies	
How	
Plant breeding in wheat, maize, rice	Genetic manipulation of all plants, all animals, microorganisms
Primary Targets	
Semidwarf capacity in response to fertilizers	Herbicide tolerance
	Natural substitution
	Factory production
Investment	
$108 million for agricultural R&D through CGIAR (1988)	Agbiotech R&D investment of $144 million in USA (1988) by 30 companies
General Impact	
Substantial but gradual	Enormous, sometimes immediate
52.9% of Third World wheat and rice in HYVs (123 million hectares)	$20 billion in medicinal and flavor/fragrance crops at risk

Table 8.3.   (Continued)

Green Revolution	Gene Revolution
General Impact	
500 million would not otherwise be fed	Multibillion dollar beverage, confectionery, sugar, and vegetable oils trade could be lost
Impact on Farmers	
Access to seeds and inputs uneven	Increased production costs
Small farmers lose land to larger farmers	Loss of some crops to factory farms
New varieties improve yield but increase rise	Input/processing efficiencies increase farmer risk
Reduce prices	Overproduction and materials diversification
Impact on Farms	
Soil erosion due to heavy use of crop chemicals	Continuation and possible acceleration of green revolution effects plus
Genetic erosion due to replacement of traditional varieties	Release of potentially uncontrollable new organisms into the environment
Species loss due to over-planting of traditional crops with maize, wheat, or rice	Genetic erosion of animals and microorganisms
Pressure on water resource due to irrigation	Biological warfare on economically important crops
Impact on Consumption	
Decline in use of high-value foods for poor people	Emphasis on feeding the rich Yuppie market
Export of food out of the region	Increased use of chemical and biological toxins
Economic Implications	
Direct contribution of $10 billion per annum to Third World food production	Contribution to seed production of $12.1 billion per annum by year 2000
Indirect contribution of $50–60 billion	Contribution to agriculture of $50 billion per annum by year 2000
Gene flow to U.S. alone contributes to farm sales of $2 billion per annum for wheat, rice, and maize.	Absorb benefit of gene flow from the Third World

Table 8.3.   (Continued)

Green Revolution	Gene Revolution
Political Implications	
National breeding program curtailed	CGIAR system subverted to corporate interests
Third World agriculture westernized	
Germ plasm benefits usurped	Genetic raw materials and technologies controlled by genetics supply industry through patents
Dependency	

Source: Development Dialogue, 1988

modities. The Pepsico project for the lab to farm to factory integration of seeds and agro-processing is an example of what the new liberalization implies. As part of this integrated project, Pepsico will start a biotechnology base agro research center for developing high-yielding disease resistant seeds of fruit and vegetable crops which the Pepsico plant will process. It took more than two years for Pepsico to get the clearance due to opposition by the public and by local industrialists. But with the new seed policy, doors have been opened for other multinationals.

The pharmaceutical giant Sandoz India has entered into an agreement with Northrup King of the United States, subsidiary of its multinational parent company, and also with the Dutch vegetable king, Zaaduine. ITC is tying up with Pacific Seeds, a subsidiary of Continental Grains from Australia. The U.S. seed giant Cargill has tied up with the Gilland Company retaining controlling interest of the company. Two other U.S. companies, Seedtec International and Dehlgien, have entered into agreements with Maharashtra Hybrid and Nath Seed Company respectively. Pioneer Hi-Bred has started the Indian Subsidiary Pioneer Seed Company. Apart from these, Hindustan Lever is negotiating with a Belgium firm while Hoechst and Ciba-Geigy are reportedly moving in with other tie-ups ("Seeds: A Hard Row to Hoe," 1989).

The Indian research stations and public sector seed producers like the National Seeds Corporation, which were until recently applauded for the green revolution, are now being reprimanded. And the government's new stance toward the public sector is being used by it to legitimize the privatization and transnationalization of the seed industry. Naturally, the scientific community is alienated. At a seminar on the new seed policy at the National Institute of Science, Technology, and Development (NISTAD) scientists of the Indian Agricultural Research Institute, the Council for Scientific and

Industrial Research, the Central Food Technology Research Institute and the National Board for Plant Genetic Resources responded critically to the new seed policy ("Scientists Seethe at Seed Policy," 1989). These scientific bodies had not been consulted before the policy was announced. Indigenous research and indigenous genetic resources have been sacrificed for corporate research and the corporate supply of genetic material. Total world retail sales in seeds per annum approximates US$136 billion, of which US$6 billion is proprietary (hybrid or patented seed). Analysts suggest that by the year 2000, the world seed market will be US$28 billion, and US$12 billion of this will be based on contributions from biotechnology. With the opening up of the untapped Indian market, this share will increase, as will the experimental ground for trying out new genetically engineered seeds with the ecological risks they carry. As a recent issue of *Development Dialogue* on the new biotechnologies points out, most of these agricultural inputs from genetic engineering are not here yet—they are arriving. However, our new seed policy has opened the door for that arrival, and has already allowed the entry of the multinationals whose corporate strategies and future profits hang on biotechnology.

The false miracle that seed companies are selling with biotechnology and genetic engineering is the possibility of liberating agriculture from chemicals and other ecological risks. However, most of the seed multinationals are also leading chemical companies. These include Ciba-Geigy, ICI, Monsanto, and Hoechst. The immediate strategy for these companies is to increase the use of pesticides and herbicides by developing pesticide- and herbicide-tolerant varieties.

While deepening corporate control of agriculture, the biotechnologies also expand the scope for this control. While markets for agro-chemical inputs and HYV seeds were restricted to regions with irrigation, the biorevolution will permit the extension of commercial agriculture to all regions, to rain-fed lands and marginal soils. The impacts of the biorevolution thus have the potential to encompass the entire rural populations of the Third World. Transnationals will gain total market control in a sector around which the life and livelihood of millions of farmers and peasants revolves. Given the private and proprietary character of the new technologies, the passage of the Plant Variety Protection Act, and patenting of genetically modified life forms, the development of biotechnologies will bring tropical genes and tropical land under the control of MNCs and will increasingly exclude Third World people from directly drawing sustenance from their land and the common heritage of living genetic wealth given by nature in abundant diversity in the tropics.

While the green revolution and biorevolution differ in scope and impact of control, they share the logic of commoditization and demand-led growth in agriculture. The continuity is provided by the agribusiness and agrochemical MNCs that controlled the green revolution indirectly but lead the biotechnology directly and overtly. If the first line of products they sold to innocent nations and farmers is already known to be a failure, should not one be at least partially skeptical about the second line of products that multinational agribusiness is pushing through biotechnologies? If the package is technologically and financially beyond the access of the ordinary cultivator and people by its research and resource intensity, biotechnologies will breed new inequalities and new ecological hazards. In the biorevolution, as in the green revolution, "improved seeds" will create a new dependence on global monopolies in the seed business.

Indigenous breeding through selection has given access to the best seeds to all, and the crop itself provides the seeds. Geertz's work on involution and Richaria's work on conserving indigenous strains have established that by maintaining control over seeds, the peasant need not sacrifice in terms of yields. It is not the yields but the transnational control that "improved" seeds improve. What is a drawback for the peasant is an advantage for the seed corporation. The hybrid seed must be bought each year from the seed merchants. The genetically engineered seed of the biorevolution will deepen peasants' dependence on MNCs. The lab, not nature, will become the sole source of seeds of the biotechnologies, and with labs shifting from universities to the corporate sector, from the public to the private domain, only those who can pay will have a right to seeds. As integration with nature as the primary genetic source is broken down, new integrations appear within MNC biotechnologies; seeds and agrichemicals are merging together. Corporate strategies are using agricultural biochemistry and biotechnology to get a new monopoly over plant breeding. As mentioned earlier, genetically engineered plant varieties are being developed by seed companies to be compatible with the proprietary plant protection chemicals manufactured by another subsidiary of the same company. Monsanto has genetically engineered a tomato variety to be compatible with one of its herbicides, Roundup. Calgene has recently obtained a patent for a modified DNA chain which enhances the herbicide resistance of plants. With a single patent, they now have exclusive rights to charge others in utilizing that property whether in tomatoes, tobacco, soybeans, cotton, and so on. Biotechnology could thus make possible the full integration of biological and chemical product lines, and thus a complete control on agriculture and on genetic resources (Patents and Plant Genetic Resources 1986).

The Pepsico project and the new seed policy are supposed to bring the latest biotechnologies to India. But it is in the nature of these technologies that they will be capital intensive and research intensive. They will be physically located in India, but controlled by multinationals of industrialized countries like Pepsico USA.

Recent pressures for liberalizing the patent laws of India are closely related to getting monopoly control, not just over plants but also over plant traits (*Proceedings* 1989). The United States has set a precedent in granting utility patents which allow claims for only part of a plant, or the genes expressing certain traits, like black flowers, tolerance to salt water, the ability to produce nitrogen, and so on. This gives the patent holder the right to exclude or collect a royalty from others reproducing any plant or selling seeds carrying the patented trait. A plant breeder wanting to utilize those genes in another variety or species would require a license. Utility patents would also make the practice of planting second generation seeds from a protected variety illegal. It is expected that utility patents will double the current seed bills of farmers. A utility patent has been granted for seventeen years to a seed company which had utilized genetic engineering to introduce the protein tryptophan into corn, thus increasing its nutritional value ("Patents and Plant Genetic Resources" 1988).

Patents and other intellectual property rights are the remaining hurdles to be crossed for large-scale distribution of biotechnology seeds by transnational corporations. For instance, a clause of the new seed policy directs all companies importing seeds to make a small quantity available to the gene bank of the government-controlled National Bureau of Plant Genetic Resources (NBPGR). The corporate giants are, of course, unwilling to accept that clause and want it removed. As Jan Nefkins, general manager of Cargill Southeast Asia Limited, pointed out, "No Company would be willing to part with what they took years and spent millions of dollars developing. It's a question of intellectual property rights" ("Seeds: A Hard Row to Hoe" 1989).

The fight over patents and proprietary rights has become an essential element of global politics in the biotechnology era. On the one hand, the United States is trying to globally introduce its patent protection system, which is heavily biased in favor of the industrially developed countries. Under the 1984 amendment to the trade act, the U.S. government considers the lack of patent protection to transnationals as an unfair trading practice, and is using trade as a weapon in the battle over patents. On the other hand scientists, industrialists, and public interest groups in countries like India are demanding a use of India's patent laws for protection of the national and public interest. The National Working Group on Patent Laws has been critical of attempts to erode national sovereignty through changes in patent laws. New economic conflicts between industrialized countries and the Third World, and between private corporate interests and the public interest are emerging with the age of bioengineering. Biotechnologies are opening up new areas for corporate profit, and even while the promise is of unprecedented prosperity, like the green revolution, it could be a prosperity with a very high price, especially for the poor.

SEEDS OF INSECURITY, SEEDS OF VIOLENCE

Globally and nationally, food grain production has been dramatically reduced due to ecological instability, including drought, induced both by climatic change associated with the greenhouse effect, and desertification through inappropriate land and water use. The momentum of grain production between 1950 and 1984, when world output grew from 624 million tons to 1,645 million tons, has waned in the late 1980s and may continue to dip in the 1990s. The world carryover stocks at the beginning of the harvest season in 1989 will not be more than 243 million tons, just enough to feed the world's population for 54 days, against 459 million tons to meet 101 days of consumption needs in 1987 (Brown 1988). In India, food grain stocks were at rock bottom at the end of 1988. The country had food stocks of barely 7.7 million tons on November 1, 1988 (i.e., 2.2 million tons of rice and 55 million tons of wheat). This was against 15.7 million tons of food grains—5.4 million tons of rice and 10.3 million tons of wheat, held by the country on November 1, 1987 ("Food Grains" 1988).

The public distribution system, which supplies subsidized food grain, requires 7 lakh tons of rice and six lakh tons of wheat every month. Besides this, grain needs are distributed through the National Rural Employment Program (NREP) and the Rural Landless Employment Guarantee Program (RLEGP), which aim at providing for the survival needs of the poorest. A large part of food grain for the public distribution system comes from Punjab. Production of surplus in Punjab for the food needs of the entire country was the objective of the first green revolution. An indication of Punjab's contribution to India's national stock is that 85.7 percent of the paddy and 57.3 percent of the wheat produced in 1985–1986 was procured by various agencies in the state.

Table 8.4.   U.S. Grain Production, Consumption, and Exportable Surplus by Crop Year, 1984–1988

Year	Production	Consumption Surplus from Current Crop (million metric tons)	Exportable
1984	313	197	116
1985	345	201	144
1986	314	216	97
1987	277	211	66
1988	190	202	− 2

Note: Does not include carryover stocks.
Sources: U.S. Department of Agriculture, Economic Research Service, "World Grain Harvested Area, Production, and Yield 1950–87" (Washington, D.C., 1988); USDA, Foreign Agricultural Service, World Grain Situation and Outlook, August 1988.

What will be the impact on the availability of staple foods as more and more land is diverted to fruits and vegetables for export, at a time when food scarcity is already a reality, both nationally and globally? Will potato chips for export feed the hungry in India who will be further deprived of grain through the public distribution system? And with pressure from the World Bank and the IMF to reduce food subsidies, how will the food entitlements of the economically and politically weakest groups be protected?

During the visit of the director of the IMF, Mr. Camdessus, in October 1988, the union minister for finance had indicated that India would be reducing subsidies for food distribution. The Finance Ministry's willingness to fall in line with World Bank/IMF policy was resisted by the Food Ministry, which saw the issue of food subsidies as essential for maintaining the public distribution system ("Fertilizer" 1988).

The experience of countries in Latin America and Africa where food riots have broken out following IMP/World Bank conditionalities for the removal of subsidies can help us anticipate the violent consequences of the new agricultural policy symbolized by the Pepsico project, which introduces new subsidies for processed food exports while removing subsidies for the domestic distribution of staple foods.

Higher farm incomes are a primary promise of the Pepsico project. Promotional literature from Pepsico and the new Ministry for Agro-processing announces that farm incomes which are around Rs7,000 per hectare from cereal cultivation may jump to Rs15,000–Rs20,000 per hectare from fruit and vegetable cultivation.

The experience of the first green revolution should teach us to treat such economic miracles with caution. The profitability in the cultivation of wheat and rice of the early period of the green revolution did not last too long, since increased inputs were needed to maintain yields of the green revolution varieties. According to a recent study, the net returns from wheat cultivation per hectare at 1970–1971 prices declined from Rs328 in 1971–1972 to Rs54 in 1981–1982. As a result, the profitability of large farmers declined and the deficits of the poor peasants have risen (Gill 1988, 1989).

The miraculous jump in farm income as promised by the Pepsico project and the new agricultural policy will be similarly short-lived even for the small group of farmers that benefits from it. Farmers who started cultivating hybrid tomatoes in the western region of India initially had incomes as high as Rs30,000 per hectare because hybrid tomatoes give yields of about 40 tons per hectare as compared to 22 tons per hectare produced by open pollinated varieties. However, hybrids are also more vulnerable to pests and disease, and in a few years income from hybrid tomato cultivation had dropped from Rs30,000 to a few hundred rupees.

Cash crops, especially for export, are subject not just to ecological risks, but to financial risks as well, because cash crops for export do not produce much cash over time. The growth of export-oriented cash crop agriculture is a primary reason for Africa's food crisis. As Lloyd Timberlake states in the context of Africa's food crisis, "the main drawback to cash crops is that over the past decade they have produced less and less cash" (Timberlake 1985). First, cash crops are encouraged over food production by an export-oriented agriculture policy. As the area under commodities for exports grows, prices fall and returns decline. As a catalyst, the Pepsico project for a new export-oriented agriculture policy will put India on the path of debt, dispossession, and agricultural decline that the export-led agricultural strategies have created in Africa and Latin America. As Clairmonte and Cavanagh observe, "The outcome, like tragedy, is ineluctable; Third World countries are literally being driven to market fatter and fatter volumes of commodities at lower and lower prices on the global market in return for higher priced goods and service imports" (Clairmonte and Cavanagh 1986).

Cash crop exports have been tried elsewhere and are a proven way to get trapped in food scarcity and spiraling debt burdens. Africa's food crisis and hunger and famine are linked directly to the underdevelopment of Africa's food production by cash crops leading to a decline in food production. Scarce resources have been diverted to each crop, undermining the cultivation of food and causing major ecological instability. As recently as 1970, Africa was producing enough food to feed itself. By 1984, 140 million Africans out of a total of 531 million were fed with grain from abroad, because by the end of the 1970s, the economies of many African nations were tied to cash crop production. Dependence on single crop commodities for export is in large measure at the root of Africa's ecological, economic, and human crisis.

Pepsico's entry will generate a similar crisis for India as the logic of diverting land from staple food to processed food exports unfolds. It took Africa less than a decade to go from food sufficiency to scarcity. It could take India less than that if the Pepsico project sets precedents, and other multinational agribusinesses move in to use India's farmland for export commodities. Food companies that are already looking at India for investment include Kellogg, Campbell, Heinz, Del Monte, Nestle, Nissan, and Swedish Match AB among many others ("Foreign Firms" 1989). The impact of integrated agribusiness projects on food entitlements of people in the Third World has been rehearsed too often for us to close our eyes to it. The issue is not the entry of a soft drink multinational, but of the control by a multinational agribusiness of India's food growing land, largely for export commodities. Is India ready to forgo its carefully built strategy for self-reliance in food?

The experience of the first green revolution shows that price incentives and subsidies for the production of new varieties of wheat and rice were simultaneously disincentives and penalties for the production of coarse grains, pulses, and oilseeds. The scarcity of oilseeds has become so severe that the government has had to create a special oilseed technology mission to increase cultivation and production. The introduction of incentives and subsidies for production of fruits and vegetables as raw material for the export-oriented agro-processing industry will similarly act as a disincentive for the production of staple food grains, aggravating the present scarcity and diseconomies.

Employment generation is a much exaggerated economic benefit associated with the Pepsico project. The project will employ only 489 people but employment generation through indirect job creation is put at 25,000 in Punjab agriculture and another 25,000 in the rest of the country. The official figures fail to take into account the large-scale unemployment that will be created by the displacement of small and marginal farmers and among the self-employed.

Industrialization of agriculture is a proven way toward aggravating rural unemployment rather than ameliorating it. Comparative research on rice-growing areas has shown that industrialization displaces labor, while alternative strategies exist which increase productivity through increase of labor inputs (Bayliss Smith 1984: 169).

Integrated industrialization of agriculture, from production to processing, will also create large-scale labor displacement and loss of skill in the informal sector where most food processing currently takes place. The Pepsico advertisers ridicule Indian foods as ethnic, "made up of traditional mango pulp, pickles and chutney." These products have suited our needs, our climate, and our skills. Joining the global monoculture of potato chips will reduce our richness of diet and destroy our food diversity. It will also lead to large-scale deindustrialization and deskilling in the traditional food processing industry, in which every home and every community in the country participates productively.

The irony of the capital-intensive, high-input agricultural strategy that was initiated with the green revolution and is being carried to the next stage with the biotechnology and food processing revolution is that it generates violence and distress not only where it fails but even where it succeeds. It creates social, political, and economic crises by generating scarcity on the one hand and generating surpluses on the other. The crisis of scarcity and the crisis of surpluses are two aspects of the same crisis generated by a non-sustainable resource and capital-intensive agriculture. Small farmers are victims of both aspects of the crisis, in the north and in the south, in industrialized countries as well as in largely agrarian societies. According to Wendell Berry,

For nothing at present is more destructive of farms and farmers than bumper crops. High production keeps production costs high and the market prices low—a bonanza (so far) for the industrial suppliers of "purchased inputs" to farmers and (so far) to the banks from which desperate farmers must borrow (at usurious interest) the increasing amounts of money necessary to bridge the gap between the depressed farm economy and an inflated industrial economy. But high production is death to farmers. Though most interested parties seem still addicted to the perception of American agricultural productivity as a "miracle," even news articles now occasionally glimpse the fact that, for farmers, a good year in corn is a bad year in dollars. (Berry 1984)

A *Newsweek* article entitled "Down and Out on the Farm" reported how farmers were being dispossessed by the "success" of increasing production (*Newsweek* 1982). In Ontario, Canada, the government has started a $6 million relief program for farmers who have been left redundant in a capital and resource intensive industrialized farming. The program is called Farmers in Transition and includes a help line (1-800-265-1511) for free, around-the-clock telephone assistance to depressed and distressed farmers ("Farmers in Transition" 1986). Suicide rates and violence have shot up in rural areas of North America as part of the crisis. As Mark Ritchie and Kevin Ristau report, "The agricultural crisis in affluent America is sowing seeds of violence, and many bitter and desperate rural people, faced with losing everything they've worked for, may become involved in one of the extremist organizations that are increasingly active throughout the countryside" (Ritchie and Ristau 1987).

Agricultural surpluses of selected commodities created artificially through high capital, energy, and resource inputs seem to generate invisible scarcity, rising distress, and conflict. The violence of Punjab seems to be the pattern associated with capital- and resource-intensive agriculture everywhere.

The first technological fix of the green revolution in Punjab brought violence instead of peace, dependence instead of self-reliance and autonomy. The second technological fix heralded by Pepsico could deepen the trends of violence and dependence because it will be more excluding, more centralizing, and more globally integrated into international markets of farm inputs and farm commodities. In the final analysis, the deepening violence and militarization of society is linked with people's loss of autonomy and loss of control over their lives. It arises as people are turned into part of the assembly line of corporate food production or thrown out as waste. The path to peace cannot come from deepening the centralizing thrust that is at the root of present discontent. Restoring a decentered and ecological system of food production is the only strategy for creating a lasting peace.

An agriculture integrated from farm to factory by the same corporate interests creates new risks and new vulnerabilities for Indian peasants and consumers. The corresponding disintegration of ecological and political processes will aggravate the discontent that already exists. Pepsi and the new agricultural policy cannot become a program for peace because it establishes centralized control over farmers' lives and introduces new instability in agricultural systems at the ecological, economic, and political levels. It cannot fulfill the promise of a hundred years of spring.

REFERENCES

Bayliss Smith, T. B. 1984. "The Green Revolution at Micro Scale." In Tim Bayliss-Smith and Sudhir Wanmali, eds., *Understanding Green Revolutions: Agrarian Change and Development Planning in South Asia*. Boston: Cambridge University Press.

Berry, W. 1984. "Whose Head Is the Farmer Using?" In W. Jackson, W. Berry, and Bruce Coleman, eds., *Meeting the Expectations of the Land*. San Francisco: North Point.

Bhattacharjee, A. 1988. "New Seed Policy: Whose Interest Would It Serve." *Economic and Political Weekly,* October 8.

Brown, Lester. 1988. *The Changing World Food Prospect: The Nineties and Beyond*. World Watch Paper 85. World Watch Institute.

Clairmonte, Frederick, and John Cavanagh. 1986. "Third World Debt: The Approaching Holocaust." *Economic and Political Weekly*, August 2.

Desai, Gunvant. 1979. "Fertilizers in India's Agricultural Development." In *Agricultural Development of India*. Bombay: Orient Longman.

"Down and Out on the Farm," *Newsweek*. 1982. April 12.

Doyle, Jack. 1985. *Altered Harvest*. New York: Viking.

"Farmers in Transition." 1986. Ministry of Agriculture and Food, Ontario.

"Fertilizer, Food Subsidies May Be Cut." 1988. *Hindu*, October 12.

"Floods Reduce Cultivable Area." 1989. *Economic Times*, January 26.

"Food Grains Stock at Rock Bottom." 1988. *Economic Times*, December 15.

"Foreign Firms Queue Up for Food Processing Tie-ups." 1989. *Economic Times*, April 2.

Fowler, Cary, et al. 1988. "Laws of Life." In *Development Dialogue*. Uppsala: Dag Hammarskjold Foundation.

Gill, M. S. 1978. "Success in the Indian Punjab." In J. G. Hawkes, ed., *Conservation and Agriculture*. London: Duckworth.

Gill, S. S. 1988. "Contradictions of Punjab Model of Growth and the Search for an Alternative." *Economic and Political Weekly*, October 15.

———. 1989. "The Price of Prosperity Problems of Punjab's Agriculture." *Times of India*, January.

Iyengar, Yegna A. R. 1944. *Field Crops of India*. Bangalore: BAPPCO.

Jha, Prem Shankar. 1986a. "The Pepsi Project." *Times of India*, September 1.

———. 1986b. "Punjab: Programme for Peace." *Hindustan Times*, 11 December.

Johl, S. S. 1985. *Diversification of Punjab Agriculture*. Government of Punjab.

Kang, D. S. 1982. "Environmental Problems of the Green Revolution with a focus on Punjab, India." In Richard Barrett, ed., *International Dimensions of the Environmental Crisis*. Boulder: Westview.

Kenny, Martin. 1986. *Biotechnology: University Industry Linkages*. New Haven: Yale.

Kumar, Pramod, et al. 1984. *Punjab Crisis: Context and Trends*. Centre for Research in Rural and Industrial Development, Chandigarh.

Menon, Usha. 1989. "Anything for a Dollar: A Close Look at the Pepsi Deal." *Delhi Science Forum*.

"Patents and Plant Genetic Resources." 1986. *Foundation for Economic Trends*. Mimeo. Washington, D.C.

Proceedings of National Seminar on Plant Laws. 1989. November 22.

"Punjab Floods Were Manmade." 1988. *Economic Times*, October 4.

Ramprasad, Vanaja. 1988. *Hidden Hunger*. Research Foundation for Science and Ecology.

Richaria, R. H. 1986. Paper presented at Crisis in Modern Science seminar, Penang, November.

Ritchie, Mark, and Kevin Ristau. 1987. *Crisis by Design: A Brief Review of U.S. Farm Policy*. Minneapolis: League of Rural Voters Education Project.

Robsenblum, John, ed. 1983. *Agriculture in the 21st Century*. New York: Wiley Interscience.

"Scientists Seethe at Seed Policy." 1989. *Economic Times*, December 1.

"Seeds: A Hard Row to Hoe." 1989. *India Today*, February 15.

Sidhu, G. S. 1988. "The Green Revolution and Rice Diseases in Punjab." Mimeo.

Timberlake, Lloyd. 1985. *Africa in Crisis*. London: Earthscan.

Wheale, Peter, and Ruth McNally. 1988. *Genetic-Engineering: Catastrophe or Utopia*. U.K.: Harvester.

9

Global Trade of Electronic Waste

For many of us, the cookie cutter definition of "modernity" and "progress" often focuses on technology, and specifically the electronic gadgets that increasingly fill our offices, homes, and pockets. These devices are the archetype of artifice; that is, they appear as if they have been beamed to earth from the far reaches of space. They thus represent an almost complete break from the natural world, but this is only the image. Our electronic ephemera are powered by fossil fuels (mostly coal), they contain petroleum-based plastics, and they possess a minilab of heavy metals. These are natural resources—little pieces of nature. When the technology is new, it looks like it will last forever. But all commodities have finite lives, and most commodities are destined to become waste. According to one study "an estimated 50 million metric tons of e-waste replete with toxic materials are generated annually as consumers replace used electronics such as computers and mobile phones with the latest models" ("Feature Focus" 2007: 47).

But globalization breathes new life into discarded electronic devices, usually as garbage that is legally bought and sold in the market. This is a particularly pernicious dynamic for poor people who sometimes accept payment to turn their backyards into havens for e-waste. In this chapter Elizabeth Grossman reports how this process often threatens environmental and human health in Asia, Africa, and Eastern Europe among poor people who have gone into the business of making money off discarded gadgetry.

Elizabeth Grossman, "Where Computers Go to Die— and Kill" (2006)[1]

A parade of trucks piled with worn-out computers and electronic equipment pulls away from container ships docked at the port of Taizhou in the Zheji-

155

ang province of southeastern China. A short distance inland, the trucks dump their loads in what looks like an enormous parking lot. Pools of dark oily liquid seep from under the mounds of junked machinery. The equipment comes mostly from the United States, Europe, and Japan.

For years, developed countries have been exporting tons of electronic waste to China for inexpensive, labor-intensive recycling and disposal. Since 2000, it's been illegal to import electronic waste into China for this kind of environmentally unsound recycling. But tons of debris are smuggled in with legitimate imports, corruption is common among local officials, and China's appetite for scrap is so enormous that the shipments just keep on coming.

In Taizhou's outdoor workshops, people bang apart the computers and toss bits of metal into brick furnaces that look like chimneys. Split open, the electronics release a stew of toxic materials—among them beryllium, cadmium, lead, mercury, and flame retardants—that can accumulate in the blood and disrupt the body's hormonal balance. Exposed to heat or allowed to degrade, the plastics in electronics can break down into organic pollutants that cause a host of health problems, including cancer. Wearing no protective clothing, workers roast circuit boards in big, uncovered wok-like pans to melt plastics and collect valuable metals. Other workers sluice open basins of acid over semiconductors to remove their gold, tossing the waste into nearby streams. Typical wages for this work are about $2 to $4 a day.

Jim Puckett, director of Basel Action Network, an environmental advocacy organization that tracks hazardous waste, filmed these Dickensian scenes in 2004. "The volume of junk was amazing," he says. "It was arriving twenty-four hours a day and there was so much scrap that one truck was loaded every two minutes." Nothing has changed in two years. "China is still getting the stuff," Puckett tells me in March 2006. In fact, he says, the trend in China now is "to push the ugly stuff out of sight into the rural areas."

The conditions in Taizhou are particularly distressing to Puckett because they underscore what he sees as a persistent failure by the U.S. government to stop the dumping of millions of used computers, TVs, cell phones, and other electronics in the world's developing regions, including those in China, India, Malaysia, the Philippines, Vietnam, Eastern Europe, and Africa.

Because high-tech electronics contain hundreds of materials packed into small spaces, they are difficult and expensive to recycle. Eager to minimize costs and maximize profits, many recyclers ship large quantities of used electronics to countries where labor is cheap and environmental regulations lax. U.S. recyclers and watchdog groups like Basel Action Network estimate that 50 percent or more of U.S. used computers, cell phones, and TVs sent to recyclers are shipped overseas for recycling to places like Taizhou or Lagos, Nigeria, as permitted by federal law. Much of this obsolete equipment ends up as toxic waste, with hazardous components exposed, burned, or allowed to degrade in landfills.

BAN first called widespread attention to the problem in 2002, when it released *Exporting Harm,* a documentary that revealed the appalling damage caused by electronic waste in China. In the southern Chinese village of Guiyu, many of the workers who dismantle high-tech electronics live only steps from their jobs. Their children wander over piles of burned wires and splash in puddles by the banks of rivers that have become dumping grounds for discarded computer parts. The pollution has been so severe that Guiyu's water supply has been undrinkable since the mid-1990s. Water samples taken in 2005 found levels of lead and other metals four hundred to six hundred times what international standards consider safe.

In the summer of 2005, Puckett investigated Lagos, another port bursting with what he calls the effluent of the affluent. "It appears that about five hundred loads of computer equipment are arriving in Lagos each month," he says. Ostensibly sent for resale in Nigeria's rapidly growing market for high-tech electronics, as much as 75 percent of the incoming equipment is unusable, Puckett discovered. As a result, huge quantities are simply dumped.

Photographs taken by BAN in Lagos show scrapped electronics lying in wetlands, along roadsides, being examined by curious children and burning in uncontained landfills. Seared, broken monitors and CPUs are nestled in weeds, serving as perches for lizards, chickens, and goats. One mound of computer junk towers at least six feet high. Puckett found identification tags showing that some of the junked equipment originally belonged to the U.S. Army Corps of Engineers, the Illinois Department of Human Services, the Kansas Department of Aging, the State of Massachusetts, the Michigan Department of Natural Resources, the City of Houston, school districts, hospitals, banks, and numerous businesses, including IBM and Intel.

Under the Basel Convention, an international agreement designed to curtail trade in hazardous waste, none of this dumping should be happening. Leaded CRT glass, mercury switches, parts containing heavy metals, and other elements of computer scrap are considered hazardous waste under Basel and cannot be exported for disposal. Electronics can be exported for reuse, repair and—under certain conditions—recycling, creating a gray area into which millions of tons of obsolete electronics have fallen.

The United States is the only industrialized nation not to have ratified the Basel Convention, which would prevent it from trading in hazardous waste. The United States also has no federal laws that prohibit the export of toxic e-waste, nor has it signed the Basel Ban, a 1995 amendment to the convention that prohibits export of hazardous waste from Organization of Economic Cooperation and Development member countries to non-OECD countries—essentially from wealthy to poorer nations. While this policy is intended to spur reuse and recycling, it also makes it difficult to curtail the kind of shipments BAN found in Lagos.

Despite a growing awareness of e-waste's hazards, the U.S. government, says Puckett, has done nothing in the past several years to stem the flow of e-trash. Given the Bush administration's reluctance to enact or support regulations that interfere with what it considers free trade and the difficulty of monitoring e-waste exports, the shipments continue. "Follow the material, and you'll find the vast majority of e-waste is still going overseas," says Robert Houghton, president of Redemtech, a company that handles electronics recycling for a number of Fortune 500 companies, including Kaiser Permanente. As Puckett says, "Exploiting low-wage countries as a dumping ground is winning the day."

Over a billion computers are now in use worldwide—over 200 million in the United States, which has the world's highest per capita concentration of PCs. The average life span of an American computer is about three to five years, and some 30 million become obsolete each year. According to the International Association of Electronics Recyclers, approximately 3 billion pieces of consumer electronics will be scrapped by 2010. Overall, high-tech electronics are the fastest-growing part of the municipal waste stream in the United States and Europe.

The EPA estimates that only about 10 percent of all obsolete consumer electronics are recycled. The rest are stored somewhere, passed on to second users, or simply tossed in the trash. The EPA's most recent estimate is that over 2 million tons of e-waste end up in U.S. landfills each year. As Jim Fisher of *Salon* reported in 2000, a toxic stew from discarded computers leaches into groundwater surrounding landfills.

Current design, particularly of equipment now entering the waste stream, makes separating the dozens of materials in electronics labor intensive. "Almost every piece of equipment is different," says Greg Sampson of Earth Protection Services, a national electronics recycler. The process almost always involves manual labor and, once the electronics are dismantled, sophisticated machinery is required to safely separate and process metals and plastics.

The fragile CRTs with leaded glass used in traditional desktop monitors and TV screens pose a particular recycling challenge. Metals are the easiest materials to recycle and the most valuable. Circuit boards typically contain gold, silver, and other precious metals. Plastics are the peskiest, as many different kinds may be used in a single piece of equipment and markets for recycled plastics are far less established than those for scrap metals.

E-Scrap News, a recycling industry trade magazine, features about 950 e-scrap processors in its North American database—a list that doesn't include nonprofits or reuse organizations. And not all electronics recyclers offer the same services. Some dismantle the equipment and recover materials themselves. But many simply collect equipment and do initial disassembly, then contract with others for materials recovery.

According to the International Association of Electronics Recyclers, this business now generates about $700 million annually in the United States and is increasing steadily. Most recyclers charge fees to process equipment. But essentially profits come from the sale of materials recovered or by selling equipment or components to those who will do so. There's also a speculative aspect to the business, especially when the scrap metal market is booming and the value of recyclable circuit boards increasing. It reached an all-time high in January 2006 at $5,640 a ton.

Some recyclers—mostly smaller shops—acquire used equipment at surplus property auctions on eBay or other such resale outlets, then resell equipment whole or in parts by the pound to what Houghton calls "materials brokers" and "chop shops." One batch of equipment may end up being sold to a series of brokers before it reaches a materials processor, and much of what these brokers deal in ends up overseas where costs are lowest. "If a company is buying your electronic scrap or untested equipment," rather than charging for this service, "it's highly likely that it's going overseas," says Sarah Westervelt of BAN.

In 2000, *Salon's* Fisher noted that U.S. computer manufacturers bucked the European trend of instigating convenient buy-back programs for used computers—a resistance that continues today. Since 2000, the Silicon Valley Toxics Coalition, an environmental group, has maintained a "report card" of computer makers' environmental progress in recycling and manufacturing. In its most recent report card, it notes that the "most alarming trends in the electronics industry in the United States continue to be staunch opposition to producer take back programs."

Currently there is no consistent, industry-wide, or government program to certify or license electronics recyclers. As a result, says Houghton, "It's extremely difficult to peel back the onion far enough to find out where the equipment goes. It may change hands two, three or four times before it leaves the country." And, he explains, "The cost of shipping a forty-foot container full of computers, relative to the value of the equipment," even at scrap prices, "is pretty low." With dealers from China to Eastern Europe and Africa ready to buy used electronics for scrap or reuse, and U.S. domestic transportation and recycling costs high, it's actually more profitable to load up a container and send it to Nigeria or Taizhou than it is to process equipment at home.

So traveling the seas in the shadows of legitimate high-tech exports are huge containers that may hold as many as a thousand used computers. They're loaded on ships at East Coast and Gulf Coast ports for Atlantic crossings, or at European ports, including Felixstowe, Le Havre, and Rotterdam, arriving in West Africa by way of Spain. Others cross the Mediterranean from Israel and Dubai or travel Asian Pacific routes from the United States, Japan, Taiwan, and Korea.

Compounding the difficulty of tracking an individual computer is the fact that several different companies—including freight consolidators at both exporting and importing ports, some located in countries distant from both buyers and sellers—are responsible for moving these goods. A recycler in Texas may well be unaware of who is unloading or receiving his goods in China or Africa. Many international freight shippers make it easy to track a whole container—just punch the number into their web site—but information about who's shipping what is not public.

Even in Europe, where e-waste exports are regulated, illegal shipments slip through. "From our work, we have no doubt that there are improper shipments of waste," says Roy Watkinson of the U.K. Environment Agency, which in October of 2005 reported that 75 percent of the containers it had inspected that month contained some illegal waste, including e-scrap. A European group, IMPEL, a network of environmental regulators, has been monitoring this trade, and has found ships loaded with damaged computer equipment sailing out of Wales bound for Pakistan in containers marked "plastics."

According to accounts by Lai Yun of Greenpeace China and Mark Dallura of Chase Electronics in Philadelphia, and news reports from China, corruption is common among customs officials there. Dallura told the *Washington Post* in 2003 that the ships discarded computers to China via Taiwanese middlemen. "I sell it to [the Taiwanese] in Los Angeles and how they get it there is not my concern," Dallura said. "They pay the customs officials off. Everybody knows it. They show up with Mercedeses, rolls of hundred-dollar bills. This is not small-time. This is big-time stuff. There's a lot of money going on in this." Today, loads of e-scrap continue to enter the country despite the Chinese government's official crackdown on these imports.

In an attempt to find out how computers belonging to federal and state government agencies—including one from a Wisconsin school district—might end up in Lagos, Nigeria, I tried to get to the bottom of what happens to the half million computers the federal government disposes of each year.

Much of the federal government's used but usable computer equipment (including cell phones) is placed with another government agency or donated to a school or community nonprofit (usually chosen and vetted by an individual agency office). The rest (the exact numbers are not known) goes to the General Services Administration—the agency that deals with the procurement, use, and disposal of government property—for public auction. State governments work similarly, usually through state surplus property offices or equivalent programs. No one I consulted had any estimate of how many computers state and local governments discard annually. What was clear is that the ultimate fate of significant quantities of government electronics is poorly documented.

Equipment left after these donations and sales is sent out for recycling. Some federal and state agencies choose their own recyclers. Some federal agencies send used computers to the recyclers awarded contracts under the EPA's electronics recycling program, called Recycling Electronics and Asset Disposition services. A number send equipment to the Federal Prison Industries' computer recycling facilities, which dismantle equipment and send parts on for materials recovery. Many state and local governments (and school districts) put their electronics recycling contracts out for bid, often choosing the company that charges the least to handle and process the equipment. This itself is a red flag. If there's no charge or prices are extremely low, especially for monitors, cautions Sampson of Earth Protection Services, "chances are high equipment is being recycled using cheap labor or by less than optimum methods."

What struck me about the GSA and other public auctions was the lack of oversight, both in terms of where used equipment might end up—potentially creating environmental hazards—and in terms of data security. BAN had scrapped hard drives that it purchased in Lagos analyzed by the Swiss firm NetMon, which found correspondence from staff at the World Bank and from Wisconsin's Child Protective Custody Agency, among others. As a result of chaotic recycling, "There's a definite concern for our security," says Eric Karofsky, senior research analyst with AMR Research, a firm that analyzes business supply chains.

Recent GSA auctions have included computers belonging to the Census Bureau, the South Texas Veterans Health Care System, the Border Patrol, the Federal Aviation Administration, and the U.S. Department of Commerce. Anyone over eighteen from a country the United States does business with, who has a valid credit card, can buy at these auctions, many of which are conducted online. Auction participants are hard to identify as their bids are recorded only by user names, but it's unlikely that anyone is buying a load of seventy-five used CPUs for personal use. And there are thousands of waiting online buyers. In the United States, a laptop sells on eBay about every forty-five seconds, reports senior category manager Stephani Regalia, who helped launch eBay's ReThink program devoted to selling used electronics.

The GSA keeps records of who's bought equipment but does not track what happens to equipment that's been sold, nor does it ask buyers why they're purchasing the electronics. "Why would we?" asks a GSA staffer in Boston. The result is that at both the state and federal level, large quantities of electronics are purchased by brokers, auctioneers, and individual dealers who often sell the equipment for export.

For example, one company that has bid at GSA auctions, CTBI Co. of

San Antonio, also works as the Morsi Corp. Mike Hancock, the company's proprietor, tells me that he sells working equipment to overseas buyers, including those in Indonesia. The scrap, he says, goes to China, Pakistan, and Canada, but another company handles those transactions, so he doesn't track things further. As far as he's concerned, none of his scrap has ended up in Nigeria. "I don't do business in Nigeria," Hancock says. "There are too many bad credit cards there."

One electronics recycler that does do business in Africa is Arizona-based ScrapComputer.com. The staff person I spoke to (who would not give me his name), in the company's Chicago office, says nothing ends up in landfills, and that working equipment is refurbished for schools or sold on eBay. But it also exports computers to India and China where, the staffer says, functional CRTs are remade into TVs. ScrapComputer also sends equipment—all working, I am told—to Malaysia and Egypt, and to West African countries including the Congo. Clearly, this is not the only company selling into Africa, but given the fluid nature of the business, it's extremely difficult to pin down which recyclers knowingly sell e-scrap with a blind eye to dumping and unsound recycling methods.

Still curious to know how a computer owned by Wisconsin's Wauwatosa School District ended up in Lagos, I tracked down the office, SWAP (Surplus with a Purpose), that handles used computers for Wisconsin school districts. Business manager Tim Sell tells me that SWAP—part of the University of Wisconsin—accounts for everything it handles. He says equipment not refurbished for donations or placed in state offices goes to the Wisconsin State Corrections Department's computer recycling facilities, which refurbish and recycle used computers.

But he bemoans the legal loopholes that make e-scrap so hard to track. "Recyclers lie to us," he says, explaining that despite assurances, equipment and parts probably do end up being handled in ways SWAP would rather it did not. When I ask about the computer in Nigeria, Sell tells me he knows that individual customers buy equipment from SWAP and stockpile it for sale to bulk buyers either here or overseas, including those who buy to sell in Africa. With so many unknowns and loopholes in the current system of accounting for used electronics sent for recycling, "I don't know how you're going to stop these exports 100 percent," says Sell.

The United States may be one of the world's biggest consumers of high-tech electronics, but unlike the European Union or Japan, it has no national system for handling e-waste. Unless a state or local government prohibits it, it's currently legal to dump up to 220 pounds a month of e-waste, including CRTs and circuit boards, into local landfills. Several dozen states have introduced e-waste bills, and a handful of U.S. states—California, Maine, Maryland, Massachusetts, Minnesota, and Washington—have recently passed substantive e-waste bills, some of which bar CRTs from their landfills. E-waste bills have also been introduced in the House and Senate, but neither would create a national collection system.

The export of e-waste has been discussed in Congress but no legislation to regulate this trade has yet been introduced. Matt Gerien, press secretary to Rep. Mike Thompson (D-Calif.), who has cosponsored an e-waste bill in the House, says, "Ironically, what brought Representative Thompson to this issue are these export problems." But neither the bill that Rep. Thompson has cosponsored with Rep. Louise Slaughter (D-N.Y.), nor the one introduced by Sen. Ron Wyden (D-Ore.) and Sen. Jim Talent (R-Mo.) would deal with exports.

Meanwhile, says Laura Coughlan of the EPA's Office of Solid Waste, the Bush administration has drafted legislation that would allow the United States to ratify the Basel Convention but is waiting for final clearance for transmittal to Congress. And the Ban Amendment, which essentially prohibits sending e-waste from wealthy to poorer countries, "has created issues for U.S. ratification of the convention," says Coughlan, who explains that no "U.S. administration has supported ratification of this amendment, and the U.S. government has been unable to reach consensus with domestic stakeholders."

Legislation in Europe has made electronics recycling mandatory throughout the European Union, as it is in Japan and some other countries. Companion legislation requires the elimination of certain toxics—among them lead, cadmium, and hexavalent chromium used in solder, batteries, inks, and paints—from electronic products, and given the global nature of the high-tech industry, these new materials standards could effectively become world standards. Many such changes have already been made and more are in the works, but the old equipment now being discarded remains laden with toxics.

As U.S. lawmakers, manufacturers, environmental advocates, waste haulers, and recyclers struggle to find a way to collect the nation's high-tech trash, Americans are left with what policymakers are fond of calling a patchwork of regulations and recycling options. This makes things as confusing for manufacturers as it does for consumers and recyclers. "At some point, the feds will have to step in and harmonize things," says Ted Smith of the Silicon Valley Toxics Coalition.

In 2005, the EPA held an electronics recycling summit. Among the issues participants grappled with, and on which there is no industry-wide or national policy, are certifying electronics recyclers and exporting electronic waste. Complaints were voiced about the difficulty of dealing with products designed with materials that make recycling complicated and expensive. But loudest of all were complaints that the United States had too many confusing and uncoordinated recycling efforts. A year later, a few more state laws regulating e-waste have been passed but little has been done to stop the steady stream of used computers, cell phones, and TVs that are ending up overseas, in dumps, polluting soil, water, and air.

REFERENCE

"Feature Focus: Environment and Gobalization: Minimizing Risks, Seizing Opportunities." 2007. In *GeoYearBook: An Overview of Our Changing Environment. A Report from the United Nations Environmental Program,* www.unep.org/geo/yearbook/yb2007/PDF/6_Feature_Focus72dpi.pdf, p. 47.

III

GLOBAL WARMING

Chris Jordan, Remains of Home

10

Globalization and the Changing Climate

Globalization is not responsible for climate change. The burning of fossil fuels by human beings has led to an increase in greenhouse gases responsible for climate change; we call such changes "anthropogenic" to distinguish them from the natural change in climate. Globalization is an economic process that entails the rapid movement of products and people around the globe. Movement requires energy, and much of this energy goes into transportation and electricity-generation infrastructures that are largely based on the consumption of fossil fuels. Unless this changes, the increasing flows of capital and products will continue to warm up the planet—a process which most people believe is having, and will continue to have, negative consequences for humanity, especially for those living in the developing south. This presents a complex ethical problem for the audience of this book—students who largely live in the northern overdeveloped countries that are historically responsible for anthropogenic climate change. To be sure, dealing with the social, political, and economic changes of rapid climate change will be one of the most important and complex problems of the globalized twenty-first century.

Nevertheless, the climate change debate has created enormous confusion and acrimony, especially in the United States, which has the distinction of being the only developed country to not sign the Kyoto Protocol. The science of climate change has fallen victim to politicization and sensationalism. In this chapter Kerry Emanuel cuts to the quick and describes what we know about anthropogenic climate change. And this is the place to start. The debate over whether or not such a thing as anthropogenic climate change exists needs to end; indeed, that conversation has been concluded by scientific consensus. We need to move past this issue and discuss the type of world we want to live in tomorrow. As Emanuel makes abundantly clear, predicting future climate change is one of the most difficult scientific problems of our generation. There are too many variables within this chaotic system to predict what will happen with a degree of certainty. And perhaps this is the reason for taking precaution. We can take some solace in the recent "greening" of politics and business—the fallout of living in a post-Katrina/*Inconvenient Truth* age. Perhaps ethanol, hydrogen, wind, and solar energy will mitigate the harmful effects of globalization. Perhaps they won't. But one thing rings out clearly: our participation in a globalized economy binds us to a meteorological system that is producing severe droughts, intensifying floods and hurricanes, and—should we lose the Greenland and Antarctic ice sheets—significant rises in sea level.

Kerry Emanuel, "Phaeton's Reins: The Human Hand in Climate Change" (2007)[1]

Two strands of environmental philosophy run through the course of human history. The first holds that the natural state of the universe is one of infinite stability, with an unchanging earth anchoring the predictable revolutions of the sun, moon, and stars. Every scientific revolution that challenged this notion, from Copernicus's heliocentricity to Hubble's expanding universe, from Wegener's continental drift to Heisenberg's uncertainty and Lorenz's macroscopic chaos, met with fierce resistance from religious, political, and even scientific hegemonies.

The second strand also sees the natural state of the universe as a stable one but holds that it has become destabilized through human actions. The great floods are usually portrayed in religious traditions as attempts by a god or gods to cleanse the earth of human corruption. Deviations from cosmic predictability, such as meteors and comets, were more often viewed as omens than as natural phenomena. In Greek mythology, the scorching heat of Africa and the burned skin of its inhabitants were attributed to Phaeton, an offspring of the sun god Helios, who, having lost a wager to his son, was obliged to allow him to drive the sun chariot across the sky. In this primal environmental catastrophe, Phaeton lost control and fried the earth, killing himself in the process.

These two fundamental ideas have permeated many cultures through much of history. They strongly influence views of climate change to the present day.

THE MYTH OF NATURAL STABILITY

In 1837, Louis Agassiz provoked public outcry and scholarly ridicule when he proposed that many puzzles of the geologic record, such as peculiar scratch marks on rocks, and boulders far removed from their bedrock sources, could be explained by the advance and retreat of huge sheets of ice. This event marked the beginning of a remarkable endeavor, today known as paleoclimatology, which uses physical and chemical evidence from the geological record to deduce changes in the earth's climate over time. This undertaking has produced among the most profound yet least celebrated scientific advances of our era. We now have exquisitely detailed knowledge of how climate has varied over the last few million years and, with progressively less detail and more uncertainty, how it has changed going back in time to the age of the oldest rocks on our 4.5-billion-year-old planet.

For those who take comfort in stability, there is little consolation in this record. Within the past 3 million years or so, our climate has swung between mild states, similar to today's and lasting from ten to twenty thousand years, and periods of 100,000 years or so in which giant ice sheets, in some places several miles thick, covered northern continents. Even more unsettling than the existence of these cycles is the suddenness with which the climate can apparently change, especially as it recovers from glacial eras.

Over longer intervals of time, the climate has changed even more radically. During the early part of the Eocene era, around 50 million years ago, the earth was free of ice, and giant trees grew on islands near the North Pole, where the annual mean temperature was about 60F, far warmer than today's mean of about 30F. There is also some evidence that the earth was almost entirely covered with ice at various times around 500 million years ago; in between, the planet was exceptionally hot.

What explains these changes? For climate scientists, the ice cores in Greenland and Antarctica provide the most intriguing clues. As the ice formed, it trapped bubbles of atmosphere, whose chemical composition—including, for example, its carbon dioxide and methane content—can now be analyzed. Moreover, it turns out that the ratio of the masses of two isotopes of oxygen locked up in the molecules of ice is a good indicator of the air temperature when the ice was formed. And to figure out when the ice was formed, the layers can be counted that mark the seasonal cycle of snowfall and melting.

Relying on such analyses of ice cores and sediment cores from the deep ocean, climate scientists have learned something remarkable: the ice age cycles of the past 3 million years are probably caused by periodic oscillations of the earth's orbit that affect primarily the orientation of the earth's axis. These oscillations do not much affect the amount of sunlight that reaches the earth, but they do change the distribution of sunlight with latitude. This distribution matters because land and water absorb and reflect sunlight differently, and the distributions of land and water—continents and oceans—are quite different in the Northern and Southern Hemispheres. Ice ages occur when, as a result of orbital variations, the arctic regions intercept relatively little summer sunlight so that ice and snow do not melt as much.

The timing of the ice ages, then, is the combined result of the earth's orbit and its basic geology. But this combination does not explain either the slow pace of the earth's descent into the cold phases of the cycle or the abrupt recovery to interglacial warmth evident in the ice-core records. More disturbing is the evidence that these large climate swings—from glacial to interglacial and back—are caused by relatively small changes in the distribution of sunlight with latitude. Thus, on the timescale of ice ages, climate seems exquisitely sensitive to small perturbations in the distribution of sunlight.

And yet for all this sensitivity, the earth never suffered either of the climate catastrophes of fire or ice. In the fire scenario, the most effective greenhouse gas—water vapor—accumulates in the atmosphere as the earth warms. The warmer the atmosphere, the more water vapor can accumulate; as more water vapor accumulates, more heat gets trapped, and the warming spirals upward. This uncontrolled feedback is called the runaway greenhouse effect, and it continues until the oceans have all evaporated, by which time the planet is unbearably hot. One has only to look as far as Venus to see the end result. Any oceans that may have existed on that planet evaporated eons ago, yielding a super greenhouse inferno and an average surface temperature of around 900°F.

Death by ice can result from another runaway feedback. As snow and ice accumulate progressively equatorward, they reflect an increasing amount of sunlight back to space, further cooling the planet until it freezes into a "snowball earth." It used to be supposed that once the planet reached such a frozen state, with almost all sunlight reflected back to space, it could never recover; more recently it has been theorized that without liquid oceans to absorb the carbon dioxide continuously emitted by volcanoes, the gas would accumulate in the atmosphere until its greenhouse effect was finally strong enough to start melting the ice.

It would not take much change in the amount of sunlight reaching the earth to cause one of these catastrophes. And solar physics informs us that the sun was about 25 percent dimmer early in the earth's history, which should have led to an ice-covered planet, a circumstance not supported by geological evidence.

So what saved the earth from fire and ice?

Life itself may help answer the riddle of the faint young sun. Our atmosphere is thought to have originated in gases emitted from volcanoes, but the composition of volcanic gases bears little resemblance to air as we know it today. The early atmosphere likely consisted mostly of water vapor, carbon dioxide, sulfur dioxide, chlorine, and nitrogen. There is little evidence that there was much oxygen until the advent of life. The first life forms helped produce oxygen through photosynthesis and transformed the atmosphere into something like today's, consisting mostly of nitrogen and oxygen with trace amounts of water vapor, carbon dioxide, methane, and other gases. Carbon dioxide content probably decreased slowly with time owing to chemical weathering, possibly aided by biological processes. As the composition changed, the net greenhouse effect weakened, compensating for the slow but inexorable brightening of the sun.

Thus early life dramatically changed the planet. We humans are only the most recent species to do so.

The compensation between increasing solar power and decreasing greenhouse effect may not have been an accident. In the 1960s, James Lovelock proposed that life actually exerts a stabilizing influence on climate by producing feedbacks favorable to itself. He called his idea the Gaia hypothesis, named after the Greek earth goddess. But even according to this view, life is only preserved in the broadest sense: individual species, such as those that transformed the early atmosphere, altered the environment at their peril.

GREENHOUSE PHYSICS

As this sketch of the planet's early climatic history shows, the greenhouse effect plays a critical role in the earth's climate, and no sensible discussion of climate can proceed without grasping its nature. (A cautionary note: the greenhouse metaphor itself is flawed. Whereas actual greenhouses work by preventing convection currents from carrying away heat absorbed from sunlight, the atmosphere prevents heat from radiating away from the surface.) The greenhouse effect has to do with radiation, which in this context refers to energy carried by electromagnetic waves, which include such phenomena as visible light, radio waves, and infrared radiation. All matter with a temperature above absolute zero emits radiation. The hotter the substance, the more radiation it emits and the shorter the average wavelength of the radiation emitted. A fairly narrow range of wavelengths constitute visible light. The average surface temperature of the sun is about 10,000°F, and the sun emits much of its radiation as visible light, with an average wavelength of about half a micron. (A micron is one millionth of a meter; there are 25,400 microns in an inch.) The earth's atmosphere emits as though its average temperature were around 0°F, at an average wavelength of about 15 microns. Our eyes cannot detect this infrared radiation. It is important to recognize that the same object can both emit and absorb radiation: when an object emits radiation it loses energy, and this has the effect of cooling it; absorption, on the other hand, heats an object.

Most solids and liquids absorb much of the radiation they intercept, and they also emit radiation rather easily. Air is another matter. It is composed almost entirely of oxygen and nitrogen, each in the form of two identical atoms bonded together in a single molecule. Such molecules barely interact with radiation: they allow free passage to both solar radiation moving downward to the earth and infrared radiation moving upward from the earth's surface. If that is all there were to the atmosphere, it would be a simple matter to calculate the average temperature of the earth's surface: it would have to be just warm enough to emit enough infrared radiation to balance the shortwave radiation it absorbed from the sun. (Were it too cool, it would emit less radiation than it absorbed and would heat up; conversely, were it too warm it would cool.) Accounting for the amount of sunlight reflected back to space by the planet, this works out to be about 0°F, far cooler than the observed mean surface temperature of about 60°F.

Fortunately for us, our atmosphere contains trace amounts of other substances that do interact strongly with radiation. Foremost among these is water, H_2O, consisting of two atoms of hydrogen bonded to a single atom of oxygen. Because of its more complex geometry, it absorbs and emits radiation far more efficiently than molecular nitrogen and oxygen. In the atmosphere, water exists both in its gas phase (water vapor) and its condensed phase (liquid water and ice) as clouds and precipitation. Water vapor and clouds absorb sunlight and infrared radiation, and clouds also reflect sunlight back to space. The amount of water vapor in a sample of air varies greatly from place to place and time to time, but never exceeds about 2 percent of the mass of the sample. Besides water, there are other gases that interact strongly with radiation; these include CO_2, or carbon dioxide (presently about 380 tons for each million tons of air), and CH_4, or methane (around 1.7 tons for each million tons of air).

Collectively, the greenhouse gases are nearly transparent to sunlight, allowing the short-wavelength radiation to pass virtually unimpeded to the surface, where much of it is absorbed. (But clouds both absorb and reflect sunlight.) On the other hand, these same gases absorb much of the long-wavelength, infrared radiation that passes through them. To compensate for the heating this absorption causes, the greenhouse gases must also emit radiation, and each layer of the atmosphere thus emits infrared radiation upward and downward.

As a result, the surface of the earth receives radiation from the atmosphere as well as the sun. It is a remarkable fact that, averaged over the planet, the surface receives more radiation from the atmosphere than directly from the sun! To balance this extra input of radiation—the radiation emitted by atmospheric greenhouse gases and clouds—the earth's surface must warm up and thereby emit more radiation itself. This is the essence of the greenhouse effect.

If air were not in motion, the observed concentration of greenhouse gases and clouds would raise the average temperature of the earth's surface to around 85°F, much warmer than observed. In reality, hot air from near the surface rises upward and is continually replaced by cold air moving down from aloft; these convection currents lower the surface temperature to an average of 60°F while warming the upper reaches of the atmosphere. So the emission of radiation by greenhouse gases keeps the earth's surface warmer than it would otherwise be; at the same time, the movement of air dampens the warming effect and keeps the surface temperature bearable.

WHY THE CLIMATE PROBLEM IS DIFFICULT

This basic climate physics is entirely uncontroversial among scientists. And if one could change the concentration of a single greenhouse gas while holding the rest of the system (except its temperature) fixed, it would be simple to calculate the corresponding change in surface temperature. For example, doubling the concentration of CO_2 would raise the average surface temperature by about 1.4°F, enough to detect but probably not enough to cause serious problems. Almost all the controversy arises from the fact that in reality, changing any single greenhouse gas will indirectly cause other components of the system to change as well, thus yielding additional changes. These knock-on effects are known as feedbacks, and the most important and uncertain of these involves water.

A fundamental difference exists between water and most other greenhouse gases. Whereas a molecule of carbon dioxide or methane may remain in the atmosphere for hundreds of years, water is constantly recycled between the atmosphere, land surface, and oceans, so that a particular molecule of water resides in the atmosphere for, on average, about two weeks. On climate timescales, which are much longer than two weeks, atmospheric water is nearly in equilibrium with the surface, which means that as much water enters the atmosphere by evaporating from the surface as is lost to the surface by rain and snow. One cannot simply tally up the sources and sinks and figure out which wins; a more involved argument is needed.

To make matters worse, water vapor and clouds are far and away the most important greenhouse substances in the atmosphere, and clouds also affect climate not only by sending infrared radiation back to earth and warming it up but by reflecting sunlight back into space, thus cooling the planet. Water is carried upward from its source at the surface by convection currents, which themselves are a byproduct of the greenhouse effect, which tends to warm the air near the surface. Simple physics as well as detailed calculations using computer models of clouds show that the amount of water vapor in the atmosphere is sensitive to the details of the physics by which tiny cloud droplets and ice crystals combine into larger raindrops and snowflakes, and how these in turn fall and partially re-evaporate on their way to the surface. The devil in these details seems to carry much authority with climate.

This complexity is limited, however, because the amount of water in the atmosphere is subject to a fundamental and important constraint. The concentration of water vapor in any sample of air has a strict upper limit that depends on its temperature and pressure: in particular, this limit rises very rapidly with temperature. The ratio of the actual amount of water vapor in a sample to this limiting amount is the familiar quantity called relative humidity. Calculations with a large variety of computer models and observations of the atmosphere all show that as climate changes, relative humidity remains approximately constant. This means that as atmospheric temperature increases, the actual amount of water vapor increases as well. But water vapor is a greenhouse gas. So increasing temperature increases water vapor, which leads to further increases in temperature. This positive feedback in the climate system is the main reason why the global mean surface temperature is expected to increase somewhat more than the 1.4°F that doubling CO_2 would produce in the absence of feedbacks. (At very high temperatures, the water vapor feedback can run away, leading to the catastrophe of a very hot planet, as mentioned before.)

The amount and distribution of water vapor in the atmosphere is also important in determining the distribution of clouds, which play a complex role in climate. On the one hand, they reflect about 22 percent of the incoming solar radiation back to space, thereby cooling the planet. On the other hand, they absorb solar radiation and both absorb and emit infrared radiation, thus contributing to greenhouse warming. Different global climate models produce wildly different estimates of how clouds might change with changing climate, thus constituting the largest source of uncertainty in climate-change projections.

A further complication in this already complex picture comes from anthropogenic aerosols—small solid or liquid particles suspended in the atmosphere. Industrial activity and biomass burning have contributed to large increases in the aerosol content of the atmosphere, and this is thought to have had a large effect on climate.

The main culprits are the sulfate aerosols, which are created through atmospheric chemical reactions involving sulfur dioxide, another gas produced by the combustion of fossil fuels. These tiny particles reflect incoming sunlight and, to a lesser degree, absorb infrared radiation. Perhaps more importantly, they also serve as condensation nuclei for clouds. When a cloud forms, water vapor does not form water droplets or ice crystals spontaneously but instead condenses onto preexisting aerosol particles. The number and size of these particles determines whether the water condenses into a few large droplets or many small ones, and this in turn strongly affects the amount of sunlight that clouds reflect and the amount of radiation they absorb.

It is thought that the increased reflection of sunlight to space—both directly by the aerosols themselves and through their effect on increasing the reflectivity of clouds—outweighs any increase in their greenhouse effect, thus cooling the planet. Unlike the greenhouse gases, however, sulfate aerosols remain in the atmosphere only a few weeks before they are washed out by rain and snow. Their abundance is proportional to their rate of production; as soon as production decreases, sulfate aerosols follow suit. Since the early 1980s, improved technology and ever more stringent regulations have diminished sulfate aerosol pollution in the developed countries, aided by the collapse of the USSR and the subsequent reduction of industrial output there. On the other hand, sources of sulfate aerosols have been steadily increasing in Asia and the developing countries, so it is unclear how the net global aerosol content has been changing over the past twenty-five years.

Important uncertainties enter the picture, then, with water (especially clouds) and airborne particulates. But the uncertainties actually go much deeper: indeed, to understand long-term climate change, it is essential to appreciate that detailed forecasts cannot, *even in principle*, be made beyond a few weeks. That is because the climate system, at least on short timescales, is chaotic.

The essential property of chaotic systems is that small differences tend to magnify rapidly. Think of two autumn leaves that have fallen next to each other in a turbulent brook. Imagine following them as they move downstream on their way to the sea. At first, they stay close to each other, but the eddies in the stream gradually separate them. At some point, one of the leaves may get temporarily trapped in a whirlpool behind a rock while the other continues downstream. It is not hard to imagine that one of the leaves arrives at the mouth of the river days or weeks ahead of the other. It is also not hard to imagine that a mad scientist, having equipped our brook with all kinds of fancy instruments for measuring the flow of water and devised a computer program for predicting where the leaves would go, would find it almost impossible to predict where the leaf would be even an hour after it started its journey.

Let's go back to the two leaves just after they have fallen in the brook, and say that at this point they are ten inches apart. Suppose that after thirty minutes they are ten feet apart, and this distance increases with time. Now suppose that it was possible to rewind to the beginning, but this time start the leaves only five inches apart. It would not be surprising if it took longer—say an hour—before they are once again ten feet apart. Keep rewinding the experiment, each time decreasing the initial distance between the leaves. You might suppose that the time it takes to get ten feet apart keeps increasing indefinitely. But for many physical systems (probably including brooks), this turns out not to be the case. As you keep decreasing the initial separation, the increases in the amount of time it takes for the leaves to be separated by ten feet get successively smaller, so much so that there is a definite limit:

no matter how close the leaves are when they hit the water, it will not take longer than, say, six hours for them to be ten feet apart.

The same principle applies if, instead of having two leaves, we have a single leaf and a computer model of the leaf and the stream that carries it. Even if the computer model is perfect and we start off with a perfect representation of the state of the brook, any error—even an infinitesimal one—in the timing or position of the leaf when it begins its journey will lead to the forecast being off by at least ten feet after six hours, and greater distances at longer times. Prediction beyond a certain time is impossible.

Not all chaotic systems have this property of limited predictability, but our atmosphere and oceans, alas, almost certainly do. As a result, it is thought that the upper limit of the predictability of weather is around two weeks. (That we are not very close to this limit is a measure of the imperfection of our models and our measurements.)

While the day-to-day variations of the weather are perhaps the most familiar examples of environmental chaos, variations at longer timescales can also behave chaotically. El Niño is thought to be chaotic in nature, making it difficult to predict more than a few months in advance. Other chaotic phenomena involving the oceans have even longer timescales, but beyond a few years it becomes increasingly difficult for scientists to tell the difference between chaotic natural variations and what climate scientists called "forced" variability. But this difference is important for understanding the human role in producing climate change.

On top of the natural, chaotic "free" variability of weather and climate are changes brought about by changing "forcing," which is usually considered to involve factors that are not themselves affected by climate. The most familiar of these is the march of the seasons, brought about by the tilt of the earth's axis, which itself is independent of climate. The effects of this particular forcing are not hard to separate from the background climate chaos: we can confidently predict that January will be colder than July in, say, New York. Other examples of natural climate forcing include variations in solar output and volcanic eruptions, which inject aerosols into the stratosphere and thereby cool the climate.

Some of this natural climate forcing is chaotic in nature, but some of it is predictable on long timescales. For example, barring some catastrophic collision with a comet or asteroid, variations of the earth's orbit are predictable many millions of years into the future. On the other hand, volcanic activity is unpredictable. In any event, the actual climate we experience reflects a combination of free (unforced), chaotic variability, and changes brought about by external forcing, some of which, like volcanic eruptions, are themselves chaotic. And part of this forced climate variability is brought about by human beings.

DETERMINING HUMANITY'S INFLUENCE

An important and difficult issue in detecting anthropogenic climate change is telling the difference between natural climate variations—both free and forced—and those that are forced by our own activities.

One way to tell the difference is to make use of the fact that the increase in greenhouse gases and sulfate aerosols dates back only to the industrial revolution of the nineteenth century. Before that, the human influence is probably small. If we can estimate how climate changed before this time, we will have some idea of how the system varies naturally. Unfortunately, detailed measurements of climate did not begin in earnest until the nineteenth century, but there are "proxies" for quantities like temperature, recorded in, for example, tree rings, ocean and lake plankton, pollen, and corals.

Plotting the global mean temperature derived from actual measurements and from proxies going back a thousand years or more reveals that the recent upturn in global temperature is truly unprecedented: the graph of temperature with time shows a characteristic hockey-stick shape, with the business end of the stick representing the upswing of the last fifty years or so. But the proxies are imperfect and associated with large margins of error, so any hockey-stick trends of the past may be masked, though the recent upturn stands above even a liberal estimate of such errors.

Another way to tell the difference is to simulate the climate of the last hundred years or so with climate models. Computer modeling of global climate is perhaps the most complex endeavor ever undertaken by mankind. A typical climate model consists of millions of lines of computer instructions designed to simulate an enormous range of physical phenomena, including the flow of the atmosphere and oceans, condensation and precipitation of water inside clouds, the transfer of solar and terrestrial radiation through the atmosphere, including its partial absorption and reflection by the surface, by clouds and by the atmosphere itself, the convective transport of heat, water, and atmospheric constituents by turbulent convection currents, and vast numbers of other processes. There are by now a few dozen such models in the world, but they are not entirely independent of one another, often sharing common pieces of computer code and common ancestors.

Although the equations representing the physical and chemical processes in the climate system are well-known, they cannot be solved exactly. It is computationally impossible to keep track of every molecule of air and ocean, and to make the task viable, the two fluids must be divided into manageable chunks. The smaller and more numerous these chunks, the more accurate the result, but with today's computers the smallest we can make these chunks in the atmosphere is around a hundred miles in the horizontal and a few hundred yards in the vertical, and a bit smaller in the ocean. The problem here is that many important processes are much smaller than these scales. For example, cumulus clouds in the atmosphere are critical for transferring heat and water upward and downward, but they are typically only a few miles across and so cannot be simulated by the climate models. Instead, their effects must be represented in terms of the quantities like wind and temperature that pertain to the whole computational chunk in question. The representation of these important but unresolved processes is an art form known by the awful term "parameterization," and it involves numbers, or parameters, that must be tuned to get the parameterizations to work in an optimal way. Because of the need for such artifices, a typical climate model has many tunable parameters, and this is one of many reasons that such models are only approximations to reality. Changing the values of the parameters or the way the various processes are parameterized can change not only the climate simulated by the model, but the sensitivity of the model's climate to, say, greenhouse gas increases.

How, then, can we go about tuning the parameters of a climate model in such a way as to make it a reasonable facsimile of reality? Here important lessons can be learned from our experience with those close cousins of climate models, weather prediction models. These are almost as complicated and must also parameterize key physical processes, but because the atmosphere is measured in many places and quite frequently, we can test the model against reality several times per day and keep adjusting its parameters (i.e., tuning it) until it performs as well as it can. But with climate, there are precious few tests. One obvious hurdle the model must pass is to be able to replicate the current climate, including key aspects of its variability, such as weather systems and El Niño. It must also be able to simulate the seasons in a reasonable way: the summers must not be too hot or the winters too cold, for example.

Beyond a few simple checks such as these, there are not too many ways to test the model, and projections of future climates must necessarily involve a degree of faith. The amount of uncertainty in such projections can be estimated to some extent by comparing forecasts made by many different models, with their different parameterizations (and, very likely, different sets of coding errors). We operate under the faith that the real climate will fall among the projections made with the various models; in other words, that the truth will lie somewhere between the higher and lower estimates generated by the models.

Figure 10.1 shows the results of two sets of computer simulations of the global average surface temperature of the twentieth century using a particular climate model. In the first set only natural, time-varying forcings are applied; these consist of variable solar output and "dimming" owing to aerosols produced by known volcanic eruptions. The second set adds in the manmade influences on sulfate aerosols and greenhouse gases. In each set, the

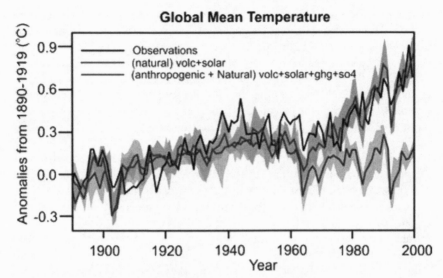

Figure 10.1.   Global Mean Temperature

model is run four times beginning with slightly different initial states, and the range among the four ensemble members is denoted by the shading in the figure, reflecting the free random variability of the climate produced by this model, while the curves show the average of the four ensemble members. The observed global average surface temperature is depicted by the black curve. One observes that the two sets of simulations diverge during the 1970s and have no overlap at all today, and that the observed global temperature also starts to fall outside the envelope of the all-natural simulations in the 1970s. This exercise has been repeated using many different climate models, with the same qualitative result: one cannot simulate the evolution of the climate over last thirty years without including in the simulations mankind's influence on sulfate aerosols and greenhouse gases. This, in a nutshell, is why almost all climate scientists today believe that man's influence on climate has emerged from the background noise of natural variability.

THE CONSEQUENCES

Projections based on climate models suggest that the globe will continue to warm another 3 to 7°F over the next century. This is similar to the temperature change one could experience by moving, say, from Boston to Philadelphia. Moreover, the warming of already hot regions—the tropics—is expected to be somewhat less, while the warming of cold regions like the arctic is projected to be more, a signal already discernable in global temperature measurements. Nighttime temperatures are increasing more rapidly than daytime warmth.

Is this really so bad? In all the negative publicity about global warming, it is easy to overlook the benefits. It will take less energy to heat buildings, previously infertile lands of high latitudes will start producing crops, and there will be less suffering from debilitating cold waves. Increased CO_2 might also make crops grow faster. On the down side, there will be more frequent and more intense heat waves, air conditioning costs will rise, and previously fertile areas in the subtropics may become unarable. Sure, there will be winners and losers, but will the world really suffer in the net? Even if the changes we are bringing about are larger than the globe has experienced in the last few thousand years, they still do not amount to the big natural swings between ice ages and interglacial periods, and the earth and indeed human beings survived these.

But there are consequences of warming that we cannot take so lightly. During the peak of the last ice age, sea level was some four hundred feet lower than today's, since huge quantities of water were locked up in the great continental ice sheets. As polar regions warm, it is possible that portions of the Greenland and Antarctic ice sheets will melt, increasing sea level. Highly detailed and accurate satellite-based measurements of the thickness of the Greenland ice show that it is actually increasing in the interior but thinning around the margins, and while there are also patterns of increase and decrease in Antarctic ice, it appears to be thinning on the whole. Meltwater from the surface of the Greenland ice sheet is making its way to the bottom of the ice, possibly allowing the ice to flow faster toward the sea. Our understanding of the physics of ice under pressure is poor, and it is thus difficult to predict how the ice will respond to warming. Were the entire Greenland ice cap to melt, sea level would increase by around twenty-two feet, flooding many coastal regions including much of southern Florida and lower Manhattan.

My own work has shown that hurricanes are responding to warming sea surface temperatures faster than we originally expected, especially in the North Atlantic, where the total power output by tropical cyclones has increased by around 60 percent since the 1970s. The 2005 hurricane season was the most active in the 150 years of records, corresponding to record warmth of the tropical Atlantic. Hurricanes are far and away the worst natural disasters to affect the United States in economic terms. Katrina may cost us as much as $200 billion, and it has claimed at least 1,200 lives. Globally, tropical cyclones cause staggering loss of life and misery. Hurricane Mitch of 1998 killed over 10,000 people in Central America, and in 1970 a single storm took the lives of some 300,000 people in Bangladesh. Substantial changes in hurricane activity cannot be written off as mere climate perturbations to which we will easily adjust.

Basic theory and models show another consequential result of a few degrees of warming. The amount of water vapor in the air rises exponentially with temperature: a seven-degree increase in temperature increases water vapor by 25 percent. One might at first suppose that since the amount of water ascending into clouds increases, the amount of rain that falls out of them must increase in proportion. But condensing water vapor heats the atmosphere, and in the grand scheme of things, this must be compensated by radiative heat loss. On the other hand, simple calculations show that the amount of radiative heat loss increases only slowly with temperature, so that the total heating by condensation must increase slowly as well. Models resolve this conundrum by making it rain harder in places that are already wet and at the same time increasing the intensity, duration, or geographical extent of droughts. Thus the twin perils of flood and drought increase substantially in a warmer world.

It is particularly sobering to contemplate such outcomes in light of the evidence that smaller, natural climate swings since the end of the last ice age debilitated and in some cases destroyed entire civilizations in such places as Mesopotamia, Central and South America, and the southwestern region of what is today the United States.

In pushing the climate so hard and so fast, we are also conscious of our collective ignorance of how the climate system works. Perhaps negative-feedback mechanisms that we have not contemplated or have underestimated will kick in, sparing us from debilitating consequences. On the other hand, the same could be said of positive feedbacks, and matters might turn out worse than projected. The ice-core record reveals a climate that reacts in complex and surprising ways to smoothly and slowly changing radiative forcing caused by variations in the earth's orbit. Far from changing smoothly, it remains close to one state for a long time and then suddenly jumps to another state. We do not understand this and we worry that a sudden climate jump may be part of our future.

SCIENCE, POLITICS, AND THE MEDIA

Science proceeds by continually testing and discarding or refining hypotheses, a process greatly aided by the naturally skeptical disposition of scientists. We are, most of us, driven by a passion to understand nature, but that means being dispassionate about pet ideas. Partisanship—whatever its source—is likely to be detected by our colleagues and to yield a loss of credibility, the true stock of the trade. We share a faith—justified by experience—that at the end of the day, there is a truth to be found, and those who cling for emotional reasons to wrong ideas will be judged by history accordingly, whereas those who see it early will be regarded as visionaries.

The evolution of the scientific debate about anthropogenic climate change illustrates both the value of skepticism and the pitfalls of partisanship. Although the notion that fossil-fuel combustion might increase CO_2 and alter climate originated in the nineteenth century, general awareness of the issue dates to a National Academy of Sciences report in 1979 that warned that doubling CO_2 content might lead to a three- to eight-degree increase in global average temperature. Then in 1988, James Hansen, the director of NASA's Goddard Institute for Space Studies, set off a firestorm of controversy by testifying before Congress that he was virtually certain that a global-warming signal had emerged from the background climate variability. At that time, less was known about natural climate variability before the beginning of systematic instrumental records in the nineteenth century, and only a handful of global climate simulations had been performed. Most scientists were deeply skeptical of Hansen's claims; I certainly was. It is important to interpret the word "skeptical" literally here. It was not that we were sure of the opposite, merely that we thought the jury was out.

At roughly this time, radical environmental groups and a handful of scientists influenced by them leaped into the fray with rather obvious ulterior motives. This jump-started the politicization of the issue, and conservative groups, financed by auto makers and big oil, responded with counterattacks. This also marked the onset of an interesting and disturbing phenomenon that continues to this day. A small number of climate scientists adopted dogmatic positions and in so doing lost credibility among the vast majority who remained committed to an unbiased search for answers. On the left, an argument emerged urging fellow scientists to deliberately exaggerate their findings so as to galvanize an apathetic public, an idea that failed in the scientific arena but took root in Hollywood, culminating in the 2004 release of *The Day After Tomorrow*. On the right, the search began for negative feedbacks that would counter increasing greenhouse gases. Imaginative ideas emerged, but they have largely failed the acid test of comparison to observations. But as the dogmatists grew increasingly alienated from the scientific mainstream, they were embraced by political groups and journalists who thrust them into the limelight. This produced a gross distortion in the public perception of the scientific debate. Ever eager for the drama of competing dogmas, the media largely ignored mainstream scientists whose hesitations did not make good copy. As the global-warming signal continues to emerge, this soap opera is kept alive by a dwindling number of deniers constantly tapped for interviews by journalists who pretend to look for balance.

While the American public has been misinformed by a media obsessed with sensational debate, climate scientists developed a way forward that helps them compare notes and test one another's ideas and also creates a valuable communication channel. Called the Intergovernmental Panel on Climate Change (IPCC), it produces a detailed summary of the state of the science every four years. Although far from perfect, the IPCC involves serious climate scientists from many countries and has largely withstood political attack and influence.

The IPCC reports are fairly candid about what we collectively know and where the uncertainties probably lie. In the first category are findings that are not in dispute, not even by *les refusards*:

- Concentrations of the greenhouse gases carbon dioxide, methane, ozone, and nitrous oxide are increasing owing to fossil fuel consumption and biomass burning. Carbon dioxide has increased from its preindustrial level of about 280 parts per million (ppmv) to about 380 ppmv today, an increase of about 35 percent. From ice core records, it is evident that present levels of CO_2 exceed those experienced by the planet at any time over at least the past 650,000 years.
- Concentrations of certain anthropogenic aerosols have also increased owing to industrial activity.
- The earth's average surface temperature has increased by about 1.2°F in the past century, with most of the increase occurring from about 1920 to 1950, and again beginning around 1975. The year 2005 was the warmest in the instrumental record.
- Sea level has risen by about 2.7 inches over the past forty years; of this, a little over an inch occurred during the past decade.
- The annual mean geographical extent of arctic sea ice has decreased by 15 to 20 percent since satellite measurements of this began in 1978.

In the second category are findings that most climate scientists agree with but are disputed by some:

- The global mean temperature is now greater than at any time in at least the past five hundred to a thousand years.
- Most of the global mean temperature variability is caused by four factors: variability of solar output, major volcanic eruptions, and anthropogenic sulfate aerosols and greenhouse gases.
- The dramatic rise in global mean temperature in the past thirty years is owing primarily to increasing greenhouse-gas concentrations and a leveling off or slight decline in sulfate aerosols.
- Unless measures are taken to reduce greenhouse-gas production, global mean temperature will continue to increase, about 2.5 to 9°F over the next century, depending on uncertainties and how much greenhouse gas is produced.
- As a result of the thermal expansion of seawater and the melting of polar

ice caps, sea level will increase six to sixteen inches over the next century, though the increase could be larger if large continental ice sheets
become unstable.

- Rainfall will continue to become concentrated in increasingly heavy but
less frequent events.
- The incidence, intensity, and duration of both floods and drought will
increase.
- The intensity of hurricanes will continue to increase, though their frequency may dwindle.

All these projections depend, of course, on how much greenhouse gas is
added to the atmosphere over the next century, and even if we could be certain about the changes, estimating their net effect on humanity is an enor-
mously complex undertaking, pitting uncertain estimates of costs and
benefits against the costs of curtailing greenhouse-gas emissions. But we are
by no means certain about what kind of changes are in store, and we must
be wary of climate surprises. Even if we believed that the projected climate
changes would be mostly beneficial, we might be inclined to make sacrifices
as an insurance policy against potentially harmful surprises.

THE POLITICS OF GLOBAL CLIMATE CHANGE

Especially in the United States, the political debate about global climate
change became polarized along the conservative-liberal axis some decades
ago. Although we take this for granted now, it is not entirely obvious why
the chips fell the way they did. One can easily imagine conservatives embracing the notion of climate change in support of actions they might like to see
anyway. Conservatives have usually been strong supporters of nuclear
power, and few can be happy about our current dependence on foreign oil.
The United States is renowned for its technological innovation and should
be at an advantage in making money from any global sea change in energy-
producing technology. Consider the prospect of selling new means of pow-
ering vehicles and electrical generation to China's rapidly expanding economy. But none of this has happened.

Paradoxes abound on the political left as well. A meaningful reduction in
greenhouse-gas emissions will require a shift in the means of producing
energy, as well as conservation measures. But such alternatives as nuclear and
wind power are viewed with deep ambivalence by the left. Senator Kennedy,
by most measures our most liberal senator, strongly opposes a project to
develop wind energy near his home in Hyannis, and environmentalists have
only just begun to rethink their visceral opposition to nuclear power. Had it
not been for green opposition, the United States today might derive most of

its electricity from nuclear power, as does France; thus the environmentalists must accept a large measure of responsibility for today's most critical environmental problem.

There are other obstacles to taking a sensible approach to the climate problem. We have precious few representatives in Congress with a background or interest in science, and some of them display an active contempt for the subject. As long as we continue to elect scientific illiterates like James Inhofe, who believes global warming to be a hoax, we will lack the ability to engage in intelligent debate. Scientists are most effective when they provide sound, impartial advice, but their reputation for impartiality is severely compromised by the shocking lack of political diversity among American academics, who suffer from the kind of groupthink that develops in cloistered cultures. Until this profound and well documented intellectual homogeneity changes, scientists will be suspected of constituting a leftist think tank.

On the bright side, the governments of many countries, including the United States, continue to fund active programs of climate research, and many of the critical uncertainties about climate change are slowly being whittled down. The extremists are being exposed and relegated to the sidelines, and when the media stop amplifying their views, their political counterparts will have nothing left to stand on. When this happens, we can get down to the serious business of tackling the most complex and perhaps the most consequential problem ever confronted by mankind.

Like it or not, we have been handed Phaeton's reins, and we will have to learn how to control climate if we are to avoid his fate.

11

The Problem of a Rising Sea-Level

The aftermath of Hurricane Katrina caused many Americans to think carefully, some for the first time, about the precariousness of ocean-side developments. The natural disaster, some commentators remarked, was actually an *unnatural* disaster in that the environmental damage was indirectly caused by rapid industrialization and the effects were mostly borne by the poorer people of New Orleans (Kelman 2006). But the New Orleans hurricane victims represent a wider group of peoples and nations across the globe who are similarly threatened by rising sea levels and an increasingly erratic climate.

The scientific and now political consensus is that the problem of global warming was largely created by the emissions released when fossil fuels are burned. Industrialization, much more than globalization, is thus the chief culprit of this environmental problem. But the two processes are inherently and historically interlinked. The fruits of the processes have predominately accrued to the world's industrialized nations, but by some cruel irony, the environmental costs of global warming will largely be borne by people in developing countries. In this chapter Julia Whitty describes some of the problems encountered by people of the South Pacific. Tuvalu and other areas of the world close to (or under) sea level are already dealing with loss of real estate as well as unpredictable and often catastrophic weather changes. It remains to be seen how industrialized nations will respond to these environmental problems that they created.

Julia Whitty, "All the Disappearing Islands" (2003)[1]

From the air the tiny islets of Funafuti atoll appear as a broken pearl necklace scattered on the blue throat of the tropical sea. No other land is in sight, only an ocean without end and its own billowy breath rising as cumulus clouds that seem far more substantive than the tiny landforms below. As the twin-engine turboprop banks for final approach, the atoll assumes the classic dimensions of a desert island—a sand outpost studded with coconut palms and surrounded by impossibly huge swells topped with wave crests longer than the island is wide. This leaves me to ponder, as Charles Darwin did, how "these low hollow coral islands bear no proportion to the vast ocean out of which they abruptly rise; and it seems wonderful that such weak invaders are not overwhelmed, by the all-powerful and never-tiring waves of that great sea."

Although Darwin eventually discovered the reef-building mechanisms of corals that keep atoll islands from succumbing to the waves, even his prescient mind never considered the dread possibilities of the twenty-first century: that global warming could cause the sea to expand and rise faster than the corals could fortify themselves against it, and that these fragile spits of sand might disappear beneath the waves that tossed them into being in the first place.

Today, roughly one million people live on coral islands worldwide, and more millions live on low-lying real estate vulnerable to the rising waves. At risk are not just people, but unique human cultures, born and bred in watery isolation. Faced with inundation, some of these people are beginning to envision the wholesale abandonment of their nations. Others are buying higher land wherever they can. A few are preparing lawsuits that will challenge the right of the developed world to emit the greenhouse gases threatening to cause the flooding of their homelands. But whatever their actions or inactions, the citizens of tropical island nations are likely destined to become the world's first global warming refugees, although they contribute only 0.6 percent of greenhouse gas pollution.

At no point is the sandy island of Funafuti higher than thirteen feet above sea level, as is the case throughout the nine coral atolls of this South Pacific nation of Tuvalu. Surrounded by the sea, the people here have been shaped by it as few others on earth. Every afternoon, rain or shine, Tuvaluan children romp in its unsupervised playground. Fishing at dusk for the night's dinner, the men cast nets weighted with coral into the surf. Islanders who lack outhouses wade into the privacy of the waves, where—they laugh and tell me—they feed the same fish that will soon feed them. Inescapably, this is a nation of waterfront property; even the plywood and corrugated tin houses standing "inland" a block or two enjoy the ambience of the ocean. No one here has ever lived a moment without hearing the thunder of surf.

"Tuvaluans are blessed," wrote former Prime Minister Faimalaga Luka. "We have the sea, and above all we have our land. [We] are closely knit through kinship, a small population, and a single binding culture. What this mixture stirs up is a sensation that runs deep, a supreme sense of place."

That place, now in danger of disappearing beneath the waves, is located halfway between Hawaii and Australia. Once part of the British empire, Tuvalu is among the smallest and most remote countries on earth, with a total land mass comprising only ten square miles, less than half the size of Manhattan and scattered over 347,400 square miles of ocean, an area larger than California, Oregon, and Washington combined. Nine thousand people live on these nine atolls, 95 percent of whom are Polynesians, having arrived variously from Samoa, Tonga, and Uvea over the past 2,000 years.

Life on a *motu* (the low island atop a coral reef) is always precarious, and when the first Polynesians arrived in Tuvalu, they found it hard going. With only sand for soil, they depended on the sea, coconuts, their pigs, and a threadbare agriculture of *pulaka* (a tarolike root). When high winds and waves from tropical storms and cyclones washed over their low-lying islands, the Tuvaluans sometimes tied themselves to spindly coconut palms, hoping the wind would spare these tenuous anchors.

Yet now, ominously, the high tides and resultant floods that used to visit Tuvalu in February are occurring nearly half the year, from November to March. And whereas in the past big cyclones rampaged through these islands only once or twice a decade—the most violent in recent memory being Cyclone Bebe, which in 1972 inundated Funafuti, killing six people, razing most buildings, flattening nearly every coconut palm—the 1990s saw seven of them. When three cyclones ripped through Fiji and Tonga in 1997, a 124-acre *motu* in the Funafuti atoll washed away. On my visit across the lagoon to see what was left, I found only a dome of petrified coral cement—the basement, as it were, for the sandy beaches and palm trees that once comprised a favorite Funafutian picnic site.

And these islands could be rendered uninhabitable by other effects of climate change. Floods and rogue waves raise the saltwater table underlying the atolls, poisoning the Tuvaluans' staple crops. Already some farmers have been forced to grow their *pulaka* in tin containers, and already some of the smaller *motus* have lost their coconut palms to saltwater intrusion. Nor are storms a prerequisite for disaster. "Last August," Prime Minister Saufatu Sopoanga tells me, "on a clear, calm day, a sudden wave surge rolled in from the sea and washed across Funafuti into the lagoon, flooding houses."

There was no apparent reason for it, and during my stay on the atoll, I find the sensation of threat to be ever present—the sea on both sides, the constant drum roll of surf, a thin strip of land between—like living on a liquid fault line.

The Tuvaluans face a difficult choice. If the seas rise and they stay in Tuvalu, they will die. But if they leave, some part of them will die. In the event of abandonment, says Sopoanga, "we'd like to stay as close to Tuvalu as possible, where we could still have the same water and the same air." Despite a prevalent Western belief that all the world would like to emigrate to its shores, the Tuvaluans feel differently. Not at all happily, they are preparing to become a nation of *fakaalofa*—their word for landless people, which literally means "deserving of pity."

Because there are no motor scooters or even push bikes in working order for me to rent, I am hitchhiking on Funafuti, although thumbs are not required here, simply a suitably heat-stricken gait. It's a good way to meet the locals, albeit only men, who immediately inquire as to my marital status. Recently a Funafutian married a *palangi* (white) woman, and his reports on the novelty of my kind are apparently piquing some interest.

Most of these men turn out not to be native Funafutians, but transplants from the outer atolls of Tuvalu. They have come here in search of economic opportunity, swelling the population of the capital to around five thousand. When I ask if they have seen many changes on the atoll since they arrived, they avoid talk of rising seas, turning instead to more immediate concerns. Eight months ago, the only road in the country was paved along a 7.5-mile span in Funafuti, and everyone agrees the island has gotten much hotter since the black tarmac usurped so much white sand. One elderly passenger complains that the Funafutians won't walk anywhere anymore, and worse yet, they won't go barefoot, but insist on wearing flip-flops. He blames this preponderance of newfangled footwear on the road too, saying the pavement is too hot to walk on, even for coral-calloused feet.

There is little or no television here, only a few hours of radio a day, and most of these drivers have never been farther than their home islands, although some have traveled to Fiji or New Zealand. But most don't have much to compare their country to, and when I mention that Tuvalu is graced with universal literacy and almost no violent crime (the only jail is currently empty)—the Funafutians smile and nod politely. It would be unseemly to acknowledge that their world is that much better than mine.

But whereas I had expected to meet a nation of people eager for me to broadcast their plight to the world, instead I am finding citizens wary of the topic of sea levels. To a person, they seem quietly disappointed that I am not a tourist. Despite the country's international airport code of FUN, virtually no vacationers make it to these islands. Perhaps the Tuvaluans are afraid that talk of flooded islands will squash any hopes that tourism will ever establish itself on their thirteen-foot-high shores. Yet I also sense something of shame, as if they feel responsible for their impending status as *fakaalofa*.

Thirty-one years ago, when Cyclone Bebe inundated Funafuti, its waves tossed coral rubble onto the windward side of the atoll, creating a rampart that still stands as the highest point on the *motu*. This rampart is now colonized by coconut palms, pandanus, and breadfruit trees, and I liked to sit here in the late afternoons and watch the sea rolling ashore. As each wave climbs and then withdraws, it rolls the coral rubble back and forth. The chattering sounds these stones make are like the noise of thousands of falling dominoes, sharply audible even above the pounding surf.

The precariousness of dominoes seems an apt metaphor for Tuvalu's fate, where changes to either sea levels or the coral cover will likely result in the entire nation succumbing to what Darwin described as the "irresistible power" of the "miscalled Pacific." Snorkeling in the lagoon each afternoon, I see evidence of the struggle already under way. Stands of *Acropora* (staghorn) corals, the densest I have seen in more than two decades of diving and filming reef life, rise in a tangle as chaotic as blackberry thickets. Yet, by my estimate, 80 percent of these reefs are dead, killed in the 1997 and 2002 El Niños, which uprooted corals in a rash of cyclones and raised sea temperatures enough to cause the most massive, fatal, worldwide episodes of coral bleaching ever recorded.

The live corals still found inside Funafuti's lagoon are all young colonies, decorating the pointy tips of the dead staghorns like gaudy blue and pink fingernails. Below them, the thicket of what was once a spectacular coral world is now choked in velvety algae and aswarm with the herbivorous species of parrotfish, surgeonfish, rabbitfish, blennies, damselfish, mollusks, and sea urchins. Together, these browsers and grazers form a bioerosive army that will eventually convert the bones of this reef to sand.

In the event that these corals—the backbone of the atoll—never recover their health, the whole island will eventually be swept away as well. Yet even with robust reefs, a rising ocean will likewise overwhelm these low-lying islands, and the most likely cause of rising oceans is rising global temperatures. Most scientists (even those employed by oil companies) now agree that the dangerous rate by which global temperatures are escalating is largely due to human activity. Forecasts predict the earth will warm 3° to 9°F over the next century—far more rapid than any previous fluctuations—with a 3°F rise akin to moving the climate bands poleward thirty feet a day. "Squirrels might be able to move at those kinds of rates, but an oak tree can't," says climatologist Ken Caldeira of the Lawrence Livermore National Laboratory. Neither can islands. At their best, the reef-building corals grow only an inch per year.

Evidence of global climate change is already mounting from the most distant reaches of the globe. The snows of Kilimanjaro are melting away. In 2002, the ice covering the Arctic and Greenland shrank by a record 650,000 square miles, while a study published in *Science* found that Alaskan glaciers were melting at more than twice the rate previously assumed, adding twelve cubic miles of freshwater to the world's oceans each year. Also in 2002, an area of ice the size of Rhode Island broke from the Larsen B ice shelf in Antarctica, where it had been firmly cemented for 12,000 years. New research reveals that the rapidly melting glaciers are even changing the shape of the planet, making the earth more oblate than spherical. Yet another study in *Science* suggests that the warming oceans may trigger intense eruptions of methane now frozen beneath the seafloor, leading to global warming on a catastrophic scale.

More alarming still, this melting creates a feedback loop difficult to escape. Because compact sea ice reflects 80 percent of the sun's heat back into space, and water absorbs 80 percent, any reduction in the ratio of ice to water further increases the warming of the oceans and the thermal expansion that will eventually raise sea levels worldwide—if it is not doing so already. "Once the process is set in motion," warns Robert Watson, chairman of the U.N. Intergovernmental Panel on Climate Change (IPCC), "it cannot be slowed down in anything less than a few millennia."

But the evidence is not without controversy. Tangled up with the science is the reality that nations prefer not to alter the fossil fuel consuming habits that make them globally powerful, even at the expense of a stable climate. Chief among these are the United States and Australia, both of which refused to sign the 1997 U.N. Kyoto Protocol—calling on the developed world to reduce greenhouse-gas emissions by 5.2 percent of 1990 levels by 2012—even though Australia is the world's highest greenhouse-gas emitter per capita, followed closely by the United States, the largest overall polluter.

Perhaps in light of this stance, in 1999 Australia was quick to trumpet its own evidence that sea levels in the Pacific are not rising after all. The report came from Australia's National Tidal Facility, which monitors a network of tidal gauges across the Pacific, including one on Funafuti. Yet much less noted was the evidence from the University of Hawaii's tidal gauge in Tuvalu—which has been recording sea levels for nearly three times as long as the Australians, and which indicates a mean one- to two-centimeter rise per decade. Mark Merrifield of the Hawaii study tells me that what's really worrying is that the maximum sea levels—the highest of the high tides—have been increasing at a much faster rate. "This might explain why the inhabitants of Tuvalu have seen more extreme flooding events than one might expect from just looking at the change in mean sea level."

Aware of the ambiguities in the science, Prime Minister Sopoanga reminds me, "Here in Tuvalu we don't need to refer to reports because we see the evidence with our own eyes every day."

Because I am on foot in Funafuti, moving slowly through the heat and the afternoon rainstorms, I have ample time to savor the ambiguities. In 2001, Tuvalu began actively lobbying Australia and New Zealand to accept its entire population as environmental refugees, a request that Australia, with its strict no-refugee policy, refused, citing its tidal-gauge data. New Zealand, on the other hand, agreed to accept the citizens of Tuvalu, although only seventy-five islanders a year—at which rate the country will not be emptied for 120 years. By that time, according to the 2001 IPCC report, the seas may well have risen more than thirty-five inches, rendering the atolls uninhabitable.

Yet paradoxically, Funafuti is building like a nation with a long-term future. A three-story government office building is under construction in the center of town. Destined to be the tallest structure in the nation, this veritable high-rise is a thank-you gift from Taiwan, which won this round in the Pacific cold war by convincing Tuvalu to formally recognize it as the real China. Nearby, a new hospital is also under construction, funded by Japan. At both sites, Tuvaluan workers lounge in the shade, while their Australian handlers march around in Blundstone boots and khaki shorts.

On much of the rest of the atoll I see new houses springing up—evidence of Tuvaluans moving to Funafuti from the outer atolls, and of the growing prosperity of the nation as a whole, as money flows in from Tuvaluans working overseas, from foreign aid organizations, and from a host of innovative money-making plans implemented by the government. Presumably in acknowledgment of the rising waters, the new houses are all being built on ten-foot stilts—notably different from traditional dwellings—and overall, this tiny nation appears to be caught in a tidal cycle of doubt, ebbing and flowing between plans to abandon the country and hopes of developing it.

Of course, the stilt houses might also be due to the rising tide of garbage. Until recently, the only refuse the Tuvaluans created was coconut husks and fish bones, and in keeping with past practices, they now throw everything from plastic bottles to beer cans and disposable diapers more or less out their front doors. Paul Scells, an Australian aid worker who's helping to establish a waste management program here, jokes that sea levels may or may not be rising, but for sure the housewives of Tuvalu are sweeping the island away. I too have heard the pleasant soundtrack of their work in the cool hour after dawn, as they brush away the leaves and fronds that have fallen in the night, and dutifully weed the tenacious green shoots growing in their yards. Apparently the people here prefer unvegetated plots (garbage or no), and the ex-pat Aussies and Kiwis who gather each afternoon for lunch on the terrace of the Vaiaku Lagi—Tuvalu's only hotel—shake their heads in shared cultural confusion. But this is what I like best about this place, and what I fear most when I imagine its eventual abandonment: a different point of view that could only survive out here. Transplanted to New Zealand, the Tuvaluans will doubtless learn to grow lawns.

Before I left home, a friend suggested that Tuvalu might have a bright future as a postapocalyptic tourist destination, and with this in mind, I find myself assessing future attractions. The lobby of the Vaiaku Lagi would make a pleasant dive site—open and airy (watery), with the guest rooms adding the thrill of exploration, all of which might be clothed in pretty corals if the sea temperatures permit. The windowless kitchen would provide an excellent daytime sleeping site for white-tipped reef sharks, while the small dining room could house a large humphead wrasse and his harem of females. Ordering a can of Victoria Bitter, I see ample room behind the bar for a moray eel, and plenty of whiskey bottles to provide homes for shy octopuses.

Because of the building boom and the accompanying population boom of Aussie and Kiwi construction workers, I've been unable to get a room at the Vaiaku Lagi, or at any of the guest houses in the village, or even at the houses of relatives of the sympathetic young woman at the front desk. Her aunties' houses are filled with family from the outer islands, who have come to Funafuti for a weekend wedding. And so I find myself three miles out of town at the Hide-Away guest house, home of Rolf Koepke, a German who came to the South Pacific forty years ago, and his Tuvaluan wife, Emily.

When they built their home on Funafuti twenty years ago, it was a novelty: a two-story palangi house, Emily says, "way out in the bush." Her Tuvaluan family was mystified as to why she would want to live so high up or so far away. Rolf insisted on moving in before the house was completed, then stepped off the unfinished second floor in the dark one night, breaking a leg so badly that he spent the next nine months in the hospital, fighting the doctor's urge to amputate.

Emily ascribes Rolf's troubles to the fact that he loves his beer too much, although he is also a good man, she says, a "working-hard man." My first night at the Hide-Away, Rolf's legs have taken another hit, as he fell off his bicycle earlier that day. Oblivious to his blood dripping onto the bed where I will soon be sleeping, he tells me that he doesn't believe a word of this rising sea level business. The Tuvaluans are building everywhere, he says, and he has personally seen no signs of rising waters, although he concedes that the climate is "all buggered up," and that none of the seasons arrive when they should anymore.

The next morning, when he looks surprised to see me there and anxious over what to do about it, he delivers me into the company of Father Camille Desrosiers, better known among his tiny congregation as Father Kamilo—a fit, seventy-four-year-old French Canadian Catholic missionary who has been on Funafuti for seventeen years, where he claims, only half jokingly, to have been forgotten by his superiors. Father Kamilo also disdains the disappearing-island theory, citing the contradiction of the building boom. But the news of even the nearby world could easily pass him by, I realize. Chatting with me at his desk in his tiny office, he tells me that letters from England arrive "pretty fast"—this as he opens a Christmas card on Valentine's Day.

Father Kamilo strives mostly in vain against the dominant Protestant Church of Tuvalu, which has been in the islands for more than a century, and whose pealing bells call its brethren to services seemingly more often than a muezzin. The church's followers—97 percent of the population—hold to a strong belief in the Genesis story, in which rainbows are proof of God's promise to Noah that he will not flood the earth again. Apparently Tuvalu's daily rainbows reinforce this belief, and whenever I hear the sound of Tuvaluan voices rising in a cappella church song, their harmonies weaving sweetly and effortlessly through the sky where rainbows blossom and fade, I can understand the comfort such faith could provide.

Somewhere in Father Kamilo's mind must be the thought that he will likely die on Funafuti, having converted few, having never been posted back to the bigger world, and having never even seen the outer atolls of Tuvalu. Perhaps he will end up like all the other Tuvaluans: buried in the private cemeteries gracing everyone's front yards, the graves surrounded by hog fencing decorated with plastic flowers. The Hide-Away has just such a cemetery, including the grave of Emily's and Rolf's eleven-year-old son, who died of leukemia in faraway New Zealand, where Rolf, in desperation, took him for treatment.

It occurs to me that after two thousand years of human habitation, a fair amount of Tuvalu's tiny landmass must be composed of the bones of its people, and when I think of the future, this thought saddens me as well. What will become of these other Tuvaluans—the ones whom the people still consider important enough to erect roofs over their graves for shade? Surely the New Zealanders will not accept the dead Tuvaluans too, or the soil they have become.

Many young Tuvaluans are already being sent away. Promising students go to universities in Fiji, New Zealand, or Australia. At any given time 750 Tuvaluans—about a quarter of the adult males—are employed as merchant mariners. When these young people return, despite being richer or better educated or both, they still have no pigs, a condition considered pitiable by the older generation.

Pigs and land have traditionally been the measure of wealth in Tuvalu. Although Emily says they love their pigs and cry when they must kill them, when two rogue pigs go rampaging through her garden, she doesn't hesitate to tell me that, by law, she has the right to kill them, which would "give us all a good excuse for a feast." Apparently slaughtering your neighbor's pigs sidesteps the sadness issue.

Because Emily is the groom's aunt, I am invited to the weekend wedding that has drawn so many people from the outer atolls. The feast is overflowing with pork, delivered whole on spits from underground *umu* ovens. In two days' time the newly married couple will go back to their university studies in Fiji. Meantime, they tear into the pig carcasses with their bare hands. Like a growing number of their countrymen, they are Tuvaluans who do not live in Tuvalu. Recent population estimates indicate that in the last two years some two thousand have fled the rising waters (or the limited opportunities) and are now scattered across the South Pacific—many in Auckland, the largest Polynesian city in the world, and a place decidedly pigless and landless, at least for refugees.

During its brief decades of independence, Tuvalu has behaved differently from its South Pacific neighbors, many of which are considered among the most corrupt nations on earth. But a democratic Tuvalu has managed its resources well: growing the national trust fund to around $30 million; licensing its Internet country code (.tv) for $12.5 million (thereby funding the country's first streetlights, the first paved road, and U.N. membership); selling commercial fishing licenses within its waters; and producing postage stamps for the international philatelic trade. Other schemes, though lucrative, were canceled—including the sale of Tuvaluan passports (after evidence that terrorists were purchasing them) and a phone sex service tied to the nation's 688 area code that once earned 10 percent of the federal budget (after Tuvalu's churches objected).

But perhaps the country's biggest revenue earner lies in the future. Currently the government is seeking partners among other island nations for a lawsuit against the United States and Australia to be brought before the International Court of Justice in The Hague, suing for damages from global warming. The reparations from such "ecological debt" could be huge, including the potential to cancel the money owed on developmental loans to the big polluters. At the very least, such lawsuits will give the World Court the means to punish the rich nations for practices that essentially amount to killing their neighbors' pigs.

There is skepticism over this lawsuit. Some see it as a cynical ploy for more foreign money. These tend to be the same people who privately mutter that garbage-strewn Tuvalu would benefit from a seawater flushing, and who appear to begrudge the Tuvaluans their clever capitalizing on the few opportunities available to them. "We hope to speak for the low-lying atolls and coastal areas of the world," says Prime Minister Sopoanga, although he admits that the suit is facing an uphill battle due to other litigants' fears that the powerful donor nations they'd be suing would seek reprisals. Still, the lawsuit is considered a threat, and Australian legal experts, at least, have advised their government to take it seriously.

Along with Tuvalu, many other island and coastal cultures have just grievances. Kiribati, Tuvalu's neighbor, has already lost two islands to the rising waters. The seas around the Carteret atolls off Papua New Guinea have cut one island in half and left 1,500 people dependent on food aid. In the Marshall Islands, World War II gravesites are washing away. Trinidad reports losing land at the rate of two to four yards per year. In the Indian Ocean, a third of the Maldives' two hundred inhabited atolls are disappearing. And in Alaska, some Eskimos are being forced to move as the tundra melts and their villages slip into the sea. Unlike other refugees displaced by wars or famines, these people on the edge of the ocean face the prospect of never again having homelands to return to.

Some help has been promised, but it pales in comparison to Western practices. In 2001, rich nations pledged $0.4 billion a year to help developing countries adapt to climate change, while spending $80 billion annually on energy subsidies, mostly for fossil fuels. In the Pacific, the frustration is apparent: "Tuvalu's voice in the debate is small, rarely heard, and heeded not at all," wrote former Prime Minister Faimalaga Luka.

Eventually the cost will be high for all nations. Regardless of any possible curbs on emissions, sea levels are predicted to rise for at least the next five hundred years, rendering a completely new map of the world, as river valleys become seas, continents fragment into islands, and thirteen of the world's twenty most populous cities submerge. During my time in Tuvalu, I find myself wondering what Darwin would have thought of it all. In the course of his long travels through the Pacific, he gleaned much about evolution and its shadow partner, extinction: "We have every reason to believe that species and groups of species gradually disappear, one after another, first from one spot, then from another, and finally from the world." Would he think the same lay in store for human cultures, and perhaps human existence, today?

Within the coming decades, the atolls of Tuvalu and elsewhere will almost certainly revert to sandbars and then nothing. Although the people themselves will not go extinct, without their home islands to anchor them, their beliefs and identity probably will, scattered person by person across the rising waters, to places where they will learn to wear real shoes and eat frozen pork—until, like Atlantis, the name of Tuvalu fades into myth.

REFERENCE

Kelman, Ari. 2006. "Nature Bats Last: Some Recent Works on Technology and Urban Disaster." *Technology and Culture* 47, no. 2 (April).

IV

POLITICS, IDENTITY, AND JUSTICE

Chris Jordan, Spent Shells

12

War and Mobilization

Only the most blindly optimistic pundit would fail to recognize the relationship between war and globalization. This was most obviously true during the wars of conquest that tied the world together with silver, gold, and African and Indian labor in the sixteenth through the eighteenth centuries. And the fruits of industrial imperialism would probably not have been so sweet without the Opium Wars, the Mutiny of 1857, and the Xulu War, among many others. The institutions that regulate the global economy today were born from the ashes of World War II in part to play a geopolitical game that pitted capitalist and socialist worlds. And this process spurred on other wars in Korea and Vietnam; the Gulf wars are only a variant on the theme.

While we justifiably concentrate on the human costs of warfare in terms of mortality, casualties, and dislocation, the environment too has had to pay a heavy price for global security. In this chapter Jessica Adley and Andrea Grant outline some of the direct and indirect threats that the global environment faces because of warfare, especially in terms of the long-term livelihoods of people who must live in these contaminated spaces. They conclude on a positive note, however, by noting how international dialogue, like that at the Earth Summits, often directly links human and economic health to the sustainability of environments that are often negatively impacted by warfare. This chapter underscores the important point that—more than the explosion of munitions—it is the *mobilization* for war during times of ostensible peace that creates the most environmental damage.

Jessica Adley and Andrea Grant, "The Environmental Consequences of War" (2003)[1]

> War is never an isolated act.
>
> —Clausewitz, 1831[2]

Although ecological disturbances brought on by war have been occurring for thousands of years, modern-day warfare has made its impact increasingly severe. Recognizing the long-term and widespread impacts caused by such degradation, experts have coined the term "ecocide," literally meaning the killing of the environment.

ENVIRONMENTAL SECURITY

From the Romans in 146 B.C. salting fields around Carthage to impair food production to the looting of Iraqi nuclear facilities, the environmental destruction resulting from war has had an enduring legacy (Chamorro 2001). While the use of Agent Orange to defoliate jungles in Vietnam and burning of oil wells in Iraq have become icons of environmental warfare, many lesser-known but no less significant acts of ecocide have been perpetrated by warring states. Among them is the extensive toll of water contamination on environmental and health security and the impact of combat on endangered species. Although by no means comprehensive, the following examples illustrate some of the different forms of environmental degradation caused by war.

DEPLETED URANIUM

Since the 1991 Gulf War, concern over the health and environmental effects of depleted uranium (DU) weapons has continued to grow. An extremely dense metal made from low-level radioactive waste, DU is principally used by the United States (but also by other countries such as Britain) in defensive military armor, conventional munitions, and some missiles (World Health Organization 2003). Its ability to penetrate the armor of enemy tanks and other targets more readily than similar weapons made of other materials has made DU extremely valuable to the U.S. military. Perhaps not surprisingly, the U.S. military has downplayed potential health risks posed by exposure to depleted uranium.

In many cases, current scientific studies have yet to substantiate links between reported health problems and the intensive use of DU weapons (World Health Organization 2003). However, other studies suggest DU is not as harmless as the United States and other "coalition forces" would like the public to believe.

"I think the evidence is piling up that DU is not benign at all," said Malcolm Hooper, an emeritus professor of medicinal chemistry at the University of Sunderland and chief scientific adviser to the U.K. Gulf Veterans Association. "The inhalation of these fine dust particles represents a health hazard that was known to the military as long ago as 1974," he said in an interview with BBC news (Kirby 2003).

The Royal Society, the U.K. national science academy, predicts that soldiers and civilians exposed to high DU levels may be at increased risk for kidney damage and lung cancer. Unfortunately, a DU cleanup and monitoring program, necessary to confirm suspected health threats, is on hold until coalition forces agree to reveal where and how much DU was used in Iraq ("Royal Society" 2003). For additional information, see the Sierra Club of Canada, www.sierraclub.ca/national/programs/atmosphere-energy/nuclear-free/index.shtml .

INFRASTRUCTURE

The degradation of infrastructure and basic services brought on by war can wreak havoc on the local environment and public health. Water supply systems, for example, can be contaminated or shut down by bomb blasts or bullet damage to pipes (Sheehan 2003). In Afghanistan, destruction to water infrastructure combined with weakened public services during the war resulted in bacterial contamination, water loss through leaks, and illegal use (UNEP 2003a). The consequence was an overall decline in safe drinking water throughout the country.

Water shortages can also lead to inadequate irrigation of cropland. Agricultural production may also be impaired by intensive bombing and heavy military vehicles traveling over farm soil (UNEP 2003b). The presence of land-mines can render vast areas of productive land unusable (Office of International Security Operations 1992).

Additional war-related problems that compound degradation of the natural and human environment include shortages in cooking fuel and waste mismanagement during and after military conflicts. During the most recent warfare in Iraq, individuals were forced to cut down city trees to use as cooking fuel (Sheehan 2003). In Afghanistan, the creation of poorly sited, leaky landfill sites resulted in contaminated rivers and groundwater (UNEP 2003a).

FORESTS/BIODIVERSITY

Throughout history, war has invariably resulted in environmental destruction. However, advancements in military technology have produced increasingly severe environmental impacts. This is well illustrated by the devastation to forests and biodiversity caused by modern warfare.

Military machinery and explosives have caused unprecedented levels of deforestation and habitat destruction. This has resulted in a serious disruption of ecosystem services, including erosion control, water quality, and food production. A telling example is the destruction of 35 percent of Cambodia's intact forests due to two decades of civil conflict. In Vietnam, bombs alone destroyed over 2 million acres of land (Wall 2003). These environmental catastrophes are aggravated by the fact that ecological protection and restoration become a low priority during and after war.

The threat to biodiversity from combat can also be illustrated by the Rwanda genocide of 1994. The risk to the already endangered population of mountain gorillas from the violence was of minimal concern to combatants and victims during the ninety-day massacre (Wall 2003). The threat to the gorillas increased after the war as thousands of refugees, some displaced for decades, returned to the already overpopulated country. Faced with no space to live, they had little option but to inhabit the forest reserves, home to the gorilla population. As a result of this human crisis, conservation attempts were impeded. Currently the International Gorilla Conservation Programme is working with authorities to protect the gorillas and their habitats. This has proven to be a challenging task, given the complexities Rwandan leaders face, including security, education, disease, epidemics, and famine (Rutagarama 2003).

CHEMICAL AND BIOLOGICAL WARFARE

One of the most striking examples of military disregard for environmental and human health is the use of chemical and biological agents in warfare. The American military's use of Agent Orange during the Vietnam War is one of the most widely known examples of using environmental destruction as a military tactic.

Agent Orange is a herbicide that was sprayed in millions of liters over approximately 10 percent of Vietnam between 1962 and 1971. It was used to defoliate tropical forests to expose combatants and destroy crops to deprive peasants of their food supply (Pesticide Action Network 1998; Eisman 2001). The environmental and health effects were devastating. The spraying destroyed 14 percent of South Vietnam's forests, including 50 percent of the mangrove forests. Few, if any, have recovered to their natural state (Pesticide Action Network 1998).

A key ingredient of Agent Orange is dioxin, the most potent carcinogen ever tested (Eisman 2001). It is therefore not surprising that Agent Orange has been linked to an array of health problems in Vietnam, including birth defects, spontaneous abortions, chloracne, skin and lung cancers, lower IQ, and emotional problems for children (Pesticide Action Network UK 2003).

Similar to toxic chemical spills, Agent Orange continues to threaten the health of Vietnamese. In 2001, scientists documented extremely high levels of dioxin in blood samples taken from residents born years after the end of the Vietnam War. Studies attribute such high levels to food chain contamination: soil contaminated with dioxin becomes river sediment, which is then passed to fish, a staple of the Vietnamese diet (Gochfeld 2001: 433–34). This is a clear reminder that poisoning our environments is akin to poisoning ourselves.

NUCLEAR

The looting of Iraqi nuclear facilities in 2003, which occurred after U.S.-led forces entered the country, has offered another blow to social and environmental security in the region. The most troubling case concerns the Tuwaitha nuclear plant, located forty-eight kilometers south of Baghdad, where an estimated two hundred blue plastic barrels containing uranium oxide were stolen. After dumping the radioactive contents and rinsing out the barrels in the rivers, poverty-stricken residents used the containers for storing basic amenities like water, cooking oil, and tomatoes. Extra barrels were sold to other villages or used to transport milk to distant regions, thus making the critical problem increasingly widespread (Browne 2003).

The mishandling of radioactive material has profound effects on the environment and on the people and animals that depend on it. Toxic substances seep into the ground (rendering the soil unsafe), disperse through the air (spreading wide-scale pollution), and taint water and food supplies. Iraq's national nuclear inspector has predicted that over a thousand people could die of leukemia (Browne 2003).

In addition to stolen radiological materials, computers and important documents have also gone missing (Rice 2003). Given the right mix of technology and materials, radiological weapons such as dirty bombs and possibly even weapons of mass destruction (WMD) could be produced. It is worth noting that uranium oxide can be refined with the proper machinery and expertise in order to produce enriched uranium, a key ingredient in a nuclear bomb ("Making a Bomb" 2003). There is concern that such materials could end up in the hands of the very terrorist groups the U.S. and U.K. military are trying to disable (Rice 2003). Unfortunately the coalition forces' failure to effectively secure nuclear sites in Iraq may well have exacerbated the situation the war was supposed to avoid: the unlawful proliferation and use of WMD.

REFORM IS NEEDED

Despite the long legacy of environmental destruction caused by warfare, the standards set by most conventions and protocols have proven inadequate in preventing and redressing environmental degradation brought on by war (Environmental Law Institute 1998). Some experts maintain that the two principal international laws that could hold wartime aggressors accountable for ecological crimes are weak and outdated. Although the UNEP labeled the Iraqi military's lighting and dumping of oil in Kuwait during the 1991 Gulf War as "one of the worst engineered disasters of humanity," the government was never tried for its scorched earth policy (Adler 2003). Some observers have called for a fifth Geneva Convention to replace existing international norms.

Additional concerns focus on the geographical and temporal constraints placed by such agreements. While only a fraction of the armed conflicts in the world are international in scope, there is a lack of domestic regulations preempting war's ecological harm (Environmental Law Institute 1998: 6). To make matters worse, international laws protecting the environment are mostly peacetime laws that are limited during conflict by the application of the Law of War, which focuses primarily on human needs (Environmental Law Institute 1998: 7; Chamorro 2003).

Enforcement has also been an issue of serious debate. Some experts maintain that mitigating environmental atrocities from warfare requires clearer standards of conduct enforced by credible authorities able to impose penalties on those guilty of violations ("Environmental Consequences of War" 2003). Such a precedent would change the way military operations perceive and use their physical environment. Rather than identifying their surroundings as providing "either logistical problems to be overcome and defeated or opportunities to be exploited," preservation of the earth's ecology would be valued for its intrinsic worth (Fisher 2003). In effect, environmental security would be treated as a desirable end in itself rather than just a means of obtaining a competitive edge.

THE SILVER LINING

The good news is that recent international environmental declarations, such as that put forward in 1992 in Rio, have denounced wartime environmental destruction (Environmental Law Institute 1998: 6). Principle 24 of the 1992 Rio Declaration states, "Warfare is inherently destructive of sustainable development. States shall therefore respect international law providing protection for the environment in times of armed conflict and cooperate in its further development, as necessary" (*Rio Declaration on Environment and Development*, 1992).

The growing realization that national security and ecological conservation are inextricably linked has made environmental security an issue worthy of consideration and protection. "The lesson of the Kosovo conflict and the

Gulf War before is that environmental consequences of war are now a legitimate topic," said senior attorney Jay Austin of the Environmental Law Institute. "It is one that is being criticized by journalists and NGOs as the consequences of those decisions unfold" (Environmental Law Institute 2003b).

Given the combination of international support and stringent mechanisms, international laws mitigating war's environmental destruction have the potential to change the face of combat and possibly discourage it from ever starting. The prospect of greater international environmental accountability when coupled with international enforcement of war crimes and human rights violations could make war less appetizing to those who would consider waging it. The times, let's hope, are a changing.

REFERENCES

Adler, Jonathan. 2003. "Saddam Hussein, Eco-Criminal." *National Review Online*, www.nationalreview.com/script/printpage.asp?ref = /adler/adler032103.asp.

Browne, Anthony. 2003. "'Iraqi Chernobyl' Uranium Fears." *The Times*, May 30, 2003, www.theaustralian.news.com.au/printpage/0,5942,6515830,00.html.

Chamorro, Susana Pimiento, and Edward Hammond. 2003. "Addressing Environmental Modification in Post-Cold War Conflict." *Sunshine Project*, www .edmonds-institute.org/pimiento.htm.

Council on Foreign Relations. 2003. "Making a Bomb," www.cfrterrorism.org/ weapons/making2.html.

Eisman, Beatrice, and Vivian Raineri. 2001. "Dioxin Damage Scientists Urge Study of the Effects of Agent Orange." US/Vietnam Friendship Association, October 4, www.mindfully.org/Pesticide/Agent-Orange-Dioxin-Damage.htm.

Environmental Law Institute. 1998. "Addressing Environmental Consequences of War," www.eli.org/pdf/background.pdf.

———. 2003a. "Addressing Environmental Consequences of War," May 29, www.eli.org/research/war.htm.

———. 2003b. "Environmental Consequences of War." ELI Associates Seminar, November 11, 1999, www.eli.org/seminars/99archive/11.11.99dc.htm.

Fisher, Richard W. 2003. "The Environment and Military Strategy." *Air & Space Chronicles*, www.airpower.maxwell.af.mil/airchronicles/ cc/fisher.html.

Gochfeld, Michael. 2001. "Recent Dioxin Contamination from Agent Orange in Residents of a Southern Vietnam City." *Journal of Occupational Medicine* 43, no. 5: 433–34.

Kirby, Alex. 2003. "UK to Aid Iraq DU Removal," news.bbc.co.uk/go/pr/fr/-/2/hi/ science/nature/2970503.stm.

Office of International Security Operations. 1993. *Hidden Killers, The Global Problem with Uncleared Landmines: a Report on International Demining*. Washington, D.C.: Department of State.

Pesticide Action Network North America. 1998. "Agent Orange and Dioxin in Viet-

nam: New Findings." *Global Pesticide Campaigner* 8, no. 4, www.panna.org/
resources/gpc/gpc_199812.08.4.10.dv.html.

Pesticide Action Network UK. 1996. "Forgotten Victims of Agent Orange." *Pesticides News* 32: 17, www.pan-uk.org/pestnews/Pn32/pn32p17d.htm.

Rice, Susan E. 2003. "Iraq's Nuclear Facilities Looted." *Globe and Mail*, May 21.

Rio Declaration on Environment and Development. 1992. www.igc.apc.org/habitat/
agenda21/rio-dec.html.

"Royal Society Calls On Coalition Forces to Reveal Where DU Has Been Used in
Iraq." 2003. *Royal Society*, www.royalsoc.ac.uk/news.

Rutagarama, Eugene. 2001. "A Conservation Triumph: The Mountain Gorillas of
Rwanda." *Science in Africa: Africa's First Online Science Magazine*, www.science
inafrica.co.za/2001/july/gorilla.htm.

Sheehan, Norman. 2003. "The Aftermath of an Invasion: A Field Report from
Nasiriyah," *Warchild*, www.envirosagainstwar.org/edit/index.php?op = view&
itemid = 80.

United Nations Environment Program. 2003a. *Afghanistan: Post-Conflict Environmental Assessment*, http://postconflict.unep.ch/afghanistan/report/afghanistan
pcajanuary2003.pdf.

———. 2003b. *A Strategy for Protecting the People and the Environment in Post-War
Iraq*, http://postconflict.unep.ch/publications/iraq_ds.pdf.

Wall, Roland. 2003. "War and the Environment: Some of the Ways That Military
Actions Can Affect the Ecosystem." *Know Your Environment*. Environmental
Associates of the Academy of Natural Sciences of Philadelphia, www.acnatsci.org/
research/kye/KYE22001.html#f3.

World Health Organization. 2003. "Depleted Uranium." Fact sheet no. 257, www
.who.int/mediacentre/factsheets/fs257/en/print.html.

13

Environmental Justice and Grassroots Globalization in the Nuclear Pacific

One of the central points made in this volume is that when globalizing forces adversely transform the environment, the marginalized, impoverished, and often-previously colonized peoples of the world suffer a disproportionate share of environmental pollution. From this perspective a change in the global environment often degrades the economic and bodily health of the people who can least afford to suffer the slings and arrows of economic "externalizations." But it would also be wrong to portray those people as passive victims. The last thirty-odd years, both at home and abroad, have witnessed the development of environmental justice movements. These are groups of people who have united to stand against the policies and companies that degrade local environments.

The Chipko movement in northern India and the U.S.-based First National People of Color Environmental Leadership Summit (1991) are two notable examples of environmental justice movements. Less known is the Nuclear Free and Independent Pacific (NFIP) movement discussed by Valerie Kuletz in this chapter. Kuletz makes crystal clear how the economics of globalization often dovetail seamlessly with a history of colonialism. More important, however, she shows how networks of colonized people are working together to improve the economic and environmental health of their homes and communities.

Valerie Kuletz, "The Movement for Environmental Justice in the Pacific" (2002)[1]

> There is no choice for us. We don't know what our future is going to be. Maybe there is only the choice to live in our contaminated land and die.

But we don't want our friends and neighbors around the world having the same problems that we are facing. . . . We have to look forward; we do not have to look back. Forward is already being damaged. I do not have to look back for the damage. I have to look forward, to reach out to my friends around the world.

—Lijon Eknilang, Rongelap, Marshall Islands

The Polynesian land, our fenua maohi, has been defiled by man's apocalyptic folly. . . . Our society has become tough, cruel, merciless and we are dominated by a new desire to make individual profits. To continue along this road is sheer nuclear prostitution.

—Jacqui Droltet, secretary-general of the Ia Mana party, speaking at a rally to commemorate Bikini Day, 1984

FUTURE SCENARIOS

Since the advent of nuclear testing after World War II, Pacific Islanders have endured the use of their oceans and islands as testing arenas for the global powers' nuclear weapons. This environmentally and socially destructive activity, which has far-reaching implications for the future of the region, was inextricably bound to colonialism. Today—in a period of so-called postcolonialism and globalization—the same regions that were used for nuclear testing have been targeted by some nuclear powers for the disposal of nuclear and toxic wastes (a trade represented by nuclear states and industry as a form of development). The current global trade in nuclear and toxic waste targeted at impoverished Pacific Island countries is held largely at bay by local, regional, and international resistance, but it remains an ongoing struggle.

This chapter explores the environmental justice movement, known as the Nuclear Free and Independent Pacific (NFIP) movement, that has emerged in response to nuclear colonialism. It seeks to identify a potential problem by interrogating the signs for future inequity and to develop insights into how environmentally destructive and socially unjust development may be alleviated. Of central concern is the targeting of Pacific Islands for socially and environmentally destructive practices (such as toxic waste burial). Identifying such activity shows the possibility of these practices being a clear and present danger. The task is to highlight these signs before they coalesce into irreversible reality. A focus on targeting, then, is a form of proactive scholarship as opposed to doing a postmortem of an already disastrous situation. Of equal importance is the identification of Pacific Islander resistance to this activity; thus, this chapter illuminates the strengths and weaknesses of the NFIP as a form of resistance to these developments.

OVERVIEW

The Pacific Island region is a geopolitical and multicultural area consisting of three major island areas: Micronesia in the northwest, Melanesia in the southwest, and Polynesia in the south. The Hawaiian islands, which are in the mid-Pacific, are included in this domain. This region consists of vast oceanic space punctuated by thousands of islands and atolls, which host many different cultures. Despite its centrality the region is not part of the celebrated Pacific rim economy. Due to its distance from most of the dominant global powers, it is an "edge" region in most senses of the word: politically, economically, and geographically. Indeed, its distance from the centers of power was one of the key reasons for its use as a nuclear testing site. When asked about the nuclear testing program in the Marshall Islands, former U.S. Secretary of State Henry Kissinger is reputed to have stated, "There's only 90,000 people out there. Who gives a damn?"

The history of nuclear colonialism (in the form of nuclear testing programs) has put in place social, political, economic, and environmental structures that make Pacific Islanders (newly independent and colonized) vulnerable to the recent pressure to accept nuclear and toxic waste. Political independence in the wake of nuclear testing comes with a legacy of dependence. As noted by many activists, the business of nuclear and toxic waste storage as a form of "development" makes independence a problematic term, since accepting such inherently destructive materials becomes an option only considered when there is a lack of economic independence. Environmentally sustainable economies, then, are among the most important forms of resistance, although, because nuclear and conventional testing regimes have disrupted traditional practices, sustainable economies (sustainable both environmentally and culturally) are not so easily revived.

The NFIP is a multidimensional social response to the use of the Pacific as a testing laboratory for nuclear weapons, the colonial and postcolonial militarization of the region, and globalization as manifested in the nuclear and toxic waste trade in particular and the acceleration of the Western neoclassical development agenda in general. In other words, it is a largely (although not exclusively) indigenous response to colonialism, neocolonialism, and certain aspects of the globalization project. As such, this movement includes within it strong place-based identity politics. Because it is also a broad network of activism it has, in some ways, redefined Pacific Island identity to move beyond its separate local arenas.

The NFIP is also a multitiered movement that functions on three distinct levels of resistance and practice: the local, the regional (composed of differently situated states), and the transregional (or global). These levels of activity are not evolutionary in the sense that one level inevitably evolves into another (such as the local into the global). Rather, movement between the levels is multidirectional. This spatial dimension of the movement makes it a promising model for other regions confronted with problems associated with the new reorganization of global power. More than simply a resistance movement, the NFIP is also a campaign that promotes "independence . . .

and true economic and social development, and environmental concerns."[2] In many ways, particularly because it has successfully mobilized intercommunity cooperation, the NFIP can be described as globalization from below.[3]

NUCLEAR AND MILITARY COLONIALISM

Within the post–World War II Pacific "theater" colonial regimes of power came hand in hand with the nuclear bomb. Under colonialism the Pacific Island region has been used as the First World's nuclear weapons laboratory and intercontinental ballistic missile testing range for over fifty years. Nuclear activity—consisting of hundreds of nuclear detonations—has occurred almost continuously from 1946 to 1996, and intercontinental missile testing continues today. In the 1940s and 1950s the United States and Great Britain tested nuclear weapons in Micronesia, Australia, and the Line Island Chain. As a result of the testing, six islands were vaporized and fourteen others were left uninhabitable. Hydrogen bombs, such as Bravo, were over a thousand times more powerful than those used on Hiroshima and Nagasaki. Needless to say, the impact of such testing has had profound consequences for Pacific Islanders and their descendants. As Darlene Keju-Johnson, a Marshall Islands woman, explains: "Since the testing . . . we have this problem of what we call 'jellyfish babies.' These babies are born like jellyfish. They have no eyes. They have no heads. They have no arms. They have no legs. They do not shape like human beings at all" (De Ishtar 1998: 24). Similarly, Marshall Islander Lijon Eknilang notes, "I know firsthand what the devastating effects of nuclear weapons are over time and over long distances, and what those effects mean to innocent human beings over several generations. I plead with you to do what you can, not to allow the suffering we Marshallese have experienced to be repeated in any other community in the world" (De Ishtar 1998: 26).

From the 1960s to the late 1990s France conducted nuclear tests in Polynesia at the atolls of Moruroa and Fangataufa in the Tuamoto Archipelago (the administrative center for nuclear operations being located in the city of Papeete on Tahiti) (Denoon and Firth 1997; Firth 1987). Throughout the last fifty years, as well as today, the region has been essentially deterritorialized and reterritorialized not only into a nuclear laboratory but also into a strategic militarized space, most recently for the U.S. star wars project (the center of which is located on Kwajalein Atoll in the Marshall Islands).

Such reterritorialization of Pacific space includes the reconstruction (at least in part) of traditional Islander identity through subjugation. For example, with the American nuclear weapons program, Marshall Islanders became American "subjects" in two ways: politically as colonial subjects, and experimentally in studies of nuclear science and the effects of radionuclides on both ecological communities and human communities. The post–World War II nuclear testing regimes in the Marshalls were in many ways typical of a colonial occupation. The difference was in the kind of raw material that was taken from the colonized site and brought back to the colonial mother country. Instead of gold, timber, or sugar, the Americans obtained scientific knowledge about radiation and nuclear weapons. Such knowledge was a valuable commodity in the cold war era. Radiation-contaminated Bikini and Enewetok atolls functioned as laboratories for an array of scientific studies. They were important sources of information in the development of ecosystems analysis, specifically the formulation of the energetic basis of ecosystems. Distinguished ecologist brothers Howard and Eugene Odum (1955) conducted ecosystems studies in these irradiated landscapes. Irradiated human subjects were studied to learn more about how the human body reacted to acute and prolonged radiation exposure. As noted by the Brookhaven National Laboratory in the U.S. Atomic Energy Commission's 1957 three-year report on the Marshall Islands of Rongalap and Utirik, "Even though . . . the radioactive contamination of Rongelap Island is considered perfectly safe for human habitation, the levels of activity are higher than those found in other inhabited locations in the world. The habitation of these people on the island will afford most valuable ecological radiation data on human beings" (Cohn 1987: 37).

Human contamination was described by the Atomic Energy Commission and the Department of Defense as a regretful but unavoidable consequence of the tests. However, according to the Greenpeace report *Pacific Paradise, Nuclear Nightmare,* 1994 releases of classified information about the test program in the Marshalls confirmed that not only has the United States been lying for forty years about the extent of contamination, but the United States deliberately exposed the Marshallese people to radiation as part of a medical experiment code-named Project 4.1. Islands have always been seen as good laboratory sites because of their isolation within vast oceanic regions. Here the "inputs" and "outputs" of the organic system are perceived as being more easily observed and controlled (Greenpeace 1994).

In Tahiti, the French nuclear testing program, called the CEP or the Pacific Experimentation Center (Centre d'Expérimentation du Pacifique), itself became the economic foundation of the Tahitian region—far surpassing tourism. The CEP's bureaucratic center in Tahiti stimulated migration of Islanders throughout Polynesia, drawing large numbers of workers into the city of Papeete. Islanders were also used extensively for low-level work at the nuclear testing sites (the atolls of Moruroa and Fangataufa) (De Vries and Seur 1997). Today, as the nuclear testing program pulls out, the Tahitian region (like the Marshalls) is left with significant environmental and social problems.

The environmental and social cost of this form of colonialism (known as nuclear colonialism) is severe and multiple: displacement of local tribes from home islands in order to conduct nuclear tests and to free up missile corridors; total destruction of tribal homelands; nuclear weapons–based economies replacing traditional self-sufficient, sustainable, and culturally appropriate economies; loss of indigenous languages, customs, and independence; disruption of community and family ties; loss of health and accompanying increases in radiation-caused child deformities, cancer, and miscarriages; increases in poverty-related illnesses such as alcoholism and suicide; severe pollution; serious overcrowding in urban centers due to mass migrations to testing centers and removals from homelands; the introduction of Western consumption desires and practices resulting in increased dependence on the colonial regime; and so forth. Most severely affected have been the Marshall Islands in Micronesia (Aelon In Majel) and the Tahitian region in French Polynesia (Te Ao Maohi). The effects are strikingly visible among the shack ghettos in the gullies of paradise in these postnuclear economies.[4]

SECOND-ORDER NUCLEARISM

It is against this background of nuclear colonialism and its aftermath that we need to understand recent efforts by representatives of the global nuclear powers and private commercial operatives contracting with nuclear states to use the Pacific as a dumping space for nuclear waste, the incineration of chemical weapons, and continued missile defense testing. It is against this background that we need to understand globalization in this region and resistance to it. Here globalization is about providing space—both isolated space and strategic space. If, as Gayatri Spivak suggests, globalization is the post-Soviet era transformation of colonialism, then the way nuclear testing under colonialism threatens to be transformed into nuclear and toxic waste disposal under the current period of globalization must be a prime example of this trend. Here, at different times, the previous colonizers and others in the nuclear arena (governments and commercial operatives) have proposed that nuclear and toxic waste be thought of by Pacific Islanders as a form of development—as a way to enter the global economy. It has been presented as their niche market, as they say in globalization discourse. Others, however, describe it as environmental apartheid (Shiva 1999: 47–69).

Examples of such targeting are numerous, although difficult to get a handle on because of their secrecy, mobility, and because those doing the targeting come from different places on the globe (many of which are not as monitored as, say, nuclear waste operatives in the United States). Private companies such as the New York investment firm KVR have attempted to obtain use of islands (Palmyra and Wake) for disposal of Russian and U.S.

plutonium wastes. The U.S.-based firm Babcock and Wilcox Environmental Service and Taipower (the state-run energy corporation of Taiwan) have attempted at different times to gain use of previously contaminated islands in the Marshalls for nuclear waste disposal (Greenpeace). France has already used the boreholes of nuclear detonations as nuclear waste dumps before sealing them over, and French parliamentarians have suggested using these same atolls for future wastes.[5] The U.S. Pangea Corporation and British Nuclear Fuels have initiated a joint feasibility study for an international nuclear waste repository in an area known as Billa Kalina in Aboriginal Australia (and aboriginal land—specifically the site of Jabaluka—is also now being used for uranium mining). In 1997 Tonga was targeted by Korean businessmen for a disposal operation reputedly named the Nuclear Waste Complete Burning Technology Research and Experimentation Center in the Kingdom of Tonga, and the list goes on, including the current problem of transboundary shipments of plutonium across Pacific waters. (France and Japan, which originate these shipments, do so in defiance of regional conventions against such activity.) What we see here are mostly private companies—transnational corporations—that are beginning to respond to an emerging global market in highly toxic materials. Most people in the United States aren't aware of these attempts to dispose of nuclear and toxic wastes—including many who consider themselves specialists in nuclear studies. This is because, first, scholars more often focus on nuclear weapons issues as opposed to waste; second, many people in the United States forget that countries such as Taiwan, Russia, and others have generated large amounts of nuclear waste; and finally, because the trade itself is fairly new (which makes a focus on targeting practices essential).[6] Indeed, because our nuclear culture now faces a nuclear waste crisis, the global trade and disposal of nuclear materials promises to be one of the most important "growth industries" in the coming decade and beyond. Thus studies on the targeting of different regions (not just the Pacific Islands) as sites for disposal are urgently needed.

THE SPACE OF ACTIVISM: THE NUCLEAR-FREE AND INDEPENDENT PACIFIC MOVEMENT (NFIP)

In the 1950s, 1960s, and 1970s it was nuclearism and its role in maintaining a communist-free Pacific that legitimated possession of Pacific Islands by the great colonial powers—particularly the United States and France. In the case of French Polynesia, nuclearism reinforced earlier forms of colonial rule.[7] However, beginning in 1975 and certainly by the 1980s, this same nuclearism (or nuclear colonialism) becomes the source of a countervailing movement. It becomes a locus for anticolonial consciousness and identity, and it becomes the source of a combined environmental and social justice movement that sweeps across the Pacific Island region in the form of the NFIP. Indeed, it is nuclearism itself that forges the links of resistance between Pacific Island nations—so much so that a pan-Islander identity politics emerged in the late 1970s, peaked during the French nuclear tests in 1996, and continues today as an active resistance to nuclear and toxic waste targeting.

My own introduction to the NFIP is a good example of the global dimension of this movement. I first became aware of the NFIP at the Nevada test site in the American West, during an annual protest (this one held in the mid-1990s) organized by the Western Shoshone Indians of the Great Basin and Mojave Deserts. As they had done with Kazakhs, who had been the victims of the Soviet Union's testing program, as well as other indigenous nuclear subjects, the Western Shoshone had invited a large contingent of Pacific Islanders (composed of people from different island nations) to join them in protest over nuclear colonialism, and to support indigenous sovereignty movements globally. (The Western Shoshone's traditional homelands have been used for over nine hundred nuclear detonations.) What I witnessed at the protest was essentially the workings of a Fourth World indigenous network, something I was to see on numerous occasions in my work with the Western Shoshone in the American Southwest—the American nuclear landscape (Kuletz 1998). Thus from the beginning I was aware of a larger field of inquiry and indeed a larger field of transregional identity linked to the international network of indigenous rights and sovereignty. This global alliance serves as a foundation or a support network for local resistance practices in the Pacific. This larger field is in some ways reminiscent of Akhil Gupta's "nonaligned movement," or imagined community, described in *The Song of the Non-Aligned World* (Gupta and Ferguson 1997). Indigeneity in this transregional, global sphere is constructed as an alternative to American and European colonialism. It is, in Derridean discourse, the maligned second term to the European/American first term within colonialist hierarchical dualism.

The NFIP also functions to inform formal governance at the regional level. Both Tahiti and the Marshall Islands (the two most prominent postnuclear cultures and economies in the Pacific), along with many other island nations, are part of a transnational Pacific Island regional network called the South Pacific Forum, which is a body of representatives from different island states that meet periodically to contend with interisland issues (in Melanesia, Micronesia, and Polynesia) relating to trade, environment, and other trans-island concerns. Prompted by the growing power of the NFIP, the 1997 South Pacific Forum meeting in Rarotonga directly stated that its members opposed the "use of the Pacific as a dumping ground for others' wastes." To ward off such activities the forum also adopted what they call the Waigani Convention, which is essentially a comprehensive ban on the importation of nuclear wastes to the region. As early as 1985, forum members had adopted the South Pacific Nuclear Free Zone Treaty, and subsequently a separate regional organization negotiated the South Pacific Regional Environment Program, a comprehensive program meant to prevent nuclear dumping in the South Pacific. So what we see here is regional action. Rather than waiting for global multilateral agreements and conventions for the regulation of toxic wastes (such as the Basel Convention, which has not been ratified by some of the most polluting states, such as the United States). Island states are attempting to address the issue of toxic dumping as a regional bloc. This constitutes a deliberate reconstruction of Pacific space—a weaving together of separate Island nations and cultures into a postcolonial regional community.

The state, of course, is the primary actor at this level of governance, and the state is not without complications. Constituting the regional body are independent, semi-independent (the Marshalls), colonized (French Polynesia), and colonial settler states (New Zealand and Australia). Differences between these differently situated governments and peoples create what could be described as stress fractures within the regional body. It is here, within the heterogeneous regional body, that differences threaten to dissolve alliances for environmental justice. It is therefore a site that requires particularly strong focus for the NFIP. For instance, indigenous independence is fundamentally threatening to white settler colonial countries like New Zealand and Australia, which constitute the most powerful members in the South Pacific Forum, as well as other regional assemblies and the Pacific Island arena in general. Because of these differences, the NFIP, which strongly supports indigenous rights and sovereignty, is perceived by some as a positive force but also a negative force. Colonial states (such as New Zealand) take great pride in the antinuclear stance of the movement and actively align themselves with it, but they do not accept the issue of independence when it is related to indigenous peoples. This part-acceptance/part-resistance to the NFIP by colonial states is consonant with the divisions between indigenous and nonindigenous environmentalism in other parts of the world where the issue of indigenous sovereignty, which is inextricably tied to indigenous environmentalism, is not always embraced by nonindigenous environmentalists. The result of this tension among Pacific Island states is a weakening of the NFIP. Even so, and in spite of these tensions, the power here of indigenous communities (through the NFIP) to influence regional interstate policy is exceptional and therefore a noteworthy model for other indigenous groups struggling with nation-states in different parts of the world.

LOCAL ACTIVISM: TAHITI
AND THE MARSHALLS

However important the global and regional levels of activism are, the real foundation of the NFIP exists at its local sites where it is grounded in the practice of survival. The following two examples show the power of the local level in this movement, one positive and one problematic.

Tahiti

The Tahitian NGO Hiti Tau (Dawn of the Bird of Peace) exemplifies the dynamic way the Pacific movement functions at the community level. I recently spent time in the town of Taravo on the island of Tahiti, at the Hiti Tau Secretariate, to observe alternative development projects in which the Maohi (Polynesians) were engaged. Here alternative development is a self-conscious form of resistance to colonialism and globalization in the form of the nuclear and toxic waste trade, as well as in the form of mass tourism controlled by transnational corporations. For without sustainable economic alternatives, the people of Tahiti are left with few options for a secure economic future. (Mass tourism and toxic waste are not considered by most Tahitians as sustainable, neither environmentally nor culturally.) This is why one Tahitian woman, Mareva Neti de Montlue, describes Hiti Tau as a source of hope: "Hiti Tau . . . for us it truly represents hope. This organization is giving people the opportunity to get themselves in hand to no longer be beneficiaries" (Hiti Tau 1998).

Hiti Tau's development projects are community identified and organized. Their goal is to create a flexible self-sufficiency that is culturally and environmentally sustainable at the local level, as well as to engage in various projects that might be successful at the regional and sometimes transregional levels. They are engaged in a variety of land/ocean-based sustainable economic ventures: growing vanilla beans using traditional rain forest planting techniques, small-scale environmentally sustainable tourism, black pearl cultivation, and the production of scented flower oils, which is controlled exclusively by women who are thus provided an avenue to reenter the production sphere, which was lost to them under colonialism. Hiti Tau exists on the island of Tahiti as well as in outlying island communities, knitting the islands of Polynesia (Te Ao Maohi) together through sustainable environmental practices. Hiti Tau is thriving, although, according to leaders I spoke with, it is no easy task to stimulate or reactivate semitraditional practices, even when they are clearly more sustainable than colonial practices. Tahitians have altered their lifestyles under the French primarily because of the cash economy that reorganized subsistence in the region toward French imports and that restructured desire and consumption practices during the French nuclear testing program. For Gabriel Tetiarahi, one of Hiti Tau's leaders and a leader in the broader NFIP movement, it is the minds of the Maohi people that have become imprisoned by colonialism, particularly in the creation of new desires and the loss of traditional practices (Tetiarahi, interview by author, 1999). Thus "independence" for him is self-sufficiency, economically as well as in terms of Tahitian identity. In the case of Hiti Tau, self-sufficiency and true independence are linked to environmental sustainability, which is inseparable from cultural sustainability. Part of this cultural independence is also expressed in a recognition of intersubjective relations between humans and nonhuman nature—a very different construction of the subject than is found in Western liberal discourse, and a fundamental aspect of their conceptions of environmental and social activism. None of this can be called strictly essentialist indigenous identity politics, including strategic essentialism. Rather, we need to see it as the local space and practice of autonomy, which calls on traditional knowledge—practical knowledge—but not to the exclusion of contemporary knowledge when it is of use to them. I would describe this as an attempt to develop flexible traditional knowledge, which is capable of expanding to include new practices and ways of knowing, or, conversely, of contracting to exclude Western influence on a case-by-case basis. As noted in item four of the Preamble to the NFIP People's Charter: "We, the peoples of the Pacific, reaffirm our intention to extract only those elements of Western civilization that will be of permanent benefit to us. We wish to control our destinies and protect our environment in our own ways."[8] Such goals have not always been realized but they nonetheless continue to instill vitality into activism at the local level.

This focus on alternative sustainable and appropriate development exists in Hiti Tau in conjunction with active antinuclear sentiments. For these Islanders, the two cannot be separated. For example, along with local development Hiti Tau also supports a relief program for the victims of the French nuclear tests. As Tetiarahi notes, "We were very active against nuclear testing because we considered nuclear testing to be a violation of human rights. . . . If nuclear testing has gone from the region its effects remain and will cause uncertainty for thousands and thousands of years. Hiti Tau has thus created Foundation 2001 for the Polynesian victims of French nuclear testing" (Hiti Tau 1998).

The Republic of the Marshall Islands (RMI)

One of the weak links on the regional level in this largely successful multidimensional environmental and social movement is found in Micronesia at the local and state levels in the Marshall Islands. One of the more serious pressure points in the movement comes in the formal relationship that Marshall Islanders have accepted with the United States, a Compact of Free Association. As both discourse and practice, the Compact of Free Association effectively disrupts the unity of the Pacific Islands regional mosaic of resistance and self-sufficiency by inserting into that region the powerful and overbearing presence of the American military. Further, the compact maintains a dependency relationship with the Marshall Islands, which inhibits local economic alternatives. For a price, under the Compact of Free Association, the Marshallese give up the right to determine military access of non-Marshallese to their oceans and atolls. The United States exercises complete control over who is allowed access to the region militarily and who is not. The Marshallese have also given up (for a price) the right to sue for future health injuries—miscarriages, deformities, cancer—resulting from the U.S. nuclear testing regime. (This is problematic since contamination by radionuclides, which alter human genetic structure, creates intergenerational illness.) Under the Compact of Free Association, the Marshallese are pushed to rent the Kwajalein atoll to the United States and only the United States, allowing the United States to reconstruct the region into the world's premier theater defense missile center. (Indeed, some have suggested that if Kwajalein military base were to close down, half the momentum for the global arms race would be lost.) And the Marshallese give up the right to stop the United States from any activity it deems necessary for its national security, which could conceivably include the stockpiling and even the testing of nuclear weapons on their atolls at some future time (Hanlon 1998). For this relinquishment of true sovereignty the Marshallese are given money, Western goods, access to the United States, and the discursively problematic claim to "independence." And the money is not substantial. The Marshallese remain among the poorest of the Micronesian peoples. As the late Amata Kabua, president of the RMI, said after signing the compact: "We lost many things in that Compact, we regret many things, but what can you do? I mean when you grow up with your brother and he's a lot bigger than you and he slaps you . . . what can you do?"[9]

We need to see this situation spatially because it is quite literally a reorganization of space (not to mention identity) linking the Marshalls to the United States and thereby breaking the unity of Pacific Island resistance to Western neocolonial power. Space here is organized along missile corridors, training theaters, and restricted zones, as well as the construction of radioactive contamination zones, such as the Bikini atoll or the Kwajalein lagoon, which has been polluted by depleted uranium as a result of the missile tests.

In the period of formal post–U.S. colonization, the Marshallese have little to sustain them, which is why they have actively entertained proposals to use their islands for nuclear waste disposal (eliciting strong criticism from other Pacific Island states). The late president Kabua has said, "It's better to earn some money out of the situation [islands left uninhabitable due to radiation contamination from nuclear testing] than having nothing." The logic of accepting nuclear waste because one's islands have been used for nuclear testing is precisely the logic of second-order nuclearism.

The postcolonial Marshallese have newly created Western desires and consumption practices, as well as an economic and psychological dependence on the United States. A walk down the trash-filled roads of Majuro atoll confirms the ubiquity of Western consumer products—disposable diapers, soda cans, and Styrofoam containers, among other things, are everywhere. Arguably it is "independence" (or the discursive doublespeak of independence deployed by the United States) that allows the United States to now justify its continued militarization of the region, and to maintain a relationship of dependency. One compares the two postnuclear local situations (Tahiti and the Marshalls) with a good deal of irony. The Tahitians are formally colonized, but in some ways are more truly independent than the "independent" Marshallese, who in some respects are more vulnerable to continued colonial exploitation. This is clearly a problem concerning nuclear and toxic waste, since dependence on the United States keeps the Marshallese from developing true sustainable economic alternatives and makes them vulnerable to targeting by a variety of nuclear states and operatives.

While this may sound like a hopeless situation, the Marshallese are not only defeated victims, first of nuclear colonialism and then of neocolonialism. There are RMI groups and individuals, such as those quoted in this chapter, who actively align themselves with the NFIP and engage in other forms of resistance. For instance, in the 1980s the Marshallese conducted sail-ins to reoccupy their land and protest forced relocation from their islands by the U.S. military. In dark humor they called the sail-ins Operation Homecoming, a play on Operation Crossroads, an earlier U.S. nuclear testing series in the Marshalls. But as with postcolonial environments in other parts of the world, colonialism has not simply disappeared with the creation of an indigenous independent government. The Marshallese have been the subjects of severe and life-threatening colonization. Neither do they have an abundance of options (environmentally) for sustainable development. Their atolls are small with limited space and vegetation—a situation quite different from French Polynesia, which has larger islands for cultivation. Aside from the possibility of a sustainable fishing industry (which has not been developed adequately, although there is some movement in that direction), the RMI situation is a decidedly difficult one. While they have decided against taking in nuclear waste for now, according to my informants in the Marshalls, they also have not completely rejected that option as a possible future development scheme.

CONCLUSION

In this brief introduction to environmental justice in the Pacific Islands there are three main issues that emerge as central to postcolonial, postnuclear Pacific resistance and the advancement of justice in this region:

- First, we recognize the continuation of colonialism within the so-called postcolonial era and its link to the discourses and practices of globalization. Nuclear and toxic waste is represented as a form of development by nuclear states and private transnational corporations as they target islands for their enterprises.
- Second, we can understand the environmental and social justice movement—the Nuclear Free and Independent Pacific movement (NFIP)—as one that addresses injustice at multiple levels of practice and governance. This model is an encouraging one as we search for new ways to contend with the negative aspects of the new free-trade market economy. The NFIP gets its strength from the grassroots. This is where resistance in the form of alternative practice is most realized, such as in the Hiti Tau example. The NFIP also functions on the regional and transregional levels, forming new blocks of resistance and strengthening when confronting the new alliances of the globalizing market, as well as strengthening global indigenous alliances and networks.
- Third, we need to be aware of the power and the problematic nature of the discourse of independence and how it can compromise regional Islander resistance to second-order nuclear colonialism. In the case of the RMI, the problematic nature of independence is represented by the Compact of Free Association, which is deployed both discursively and with active reterritorialization practices in the Marshalls domain. As a discursive and legal form of legitimization the Compact of Free Association allows the United States to enter the Pacific region to disrupt the formation of pan-Islander resistance, to disrupt the Pacific mosaic of alliance. The compact is problematic for these reasons and because Marshallese are divided on its usefulness to their country. While it does allow the Marshallese a form of political independence and does provide more autonomy than they had under colonialism, it is also controversial and contested from within the RMI.

For many Pacific Islanders their status is peripheral economically. They feel the constant pressure of the nuclear powers, they have a history of nuclear sacrifice, and—for complex cultural reasons—Western development strategies have not always provided them with sustainable economic alternatives. This is why the example of Hiti Tau is so important, since it provides a model for appropriate sustainable and socially just development. And, while not as apparent as in Tahiti, there are Marshallese who are working to move in this direction.

The question for these countries concerns whether or not there are viable alternatives to accepting nuclear and toxic wastes or entering Compacts of Free Association that continue militarization in their homelands. Supporters of the NFIP are aware of this and ask, How can the people of the Pacific be truly independent in the shadow of nuclear contamination and outside militarization? The NFIP has done an impressive job of keeping nuclear and toxic wastes out of their region. But as the demand for new disposal sites increases, they will have to continue to be vigilant, and continue to press for independence without nuclearism. In this way we may better understand why the environmental justice and independence movement in the Pacific is called the Nuclear-Free and Independent Pacific movement. For supporters of the NFIP, there can only be independence in a nuclear-free environment.

REFERENCES

Cohn, Susie, et al. 1987. *Pacific Paradise/Nuclear Nightmare: Women Working for a Nuclear Free and Independent Pacific.* London: CND Publications.

Denoon, Donald, and Stewart Firth, eds. 1997. *The Cambridge History of the Pacific Islanders.* Cambridge: Cambridge University Press.

De Vries, Peiter, and Han Seur. 1997. *Moruroa and Us: Polynesians' Experiences during Thirty Years of Nuclear Testing in the French Pacific.* Lyon, France: Centre de Documentation et de Recherche sur la Paix et les Conflicts.

Firth, Stewart. 1987. *Nuclear Playground: Fight for an Independent and Nuclear Free Pacific.* Honolulu: University of Hawaii Press.

Greenpeace. 1994. *Pacific Paradise, Nuclear Nightmare: A Critique of the Proposal to Use the Marshall Islands as a Nuclear Waste Dump.* Auckland, N.Z.: Greenpeace.

Gupta, Akhil, and James Ferguson. 1997. *Culture, Power, Place: Explorations in Critical Anthropology.* Durham, N.C.: Duke University Press.

Hanlon, David. 1998. *Remaking Micronesia: Discourses over Development in a Pacific Territory, 1944–1982.* Honolulu: University of Hawaii Press.

Hiti Tau. 1998. *Hiti Yau.* World Council of Churches Pacific Desk. Video.

Ishtar, Zohl de, ed. 1998. *Pacific Women Speak Out for Independence and Denuclearisation.* Christchurch, Aotearoa/N.Z.: Women's International League for Peace and Freedom; Christchurch: Disarmament and Security Centre.

Kuletz, Valerie. 1998. *The Tainted Desert: Environmental and Social Ruin in the American West.* New York: Routledge.

Odum, Howard, and Eugene P. Odum. 1955. "Trophic Structure and Productivity of a Windward Coral Reef Community on Eniwetok Atoll," *Ecological Monographs* 25: 291–320.

Shiva, Vandana. 1999. "Ecological Balance in an Era of Globalization." In Nicholas Low, ed., *Global Ethics and Environment.* London: Routledge.

14

Multinationals, China, and the Environment

Three institutions—the World Bank, the International Monetary Fund, and the World Trade Organization—represent in myth and reality the economic processes of globalization. The first two were developed in the 1944 Bretton Woods Agreement to plan for the economic role of Western capitalism in the postwar world; the WTO was created in 1995 to help flatten the earth by removing barriers to free trade. These institutions claim that their work helps to raise the economic security of the world, and this may be true when viewed from a specific perspective. But these are also controversial institutions that raise the ire of people who see the costly side of globalization.

Nowhere is this more evident than in China's burgeoning economy. China's recent inclusion in the WTO has signaled the country's growing involvement in manufacturing and global trade. But this growth comes at a cost in terms of social and environmental instability. In this chapter Abigail Jahiel provides one of the first analyses of the impact of WTO policies on China's environment and people. As has been the case with the World Bank and the International Monetary Fund, there is a large gap between the promises and the realities of unfettered global trade.

Abigail Jahiel, "China, the WTO, and Implications for the Environment" (2006)[1]

On December 11, 2001, China formally entered the World Trade Organization (WTO). This movement promised among other things to further liberalize the Chinese economy, accelerate economic growth, increase the country's international prestige, and enhance the flagging legitimacy of the

Chinese Communist Party. While the implications of WTO membership for the economy, society, and politics have been heatedly debated in the period surrounding China's accession (Wang 2000; Fewsmith 2001; Harwit 2001; Langlois 2001; Lee 2001; Hsiung 2003; Bhalla and Qiu 2004), far less attention has been paid to the environmental implications of membership.[2] Yet two decades of rapid economic development under China's "open door" policy prior to WTO entry intensified the country's earlier environmental degradation and resulted in serious strains on the country's resources and ecosystems. Today China faces a host of domestic environmental problems and contributes mightily to global ones, posing potentially significant political challenges. The environmental implications of its entry into the WTO thus merit close study.

Prior to WTO membership, officials in the Chinese State Environmental Protection Administration (SEPA) discussed the challenges WTO entry might pose for environmental protection. On balance their conclusions were optimistic (interview by author, May 13, 2002; Ye 2002). Along with researchers at SEPA's Policy Research Center for Environment and Economy (PRCEE), they projected that industrial pollution would decrease and that the rural environment would benefit (*Guojia* 2002; Hu and Meng 2002). Though potential problems were noted, the consensus was that proactive steps could be taken to avoid negative outcomes.[3] These optimistic conclusions were not surprising given the pressures imposed by a Communist Party that repressed dissent, embraced neoclassical economics, and staked its future on the promised benefits of WTO membership. Today, however, it is clear that even as entry into the WTO has spurred economic growth, the ecological implications have been more harmful than most observers anticipated. These conditions have exacerbated not only China's profound environmental challenges but its political ones as well.

This chapter explores the arguments on both sides of the trade and environment debate. It looks first at the theoretical literature on the subject and then at China's history with trade liberalization prior to WTO entry, and finally at the environmental effects and related social and political repercussions of WTO membership. The distinct impacts of economic growth, trade liberalization, and other results of WTO membership are noted, but emphasis is placed on the composite effect of these factors as most important for the environment. The chapter concludes with an assessment of the political dilemma faced by the Chinese state in responding to these deepening environmental harms.

TRADE AND ENVIRONMENT: THE LOGIC OF LIBERALIZATION

A sharp debate exists over the implications of trade liberalization for the environment (Weber 2001; Williams 2001). On one side are those who, like the Chinese state, view free trade primarily as a catalyst for environmental improvement. These individuals argue that trade liberalization:

1. leads to economic growth, which is a precondition for acquiring the technical and institutional capability to address pollution (the wealth argument);
2. reduces costs of imports and thus provides greater access to cleaner production techniques (the technology argument);
3. removes subsidies and trade barriers, encouraging structural changes to the economy and exchange on the basis of comparative advantage and efficient use of resources (the structural change/efficiency argument) and;
4. promotes environmental legal reform to prevent rejection of products for sale overseas (the regulatory race to the top argument).

On the other side are those who view trade liberalization as antithetical to environmental protection. They argue that:

1. the expansion in output comes at a cost to the environment (the scale argument);
2. comparative advantage can negatively affect the environment if a country's industrial structure and natural endowments favor specialization in pollution-intensive industries (the pollution haven argument); and
3. trade liberalization encourages the reduction of environmental standards as countries compete for foreign investment (the regulatory race to the bottom argument).

While this chapter will not primarily address this debate empirically (Desombre and Barkin 2002; Neumayer 2004), these arguments provide a framework for understanding and assessing the environmental effects China has experienced as a result of increasing trade liberalization, first under the "open door" policy and then following WTO membership.

TRADE LIBERALIZATION AND THE ENVIRONMENT PRIOR TO WTO ACCESSION, 1978–2001

Central to China's vast economic expansion prior to WTO accession was the gradual liberalization of trade and investment policies. Between 1978 and 2000, China's foreign trade grew twenty-four fold from US$20 billion to US$474 billion; annual average foreign direct investment (FDI) reached

US$42.7 billion; and by the beginning of the twenty-first century, exports and foreign investment generated 40 percent of China's GDP.

These changes in China's political economy had a broad impact on the environment. China's "open door" policy allowed for greater access to less-polluting technologies, pollution abatement equipment, and advanced environmental management practices (Hu and Yang 2000; CCICED 2001). Pursuit of comparative advantage encouraged China to "reallocate its resources away from capital, land, and energy-intensive dirty industries to labor-intensive cleaner industries" (Chai 2002: 30). This reallocation, in turn, led to a notable decrease in the pollution intensity of manufacturing industries between the early 1980s and the late 1990s—at least among state-owned firms and larger companies.[4] In addition, the open door policy attracted foreign funds to address specific problems.[5] Increased contact in the international arena also heightened awareness of and commitment to addressing environmental problems. This contributed to China's efforts to strengthen its regulatory environmental regime by developing an extensive environmental protection apparatus and a host of environmental laws, regulations, and policies (Jahiel 2000). In addition, by the 1990s China was urging firms to adopt international ISO 14000 standards to compete better internationally and was developing an organic foods industry and a green labeling process (Ross 2000; Theirs 2000).

In spite of these positive developments, the first two decades of rapid economic growth and trade liberalization significantly expanded China's already notable ecological problems (Smil 1993; Sanders 1999; Edmonds 2000; Muldavin 2000). In a comprehensive study of the Chinese manufacturing sector from 1978 to 1999, Chai found that even as China shifted its export portfolio toward cleaner production industries and adopted cleaner technologies, the negative environmental effects of the vastly increased scale of trade far exceeded the positive. In fact, "the rate of increase of water, air and soil pollution went almost hand-in-hand with that of Chinese manufactured export expansion" (Chai 2002: 32).

Pursuit of the export market also led to vast exploitation of the country's natural resources. In order to feed and clothe overseas epicurean tastes for exotic herbs and cashmere sweaters, fragile grasslands in Inner Mongolia were overcultivated and overgrazed. To increase cash crop yields, fertile lands in coastal areas fell subject to heavy applications of chemical pesticides and fertilizers. Delicate inland landscapes and hillsides were mined for nonferrous metals and rare minerals, exposing populations to dangerous and even radioactive materials (Wang 2001). And coastal zones were overharvested to feed the world's rapidly growing seafood industry (Feigon 2000; CCICED 2001).

China also found comparative advantage in the transfer of pollution, both from dirty industries and the waste trade (Wang 2001). According to a 1995

SEPA study, 30 percent of all foreign-invested ventures in China were engaged in heavily polluting industries (*Guojia* 2002)—including ones involved in the production and consumption of ozone-depleting substances (ODSs), whose manufacture and use were banned in the industrialized world under the Montreal Protocol (CCICED 1997).[6] With regard to the waste trade, wastes (including plastic bags, bottles and agricultural sheets, dirty diapers, sanitary napkins, food, paper, hospital wastes, radioactive scrap metals, electronic wastes, and unidentified chemicals) imported chiefly from industrialized countries, were accepted by Chinese entrepreneurs as lucrative business ventures; in others, wastes entered under the exporter's pretext that they were recyclable materials or resources (Greenpeace 1997; interview by author, July 7, 1997). Between 1990 and 1997 the value of imported hazardous wastes alone grew almost 140 fold from just under US$14 million to US$19 billion (Ren 2001). Tough new laws implemented in 1997 made trade in certain wastes punishable by up to ten years in prison or a fine of RMB 500,000, yet the waste trade persisted. In several coastal villages, China's poor continued to make their living scavenging through highly toxic electronic wastes to retrieve precious metals and other materials, at great cost to their personal health and to the health of local ecosystems (BAN 2002).

The situation between 1978 and 2001, *prior to* entry into the WTO, suggests, then, that early efforts at trade liberalization and engagement in the global economy shifted the distribution of China's manufacturing industries somewhat away from the most heavily polluting industries and technologies, increasing the economy's efficiency. Greater global engagement drew increased regulatory attention to the environment. However, these benefits to the environment were more than offset by the scale of growth and the international incentives to pursue China's comparative advantage in ecologically destructive ventures and dirty industries and trades. Moreover, even though trade liberalization did not lead to a regulatory race to the bottom— the body of environmental law grew—an environmental race to the bottom took place as a result of failure to implement new laws and policies. In seeking comparative advantage, Chinese entrepreneurs—and complicit local government officials—were willing to let China effectively become a waste haven, reducing environmental quality and ecosystem health for financially prosperous ventures, even as central government officials were working to climb the environmental regulatory ladder. How has this situation changed under WTO membership?

ACCESSION TO THE WTO AND ITS ENVIRONMENTAL IMPACT: 2002 AND BEYOND: INITIAL PROJECTIONS

Under its accession agreements, China was required to reduce its import tariffs, end all export subsidies, lower or eliminate import quotas, and open certain sectors of the economy to foreign trade. Structural changes to the economy were expected to follow, with short-term economic dislocations resulting from the failure of uncompetitive sectors and the development of other sectors with global comparative advantage. Expected to feel the hardship most were the capital-intensive heavy industries (e.g., automobile, shipbuilding, machine, steel, chemical, pharmaceutical, and petrochemical), the paper industry, township and village enterprises (TVEs), and the grain and cotton sectors of the agricultural economy (Sun 2000; Lee 2001; Harwit 2001; Mai 2002; Yeung 2002). Projected to prosper were the labor-intensive industries and agricultural sectors (e.g., textile and garment, shoe, household electronics, bicycle, fruit, vegetable, horticulture, meat and fish) and the service and financial sectors (Wang 2000; Fewsmith 2001; Ren 2001).

Environmental officials and policy analysts from China and abroad anticipated notable ecological benefits. In keeping with the logic of trade liberalization, they suggested that (1) the elimination and reduction of subsidies, tariffs, and the like would lead to the import of superior environmental protection equipment and less polluting industrial and agricultural technologies (CCICED 2001; Guojia 2002; interview by author, May 13, 2002); (2) heightened international competition would bring environmentally beneficial structural adjustments to the Chinese industrial and agricultural economies (Guojia 2002; Hu and Meng 2002); (3) greater access to low-priced foreign goods would increase imports of consumer products and raw materials, reducing domestic energy consumption, pollution emissions, and impacts on natural resources through avoided production costs (Oberheitmann 2002); and (4) increased imports would force China to strengthen its legal code to avoid an influx of pollution-intensive or environmentally harmful products (interview by author, May 28, 2002; Ye 2002), while green trade barriers and the threat they posed to exports would convince industry managers to consider environmental issues as life-and-death issues for their firms (Guojia 2002),[7] and demand the adoption of stricter domestic environmental, health, and safety codes based on international standards (Ferris and Zhang 2002; interview by author, May 13, 2002). As one report summarizes the impact, echoing these optimistic projections, "When trade and environmental policies are well coordinated, trade and investment liberalization can be conducive to saving resources, improving efficiency, restructuring industry, improving the environment and sustaining the growth of China's economy" (CCICED 2001: 7).

THE REALITIES

For the most part, however, the overall environmental benefits projected have not materialized. Economic growth has indeed outstripped earlier projections, and certain structural adjustments, technological changes, and legal and cultural developments have been beneficial for the environment. Nevertheless, some of the greatest economic advances in both the industrial and agricultural sectors are seriously exacerbating China's most severe environmental problems—and some of the world's greatest ecological crises as well. Moreover, they are creating serious political challenges.

Within the first three years of WTO entry, FDI in China grew almost 30 percent, foreign trade doubled, exceeding US$1 trillion, and China surpassed Japan to become the world's third largest importer. As a result, the economy has continued to expand rapidly, growing at an annual rate of 9.5 percent. These macro-economic trends have propelled further restructuring of the economy. Low labor and material costs have provided the comparative advantage anticipated in a number of industrial and agricultural sectors. Growth has been particularly electrifying in the export-oriented, labor-intensive textile industry, where wages are 20–40 times lower than in developed countries and two to four times lower than in many developing ones, and where WTO-related protocols have brought an end to the three-decade-old quota system (Cheng and Shen 2004).

Counter to predictions, China's automobile industry has also experienced rapid growth (Pan et al. 2004). Competition associated with the sharp drop in automobile tariffs and increase in import quotas under the WTO,[8] as well as the influx of FDI in this previously inefficient sector and continued government support for this key industry, have reduced prices for motor vehicles, increased consumer demand, and contributed to this industry's massive growth.

In agriculture, labor-intensive industries like fruit and vegetable production, horticulture, animal husbandry, and aquaculture have thrived, spurred on by favorable global economic incentives, preferential government policies, and increased foreign investment. Not only are farmgate costs for certain crops a fraction of costs in California (Rosen et al. 2004), but the Chinese government has worked to accelerate the modernization of agriculture by (1) promoting improved crop strains (including biogenetically engineered crops; see Keeley), high-value products, and advanced technology; (2) encouraging the development of large-scale agricultural corporations; and (3) courting foreign investment in these efforts. The growth of the aquaculture industry, aided by a pronounced inflow of FDI, has been particularly striking: China is presently the largest producer and exporter of marine products in the world (Zhao et al. 2004).

As for the environment, no comprehensive studies are yet available on the number of heavily polluting firms that have closed as a result of increased international competition. However, the government continues to encourage phase-outs and updates of outdated technology as well as plant closures in the metallurgy, construction, chemical industry and energy sectors. To stay competitive, the steel and automobile industries have also had to adopt newer technologies. In addition, economic expansion has been particularly robust in the less energy-intensive light industry sector, and China's environmental protection and cleaner production industries have continued to grow and attract foreign investment, as has the green food sector.

Legal and cultural changes that favor the environment are evident too. Many new environmentally beneficial laws and standards are being promulgated in response to pressures created by WTO trade liberalization (discussed below). International environmental organizations are becoming more involved in China's ecological preservation efforts, and public involvement in environmental NGOs, although still limited, is growing. The central government has indicated greater recognition of the severity of China's environmental situation in its trial adoption of a "green GDP." Finally, SEPA appears to be assuming a much more aggressive stance toward polluters, announcing in January 2005 a halt on thirty key projects (26 in the power sector) for failure to comply with environmental impact assessment laws.

Nevertheless, the actual environmental impact of those sectors that have prospered most under the WTO demonstrates the significant harm engagement in this trade regime has brought. I will explore the industrial and the agricultural sectors below.

THE INDUSTRIAL SECTOR

Unit for unit one would expect that as the economy has continued to move away from capital-intensive heavy industries to labor-intensive light industries and the service sector, pollution emissions would fall. But as Chai's study of the manufacturing sector during the 1980s and 1990s demonstrates, what is critical for the environment is the scale or extent of overall economic growth, not solely the shift in balance between various sectors. If the heavily polluting capital-intensive sector shrinks proportionately to the economy as a whole, but the less polluting labor-intensive sector grows substantially, the total amount of emissions may nevertheless rise—even as the pollution intensity of individual firms decreases.

This phenomenon is, in fact, what we are witnessing. The scale of light industry growth is so large that it is having an overall negative impact on the environment. The sheer increase in output of this sector has caused a rapid increase in energy demand throughout the economy (Jiang et al. 2004). Moreover, to meet this increased demand, economic pressures have encouraged the growth of the part of the energy sector that is most environmentally destructive: the small coal mining ventures or TVEs originally predicted to falter from increased competition following WTO entry (Jiang et al. 2004).[9] The boom in the manufacturing sector is thus responsible for air pollution increases on some indicators (both regional and global), water pollution increases (with the exception of BOD) and further soil degradation due to its greater reliance on "dirty" coal. But the growth of the manufacturing sector negatively affects the environment in many other ways as well, as is demonstrated by the textile and automobile industries.

Textiles

The ecological footprint of textile production is large. From chemicals used in the printing and dyeing processes to heavy consumption of water in the manufacturing process and the generation of large volumes of difficult-to-treat wastewater, the production of textiles creates many environmental problems. Even before it becomes fabric, cotton and synthetic fiber production takes its toll on the environment. Conventional cotton production requires high inputs of water and more pesticide use per unit of production than any other crop; a shift to genetically modified cotton, while potentially reducing pesticide use, holds unknown environmental impacts that have sparked huge debates about biosafety; the manufacture of synthetic fibers draws on limited petroleum reserves and produces toxic by-products.

In China, the environmental impact of textile production is especially great. Due to inferior technology, "water consumption per unit of production is about 50 percent higher than in developed countries." In addition, "dyes made in China usually have lower dye uptake and dye residual in wastewater is higher." Thus "the sewer discharge per product is nearly double the amount discharged in developed countries," and the textile industry is one of the major contributors of industrial sewage (Cheng and Shen 2004: 182).

Some of these problems may be mitigated in the future. With entry into the WTO, Chinese tariff rates for imports of foreign-produced dyes, cotton, and textile machinery are dropping and access to superior production technology and to foreign capital is improving. In addition, in response to the global trade regime, China has developed a series of environment-related standards for both finished products and production processes and has encouraged technological changes which result in more environmentally friendly production.[10] For example, Chinese textile factories switched to EU dyes when products with highly polluting Azo dyes were rejected from German markets, exacting huge financial losses (interview by author, May 15, 2002).

Several factors, however, suggest that these benefits are limited, and that the continued surge in the textile sector will be environmentally harmful. First, cotton production in China is not slowing, though imports are increasing.[11] While Bt cotton accounted for 66 percent of Chinese production in 2004, potentially eliminating use of some potent pesticides, the long-term ecological impacts remain to be seen. Second, like the coal industry, within the textile industry small firms have prospered, accounting for about 85 percent of all cotton textile manufacturers. The threshold for entrance into this sector is low due to limited financial and technical requirements; moreover, since WTO accession, foreign investment in small plants has increased (Cheng and Shen 2004). But small firms are equipped with inferior technology and thus scholars believe that "the cumulative [negative] impacts on the environment [of such firms] may be even greater than those of larger enterprises" (Cheng and Shen 2004: 201). Finally, the development of these firms is difficult to regulate and monitor, due to a shortage of rural environmental protection personnel and to economic pressures to approve projects quickly and overlook environmental factors. In May 2002, a Wuhan Environmental Protection Bureau official in charge of approving new industrial ventures explained:

> [With entry into the WTO,] the approval process has to speed up. Many companies want to set up apparel businesses . . . [or] dying factories. They set up very quickly, but they can't really deal with the environmental problems. There are numerous cases of such factories applying for approval. . . . And the tenth five-year plan explicitly calls for expanding production in high quality textiles. . . . So this creates a great challenge for us. The environmental impact assessment regulations require us to complete the process and notify the enterprise within 60 days. But companies want the approval much faster. There's a lot of pressure [on us]. (Interview by author, May 22, 2002)

The difficulties for environmental officials are further aggravated by the dismantling of much of the industrial ministerial structure of the planned economy, in part as preconditions for admission into the WTO. In the past, the now defunct Ministry of Textile Industry acted as an institutional ally, aiding the EPB in enforcement (Cheng and Shen 2004).

Automobile Industry

The environmental ramifications of the feverishly growing automobile industry are at least as daunting as the textile industry. In this case, however, while the manufacturing process is environmentally destructive, it is the consumption of the product that is most polluting. Car emissions are now the major source of pollution in China's large cities, contributing heavily to human health and atmospheric problems. Moreover, due to inferior technologies and congested roads, automobile emissions per vehicle are estimated to be ten times higher than those in developed countries. Yet, as noted elsewhere, the Chinese government continues to regard automobile production as critical to the country's economic development, and sales of automobiles are expected to rise (Pan et al. 2004).

As with the textile industry, the environmental impacts of automobiles may be mitigated. Since entry into the WTO, the Chinese government has developed stricter emissions standards based on EU models. Beginning in 2002, all new cars were required to meet European I standards; in 2004, China began implementing European II standards; and European III standards have been set for enforcement in 2007 (Pan et al. 2004; *China Daily*, April 28, 2005). These standards are notable improvements from previous regulations, though they do not strictly regulate trucks, whose numbers have also grown. It remains to be seen to what degree China will persevere in adopting—and especially enforcing—the highest international emissions control technologies and standards. Not only will the government have to contend with those within China who try to skirt the law in various ways (Pan et al. 2004), but it will have to hold firm against foreign investors who try to reduce costs by transferring older technologies.

Even if more stringent regulations and newer technologies for the motor vehicle sector are enforced, a computer simulation of automobile emissions under present market trends leads Pan and colleagues to conclude that the sheer scale of increased production "will result in heavier [air] pollution . . . simply because reduction [of emissions] per car is easily offset by the increase in the number of cars." Coupled with the environmental impact of higher emissions is the increased demand for more of China's scarce arable land to build roads (Pan et al. 2004: 110–11).

THE AGRICULTURAL SECTOR

The impact on the environment of WTO-induced changes may be even more harmful in the agricultural sector. Here claims of the environmental benefits of structural shifts toward labor-intensive ventures are not well supported; nor is it clear that technological modernization will be an improvement. While WTO accession is even more likely to prompt legal reform in this sector (due to direct health concerns), again problems of scale, shortcomings of technology, and institutional weaknesses may have a far more destructive impact on the environment than the many changes in laws suggest (Jahiel 2003).

Fruit, Vegetables, Horticultural Products, Aquaculture, and More

Prior to accession, WTO-induced market factors encouraging the development of labor-intensive cash crops, livestock and aquaculture ventures and discouraging production of land-intensive grain crops were widely projected to be beneficial to the environment (World Trade Organization 1997; Sun

2000; Ren 2001; Wang 2001, Guojia 2002; Hamburger 2002; Hu and Meng 2002). In line with the logic of liberalization, they were expected to:

1. minimize toxicity of chemical pesticides (as prices of low-toxicity foreign products dropped and strict environmental and health standards upheld by trading partners spurred legal changes in China);[12]
2. reduce application of environmentally degrading chemical fertilizers (with the shift toward animal husbandry and aquaculture);
3. make rural environmental problems easier to control (as farmers shifted from ventures that generate non–point source pollution such as grain production to ones that generate point source pollution such as animal husbandry);
4. promote production of pesticide-free organic crops and biogenetically engineered crops;
5. inhibit population-induced pressures to extend farming on marginal lands (as grain imports increased); and
6. encourage ecosystem restoration (as farmers abandoned grain production and followed policies to convert farmland back to forests or lakes).

All of these factors were projected to benefit water resources, rural ecosystems, and human health.

In most respects, however, the reality has been far different. Use of chemical pesticides and fertilizers has continued to rise since entry into the WTO. China is now a major importer, producer, and consumer of pesticides, and the largest importer, producer, and consumer of chemical fertilizers in the world (Hu 2004). In 2004, Chinese farmers applied twice as much fertilizer to their fields as Americans (Earth Policy Institute 2005), though the United States has over four times the arable land. This rise in chemical inputs is due in part to the shift toward cash crops, which are far more chemical intensive than grain crops, and also to the more limited supply of agricultural labor for weeding, as rural residents seek more lucrative off-farm work (Hamburger 2002; interview by author, June 3, 2004). It is paralleled by increased use of hormones and antibiotics in the growing large-scale livestock and aquaculture industries.

WTO membership may ameliorate the environmental harms of such agricultural chemicals. The increasing use of not only potentially hazardous pesticides, antibiotics, and hormones, but proven toxins banned for use abroad—and in some cases in China—has created problems for trade and pressures to reduce use. Since accession, many Chinese agricultural exports have been prohibited entry to foreign ports. In 2001, half of China's tea exports were barred from sale in the EU because of new EU regulations reducing pesticide tolerance levels for tea by one hundred times (Hamburger 2002); in 2002, the EU suspended imports of all Chinese animal products (including farm-raised shrimp and fish) after detecting excess residues of veterinary medicines (AFX.com, October 18, 2004). Later that year, Japan restricted imports of frozen spinach from China because of high pesticide residues (Japan Economic Newswire, 2003). Such actions have resulted in huge economic losses for China, amounting to billions of dollars (*China Daily* 2005). As a result, international food safety and environmental health codes have begun to influence Chinese laws and policy practices. For example, in 2001, following the loss of US$125 million to tea farmers in Zhejiang, provincial officials there set up an organic certification program (Hamburger 2002), and central government officials initiated a national campaign to control pesticide residues and harmful substances. By 2003, with such incidents rising, the Chinese press reported that governments at various levels had initiated over two hundred national and local laws, regulations, and standards dealing with food safety (*Xinhua General News Service* 2003).

Nevertheless, evidence suggests that institutional weaknesses impede implementation. These include a lack of environmental protection officials charged with monitoring agricultural work, generally poor central control over rural governance, and discrepancies between laws governing domestic and international trade. Interested in obtaining high yields, Chinese farmers still routinely use high doses of potent chemical pesticides and other toxic agents, especially on products for domestic consumption. In June 2003, the Ministry of Agriculture announced it was stepping up the pesticide residue campaign adopted two years earlier, apparently because compliance had been lax. Still, by March 2005, following a spate of dangerous domestic food scandals (some resulting in deaths), food safety remained a major concern of delegates to the National People's Congress (*Financial Times Information* 2005); as a result, wealthy Chinese are now buying imported food (*Standard* 2004)—and may well be justified in doing so. A close reading of regulations reveals that while entry into the WTO might encourage Chinese legislators to adopt stricter foreign food safety codes, international market constraints do not always translate to domestic markets. Regulations issued by Shandong province to tighten control on pesticide residues specifically target "businesses involved in vegetable exports" that are required to "set up strong monitoring systems, and only purchase vegetables from registered production bases" (Xinhua General News Service 2003). The same rules do not seem to adhere to domestic production.

As for the claim that an increase in large-scale animal husbandry ventures might make rural environmental problems easier to control, the U.S. experience with a far more developed environmental regulatory apparatus would suggest otherwise. Large livestock ventures in the United States have created huge solid waste, air, and water pollution problems with adverse impacts on rural ecosystems, drinking water supplies, and human health, and they have proven difficult to regulate (Taquino et al. 2002).

The negative impacts for the environment may be most pronounced in the aquaculture sector. Here massive quantities of nutrients and chemical byproducts from feed stock, veterinary products, and disinfectants in developed coastal regions have led to high levels of eutrophication, fish deaths, disruption of coral reefs, and a shift in the balance and type of phytoplankton, causing red tides that drastically transform China's coastal ecosystems and affect the entire food chain. Moreover, Zhao and colleagues conclude, "Not only is the frequency of red tides increasing and the size of the area affected growing year by year, but also poisonous species [which bioaccumulate] are becoming evident" (Zhao et al. 2004: 90–91, 101). In fact, the number and intensity of such red tides along China's coasts has risen dramatically, with ninety-six reported in 2004, up 83 percent from the previous year (Xinhua Economic News Service 2005). These changes explain the increasing quantities of Chinese aquaculture products rejected by WTO trading partners. Other projected rural environmental gains from trade liberalization have not yet materialized. The scale of the organic agriculture sector is too small to have a significant impact on pesticide use; genetically engineered crops, though increasing in number, pose unknown biosafety threats; and although international environmental NGO work to preserve Chinese habitat has increased, political and economic factors have had a greater impact on land use. Specifically, the economic gains to be made through development of the manufacturing and service sectors under a liberalized economy have led some local government officials to seize land from farmers to create "development zones" or other endeavors, accelerating the loss of productive farmland.

In addition, WTO accession has increased the vulnerability of China's biodiversity. As trade has blossomed, so has the number of exotic and potentially invasive species unintentionally introduced into China. In 2001, flowers imported from the Netherlands inadvertently carried a nonnative insect that spread throughout Yunnan province, affecting the unique ecosystem and devastating the new booming horticulture industry (Wu 2002). Though SEPA has considered legal changes necessary to forestall the further spread of invasive species, with limited technology and manpower and vastly increased imports, it is hard to monitor this problem. The complex and fragile nature of ecosystems along with the difficulty of enforcing policies aimed at sustaining them, has led one agronomist to conclude that the ecological problems posed by accession to the WTO will be extensive and long term, and the overall negative impacts will far outweigh the positive (Liu 2002).

WIDER IMPLICATIONS

The Global Environment

It would be a mistake to view the ramifications of WTO entry solely with regard to its effects on China. The lowering of trade barriers, at precisely the time when China has reached midlevels of development and income, is spreading environmental effects beyond the country's borders. Following severe floods in 1998 due to deforestation, the country enacted and enforced a strict forestry conservation policy. Yet since WTO-entry, China has been able to meet its rapidly rising domestic demand for wood products and has become a major international base for furniture production and wood processing. This is because the reduction of tariffs and elimination of quotas under the WTO has allowed for a rapid growth in timber imports (Sun 2004). While imports have eased pressures on Chinese forests, much of this wood comes from areas of the world practicing poor forest stewardship, such as Indonesia, Malaysia, Myanmar, Cambodia, Russia, and various South American and African countries, and is often illegally purchased (Sun 2004; *Guardian* 2005). As Sun sums up, "Economic globalisation and trade liberalization have promoted globalised resource allocation, and have made it possible that one country transfers stress on its forests to other countries via international trade" (Sun 2004: 68). A 2005 World Wildlife Fund report highlights the severity of this transfer, warning that "surging demand [in China] threatens to have a devastating impact on forests around the world" (Agence France Presse 2005).

Timber is but one example of how WTO entry has encouraged China to seek cheap raw materials overseas for processing at home. Increasingly, Chinese firms are tapping into natural resources in Africa, the Middle East, South America, Southeast Asia, and Russia, and investing in various mining and oil exploration ventures there. By doing so, certain environmental conditions in China may improve as the country's economy continues to grow (as happened with forests); but the voracious appetite of the Chinese manufacturing economy and its overseas customers from the industrialized world serves to exacerbate environmental problems elsewhere, much as development in the north has for decades brought ecological destruction to countries in the south and to the global ecosystem more broadly.

Socioeconomic Changes

While the lowering of trade barriers created by WTO membership is directly responsible for many of the environmental harms discussed above, intensifying socioeconomic changes brought about by WTO membership indirectly compound these problems. As a result of increased wealth and of structural adjustments to the economy since WTO entry, the income gap in China is widening, intensifying consumerism on the one hand and relative deprivation on the other, both of which threaten the environment.

The aggregate growth of the economy and the boost in incomes for those who have benefited from WTO entry have meant that China has now surpassed the United States as the world's largest consumer (Brown 2005).

Wealthy Chinese, still a small proportion of the population, are notably responsible for the rise in atmospheric pollution from automobiles, the loss of arable land for roads and golf courses, the threat to various endangered species for culinary delights, and the increased consumption of electricity, water, and other resources for modern houses full of electronic conveniences.

At the other end of the spectrum, the increase in relative deprivation (*Austin American Statesman* 2004), with falling consumer purchasing power for many, also poses environmental threats.[13] Unemployment in both urban and rural areas remains high; in addition, Chinese farmers have to contend with new competition from international markets and with greater incentives for local officials to seek economic gains. Experience in other parts of the world and in China suggests that when people's livelihoods are threatened and they perceive uncertainty regarding their future, they often resort to strategies that degrade the environment in order to survive (Blakie and Brookfield 1987; Redclift 1989; Gadgil and Guha 1995; Muldavin 2000). Such threats in part account for many of the problems already identified.

Conflicting Political Imperatives

Socioeconomic factors like these have for some time contributed to political imperatives propelling local leaders to engage in environmentally destructive ventures. The success of government officials in China is still measured overwhelmingly on the basis of local economic prosperity and social stability. Over the reform era, growth-oriented norms and economic opportunities have led local leaders to welcome polluting firms for the local employment opportunities and financial benefits they bring, as well as for the personal gains. Since WTO entry, in those parts of China "left behind" and grappling with intensifying economic pressures, the political imperative to pursue such developmentalist strategies, even at a cost to the environment, has heightened. Throughout China, the opportunities to reap large financial rewards from investment ventures has also grown, leading to the previously mentioned local government seizure of farmers' lands for development zones or projects. Many such ventures have supported heavily polluting industries that have destroyed the soils and streams of surrounding communities. Recently, opposition chiefly to industrial pollution, land seizures, corruption, and income differentials has led to a massive rise in protests in the countryside, estimated at 74,000 in 2004, up 28 percent from the previous year (*Chicago Tribune* 2005).

Politically, then, the Chinese government today faces a real dilemma. On the one hand, it has pursued developmentalist policies congruent with those of the WTO, policies which prioritize maximum efficiency and economic growth. On the other hand, these very policies have intensified socioeconomic disparities, heightened self-serving actions by local political leaders, and increased environmental harms in the countryside, leading to a surge of social discontent. Since at least the Tian'anmen Massacre in 1989, the Chinese Communist Party has rested its legitimacy and the regime's stability primarily on its ability to "deliver the goods." The need to expand economic growth factored heavily in the state's determination to enter the WTO. Now delivering these goods at the expense of farmland and the environment is precisely the factor undermining social stability and, with it, the state's legitimacy.

CONCLUSION

If the Chinese Communist Party hopes to maintain social order, and if China's contribution to local and global environmental degradation is to be reduced, the present development trajectory will need to be addressed. While this study demonstrates that membership in the WTO has increased wealth and brought with it technological and legal advances which might conceivably improve environmental quality, it also demonstrates that in important ways, other factors related to WTO membership have offset these benefits, and further challenged political stability. In particular, (1) the sheer scale of growth has overshadowed potential improvements from structural change; (2) weaknesses in regulatory enforcement have diminished the effects of legal advances; (3) environmental improvements at home, in some cases, have come at the expense of environmental harms abroad; (4) socioeconomic changes have increased both environmentally destructive consumption and production; and (5) conflicting political imperatives have led local officials to undertake economic ventures with noted ecological costs—not to mention social and political ones. All of these developments have roots in the normative premise of the WTO—its prioritization of economic growth—which has reinforced the ideological foundation of China's reform era (Jahiel 2000).

Now at a crossroads, the Chinese regime has three avenues of resort. First, it could continue to pursue rapid economic growth under the WTO, satisfying the consumer desires of a part of the population while attempting to stave off social unrest through repression, cooptation, and the transfer of ecological destruction to yet poorer parts of the world. Second, it could respond to popular protest with new measures aimed at strengthening regulatory enforcement, and prohibiting production in all environmentally destructive industrial and agricultural practices, even if these appear profitable under the present trade regime. Third, it could fundamentally shift its development trajectory in ways that benefit the local and global environments. This last alternative would include: (1) fully taking into consideration the environmental and human health costs of rapid economic growth when determining the country's comparative advantage; (2) prioritizing environmental protection as an equally important measure of political success as economic and social prosperity; and (3) abstaining from practices overseas which would be environmentally destructive at home. The central government appears wedded to the first alternative, while the State Environmental Protection Administration seems to be moving toward aspects of the latter two, threatening to hold large development projects to the law, urging greater attention to environmental achievements in administrative evaluation, but also discussing the need to calculate growth on the basis of a green GDP. As always, though, it remains to be seen if and how these measures will be implemented. Significantly, as yet there is no indication that these ideas are actively being linked to China's international trade policies and notions of comparative advantage, nor, fundamentally, to society's notion of prosperity. Moreover, WTO membership is unlikely to encourage these changes. Although to date, the WTO has largely respected existing environmental laws, talk about incorporating the environment within the legal framework of the WTO under the Doha Round has not progressed. Moreover, the economic growth paradigm of the WTO has encouraged its members to "support a greening of WTO rules only partially and only where it furthers their own interests" (Neumayer 2004: 1), with continued adverse effects on the environment. China is now one of these members, and it is playing by the rules set by its predecessors. Unless China makes a strong commitment to pursue growth in its own best environmental interest and prevent the transfer of environmental problems overseas—a commitment the industrialized countries have largely avoided over time, even as the country responds to powerful political pressures by better managing its environmental impacts at home—we can expect it to cast a longer and longer environmental shadow abroad.

REFERENCES

Asia Pulse Analysts. 2004. *Profile: China's Cotton Industry.* January.

Basel Action Network [BAN]. 2002. *Exporting Harm: The Techno-Trashing of Asia.* February.

Bhalla, A., and S. Qiu. 2004. *The Employment Impact of China's WTO Accession.* London: Routledge Curzon.

Blakie, P., and H. Brookfield. 1987. *Land Degradation and Society.* New York: Methuen.

Brown, L. 2005. "China Replacing the United States as World's Leading Consumer." *Eco-economy Update 2005,* www.earth-policy.org/Updates/Update45.htm. (accessed February 16 2005).

Chai, J. 2002. "Trade and the Environment: Evidence from China's Manufacturing Sector." *Sustainable Development* 10: 25–35.

Cheng, L., and X. Shen. 2004. "Textiles." In CCICED 2004, 179–206.

China Council for International Cooperation on Environment and Development [CCICED]. 1997. *Pollution Havens and Ozone Depleting Substances Control in China, Report for the First Meeting of Phase II.* Winnipeg: International Institute for Sustainable Development [IISD].

———. 2001. *China and International Cooperation on Trade and Environment: Final Report Phase II.* Winnipeg: IISD.

———. 2004. *An Environmental Impact Assessment of China's WTO Accession.* Winnipeg: IISD.

Desombre, E., and J. S. Barkin. 2002. "Turtles and Trade: The WTO's Acceptance of Environmental Trade Restrictions." *Global Environmental Politics* 2, no. 1: 12–18.

Earth Policy Institute. 2005. "Oil and Food: A Rising Security Challenge." *Environmental News Network.*

Edmonds, R., ed. 2000. *Managing the Chinese Environment.* Oxford: Oxford University Press.

Feigon, L. 2000. "A Harbinger of the Problems Confronting China's Economy and Environment: The Great Chinese Shrimp Disaster of 1993." *Journal of Contemporary China* 9, no. 24: 323–32.

Ferris, R., Jr., and H. Zhang. 2002. "The Challenges of Reforming an Environmental Legal Culture: Assessing the Status Quo and Looking at Post-WTO Admission Challenges for the People's Republic of China." *Georgetown International Environmental Law Review* 14, no. 3: 429–60.

Fewsmith, J. 2001. "The Political and Social Implications of China's Accession to the WTO." *China Quarterly* 167 (1: 573–91.

Gadgil, M., and R. Guha. 1995. *Ecology and Equity: The Use and Abuse of Nature in Contemporary India.* London: Routledge.

Greenpeace. 1997. "China: The Waste Invasion: Hazardous and Other Waste Imports to China and Hong Kong 1993–1999," www.eldis.org/static/DOC4499.htm (accessed May 31 2005).

Hamburger, J. 2002. "Pesticides in China: A Growing Threat to Food Safety, Public Health, and the Environment." *China Environment Series* 5.

Harwit, E. 2001. "The Impact of WTO Membership on the Automobile Industry in China." *China Quarterly* 167: 655–70.

Hsiung, J. 2003. "The Aftermath of China's Accession to the World Trade Organisation." *Independent Review* 8, no. 1: 87–112.

Hu, T. 2004. "Agriculture." In CCICED 2004, 25–44.

Hu, T., and F. Meng. 2002. "Zhongguo jiaru WTO yu nongye de huanjing yingxiang [China's accession to the WTO and the environmental impacts of agriculture]." Paper presented at the International Conference on China's Entry into the WTO: Economic and Ecological Challenges and Opportunities, Kunming, China, May 20.

Hu, T., and W. Yang. 2000. *Environmental and Trade Implications of China's WTO Accession: A Preliminary Analysis.* Winnipeg: IISD.

Hu Tao, senior policy analyst, PRCEE. Interview by author, Beijing, May 15 2002.

Jahiel, A. 2000. "The Organisation of Environmental Protection in China." In R. Edmonds, ed., *Managing the Chinese Environment,* 33–63. Oxford: Oxford University Press, 2000.

———. 2002. "The Environmental Impact of China's Entry into the WTO." Unpublished manuscript.

———. 2003. "Green Agriculture and Green Trade Barriers: WTO Benefits to the Chinese Countryside Reconsidered." Paper presented at the annual meeting of the Association for Asian Studies, March 29.

Jiang, K., X. Hu, D. Guo, and L. Cheng. 2004. "Energy." In CCICED 2004, 139–75.

Langlois, J., Jr. 2001. "The WTO and China's Financial System." *China Quarterly* 167, no. 1: 610–29.

Lee, K. W. 2001. China's Accession to the WTO: Effects and Social Challenges." *China Perspectives* 33: 13.

Liu, B. 2002. "WTO and Biodiversity Protection." Paper presented at the International Conference on China's Entry into the WTO, Kunming, China.

Lu Chuntao, Henan Provincial Agricultural Research Institute. Interview by author, Zhengzhou, June 3, 2004.

Mai, Y. 2002. "The Petroleum Sector after China's Entry into the WTO: Can the Chinese Oil Giants Survive Market Competition?" *China Perspectives* 41: 24.

Muldavin, J. 2000. "The Paradoxes of Environmental Policy and Resource Management in Reform-Era China." *Economic Geography* 76, no. 3: 244–71.

Municipal EPB official. Interview by author, Wuhan, May 22, 2002.

Neumayer, E. 2004. "The WTO and the Environment: Its Past Record Is Better Than Critics Believe, But the Future Outlook Is Bleak." *Global Environmental Politics* 4, no. 3: 1–8.

Oberheitmann, A. 2002. "Energy Production and Related Environmental Issues in China." *China Perspectives* 40: 37–49.

Pan, J., H. Hu, F. Yu, and L. Cheng. 2004. "Automobiles." In CCICED 2004, 107–36.

Pollution Control Department of SEPA. 2002. *Jiaru WTO dui wuran kongzhi gongzuo de yingxiang yu jianyi* [The impact of entry into the WTO on pollution control work, and suggestions], internal document, March-April.

Redclift, M. 1989. "The Environmental Consequences of Latin America's Agricultural Development: Some Thoughts on the Brundtland Commission Report." *World Development* 17, no. 3: 365–77.

Ren, G. 2001. "Jiaru WTO dui Zhongguo huanjing baohu de yingxiang fenxi [An analysis of the environmental protection impacts for China of entry into the WTO]." Manuscript, Peking University.

Rosen, D., S. Rozelle, and J. Huang. 2004. *Roots of Competitiveness.* Washington, D.C.: Institute for International Economics.

Ross, L. 2000. "China: Environmental Protection, Domestic Policy Trends, Patterns of Participation in Regimes, and Compliance with International Norms." In R. Edmonds, ed., *Managing the Chinese Environment*, 85–111. Oxford: Oxford University Press 2000.

Sanders, R. 1999. "The Political Economy of China: Environmental Protection Lessons of the Mao and Deng Years." *Third World Quarterly* 20, no. 6: 1201–15.

Senior SEPA official. Interview by author, Beijing, May 22, 2002.

SEPA official, Division of Law and Regulation. Interview by author, Beijing, May 15 2002.

Smil, V. 1993. *China's Environmental Crisis: An Inquiry into the Limits of National Development.* London: M. F. Sharpe.

Sun, C. 2000. "WTO and Chinese forestry: An Outline of Knowledge and Knowledge Gaps." *Sinosphere* 3, no. 3: 18–23.

———. 2004. "Forestry." In CCICED 2004, 47–72.

Taquino, M., D. Parisi, and D. Gill. 2002. "Units of Analysis and the Environmental Justice Hypothesis: The Case of Industrial Hog Farms." *Social Science Quarterly* 83, no. 1: 298–316.

Theirs, P. 2000. "China's Green Food Label and the International Certification Regime for Organic Food: Harmonized Standards and Persistent Structural Contradictions." *Sinosphere* 3, no. 3: 8–18.

Wang, H. 2001. "Huanjing wenti: Rushihou de waimao jiaodian: Fangwen guojia huanbao zongju fujuzhang Wang Yuqing [The environmental question: The foreign trade focus after entering the WTO: An interview with SEPA Vice Administrator Wang Yuqing]." *Keji Rihao: Science and Technology Daily*, November.

Wang, S. 2000. "The Social and Political Implications of China's WTO Membership." *Journal of Contemporary China* 25: 373–405.

Weber, M. 2001. "Competing Political Visions: WTO Governance and Green Polities." *Global Environmental Politics* 1, no. 1: 92–113.

Williams, M. 2001. "Trade and the Environment in the World Trading System: A Decade of Stalemate?" *Global Environmental Politics* 1, no. 4: 4–6.

World Trade Organization, Commission on Trade and Environment [CTE]. 1997. *Environmental Benefits of Removing Trade Restrictions,* November 7.

Wu, X. 2002. "The Implications of China's Entry into WTO on Environmental Protection." Paper presented at the International Conference on China's Entry into the WTO, Kunming, China.

Ye, R. 2002. "China's Entry to the WTO and Environmental Protection." Paper presented at the International Conference on China's Entry into the WTO, Kunming, China.

Yeung, G. 2002. "The Implications of WTO Accession on the Pharmaceutical Industry in China." *Journal of Contemporary China* 11, no. 2: 473–93.

Zhao, Y., H. Zheng, M. Bai, and X. Lin. 2004. "Aquaculture." In CCICED 2004, 75–104.

15

Globalization and the Burden of Critical Theory

When Columbus first saw the forests of the Caribbean, he commented on what wonderful ship masts the trees would make. The event expresses an attitude, or an ideology, by which nature exists to serve the needs of human beings—namely, human beings can and must dominate the natural world. This idea is also expressed in the Bible, in the passages where God gives man the dominion over nature.[1] Another entrenched idea that is given biblical legitimacy is man's domination of woman. In this chapter, Jasmin Sydee and Sharon Beder examine the ecofeminist premise that there is a strong connection between the idea of male domination of both nature and women; that is, "the rape of the earth" intrinsic to globalization and the Western model of development is a metaphor for the rape of women. Thus for ecofeminists the environmental crisis and the subjugation of women are, as they put it, "two symptoms of the same illness."

Sydee and Beder critically examine the various forms of ecofeminist arguments and the similarities and differences among them, including the claim that women are uniquely situated, culturally and biologically, to renew our links to nature. Also common to ecofeminist approaches is the idea that to address our environmental problems we must also address other symptoms of hierarchy and domination including racism, classism, and heterosexism among others. In short, we must come to understand the social, political, and historical factors that gave rise to patriarchal capitalism and male domination. Such an understanding, selectively informed by the ecofeminist critique, will enhance our ability to deal with the negative effects of globalization, especially—as Sydee and Beder point out—those effects pertaining to women and children.

Jasmin Sydee and Sharon Beder, "Ecofeminism and Globalization: A Critical Appraisal" (2001)[2]

Ecofeminists identify globalization as an outgrowth of capitalism which, according to their analysis, is the locus of social and environmental crises. They argue that the essential characteristic of capitalism is its patriarchal nature. They claim that the material and discursive institutions of patriarchal capitalism require the systematic domination and exploitation of both women and nature.

However, this materialist emphasis is not common to all ecofeminist thinkers. Certain paths of ecofeminist thought are almost wholly spiritual, as theorists and activists explore the holistic value of reality and raise it to a sacred realm. These spiritually oriented ecofeminists seek to celebrate women and their association with nature as a source of strength, power, and virtue. They argue that reconnecting humans with nature, and modeling communities and self-actualization on the patterns and webs of nature has vast political and structural implications, and, in itself, is inherently spiritual. These ecofeminists wish to break the hierarchies that have been created around difference to reimmerse humans in nature.

A materialist ecofeminist analysis has been developed in part as a critique of this spiritual ecofeminism. It sees spiritual ecofeminism as failing to come to terms with the effects of capitalism, such as the perpetuation of sexism and environmental damage. In particular, material ecofeminists are critical of the tendency of spiritual ecofeminists to endorse essentialism—the view that men and women are essentially and inherently different in character and nature.

For materialist ecofeminists, the fundamental contradiction of capitalism is not between capital and labor but between production and reproduction. Valued and economically recognized, male labor is separated off from invisible domestic female service. This is thought to be the deepest contradiction of patriarchal capitalism because women's reproductive labor remains in nature while men's productive labor is removed from nature. Their close connection with nature is said to put women in the position of being able to liberate humanity and nature from capitalist domination in order to create new, healthy societies.

While opening up valuable ground for dialogue and providing insights into the effects of globalization, ecofeminist analyses are limited in their ability to address the underlying causes and major driving forces of globalization. This is because ecofeminism insists on the primacy of gender as the determinant of social organization, attempts to separate women from culture and identifies patriarchy as the defining characteristic of capitalism. This chapter will outline the ecofeminist critique and what it has to offer before presenting a more compelling view of the defining characteristics of capitalism.

(RE)WEAVING AN ECOFEMINIST WORLDVIEW

Ecofeminism is premised on the social critique that the domination of women through patriarchy and the domination of nature through the Western model of development are intrinsically linked. "The rape of the earth, in all its forms, becomes a metaphor for the rape of woman, in all its many guises" (Plant 1989: 5). Therefore the ecological crisis and the subjugation of women are two symptoms of the same illness. Globalization is of particular concern to ecofeminists as an extension of the capitalist project which further consolidates the power of transnational companies (TNCs) and more deeply entrenches the socioeconomic institutions that enforce the domination over women and nature. This chapter will focus on a material (or socialist) ecofeminist analysis due to its ability to critique capitalism, yet a wider understanding of ecofeminism as a movement will also be used to further illuminate the ecofeminist position on globalization.

Ecofeminism developed as a theory and an activist position in response to the feminist, ecological, and peace movements and as recognition of the strength of female participation in grassroots activism. The term "ecofeminism" was coined in 1974 by Francoise d'Eaubonne when she "called for a feminist revolution to ensure ecological survival" (Howell 1997: 231). Since the mid-1970s there has been a rush of publications, conferences, organizations, actions, and celebrations recognizing and exploring connections between women, nature, and social change (Salleh 1997: 232–33). Like feminism, however, ecofeminism is an umbrella term entailing positions and standpoints as diverse as goddess worship, lesbian separatism, Christian ecofeminism, and socialist ecofeminism. This diversity is not a contradiction but is at the very heart of the theory and practice of ecofeminism.

All ecofeminists identify the failure of the feminist movement and the ecological movement to make significant headway as a failure to recognize the common cause of both problems. There is a systematic domination, they claim, over both women and nature, underpinned by a conceptual set of dualisms. These dualisms would be familiar as man/woman, mind/body, reason/emotion, human/nature, active/passive, and so forth. The importance lies not just in the presumption that reality does in fact occur in binary opposite sets, but that the former in each pair is believed to be justifiably superior to the latter. Both "woman" and "nature" fall on the same side in the dualism sets, defined as that which is not "man" or "human." In this system women and nature are subordinated as other and are legitimately treated as such (Howell 1997: 232–33; Warren 1990: 126–32, 139).

As both forms of domination and all others that conform to this pattern are bound by the same conceptual logic, each must be addressed in order to address the others. Therefore, the ecological crises cannot be challenged without challenging patriarchy and vice versa. In this way ecofeminism offers a critique of mainstream social movements. Ecofeminism insists on breaking apart these dualisms to (re)create a society of reciprocity and mutuality without hierarchy or domination. For this reason all systems of domination, including racism, classism, and heterosexism among others, must also be overcome as they stem from the same logic of domination (Howell 1997: 232; Hicks 1996: 3).

As dualism and value hierarchy are to be overcome, diversity is necessarily valued, as no one voice or group of voices will be able to say who or what has the most value. This idea is affirmed by ecology, which shows that diversity and mutuality and reciprocity are beneficial for the survival of the whole (Howell 1997: 235). This valuing of the importance of difference ("truth" is contextual and plural) is argued to avoid the postmodern trap of relativism, where truth dissolves into nothing. Ecofeminists speak of reality being like a patchwork quilt, for example, in which there are boundaries but no absolute story within (Warren 1990: 138–39). Simple patterns and mosaics of pieces that individuals and groups have contributed will form the interior. These boundaries are defined by the lack of domination, contextualism, pluralism, diversity, the championing of marginalized voices (e.g., the experiences of women), and an emphasis on understanding oneself in relationship to others (Warren 1990: 134–38).

This last comment is most important to ecofeminism. What is meant by "self in relationship to others" is that we must recognize the integrity of our own personal center (i.e., our own body and consciousness), and in doing so we can recognize and value that of others. Furthermore, just as we can understand and learn about ourselves and who we are through our relationships with other people (family, friends, loved ones, colleagues, even enemies), so too we can understand that we are also in relationships with the natural world and the things it entails. We can learn about ourselves through our interactions and relationships with those entities, both living and nonliving, and their relationships with each other as well. In this way an ecofeminist image of nature is also an image of society, as the two are intrinsically linked (Howell 1997: 232). In contrast to deep ecology, the two are defined by ecofeminists as separate entities, but they are also symbiotic. Nevertheless, nature's autonomy is recognized (Plumwood 1995: 155–58).

Ecofeminist spirituality or theology is diverse, drawing from many traditions, including ancient European, Asian, and African mythologies, from Native American belief, from neo-pagan Wiccan belief, from Christianity and other established religious traditions (Plumwood 1995: 311–13; Howell 1997: 233–35; Plant 1989: 1–4). Nevertheless, across the diversity that ecofeminism supports there seems to be a common assertion of women's spirituality as a primary good, having its own inherent nature and integrity, and being fundamentally grounded in nature.

AN EMBODIED MATERIALISM

Although materialist ecofeminism (sometimes called socialist ecofeminism) developed in part as a critique of spiritual ecofeminism, a materialist analysis always has a fluid relationship to a spiritual or ethical analysis, and the boundary between the two isn't firm. Yet for materialist ecofeminists, the breaking apart of duality is only the first stage in liberation. Spiritual ecofeminists tend to simply turn the conceptual duality on its head to illustrate that the female connection to nature is in fact a source of power and strength rather than a justification for subordination and exploitation. Therein lies a tendency for women to claim to be "closer to nature" and therefore to be the ecological and social leaders for humanity. This opens ground for charges of essentialism (Mies 1993: 16–20; Morgan 1982).

Further still, many women are concerned that the emphasis spiritual ecofeminism places on an ethic for change ignores the effects and power of capitalism in shaping the lives of women and shaping the globe. Without this dimension, it is argued that solutions for change remain too rooted in self-realization and individual and community change and prevent ecofeminism from coming to terms with the socioeconomic relationships between north and south or internal national ethnic relations (Mies 1993:16–20; Barry 1998: 150–53). White middle-class ecofeminists fail to realize that the affluence and lifestyle choices they are embracing have been afforded to them through the continued exploitation of the "sisters" in the south. Their (re)discovery is being sourced through appropriating the knowledge and experiences of women still treated as Other. Indigenous women, African American women, and women from the south, it is argued, are still excluded, by material economic forces, from any "reweaving" that is occurring.

Materialist ecofeminists have attempted to shift the emphasis of analysis from naturalizing differences to analyzing the material forces that shape the relations between men, women, and nature, in an attempt to sidestep the problems of essentialism and exclusion.

For materialist ecofeminists the locus of domination lives in patriarchal capitalism. This is the social-economic system that has crystallized the centuries of thought, ideology, and tradition (Salleh 1997; Merchant 1980) that have created dualisms and used them to systematically exploit women and nature by a single logic. Many ecofeminists premise their material analysis on the dichotomy of production and reproduction. Due to the necessary exclusion of women's reproductive labor from the formal economy, most women already live in an alternative reality and have a different relationship with nature to men. The female social experience is one in which time is not commodified as it is for males, because their work is a twenty-four-hour experience filled with life affirming and organic practices such as child raising, caring, creating home and community. This allows women the privilege of *embodying* the aspects of culture that are still firmly rooted in nature. Therefore women are uniquely qualified as the historical agents who can liberate human kind and the natural world from immanent crises (Salleh 1997; Barry 1998: 150–51).

EFFECTS OF GLOBALIZATION

For materialist ecofeminists globalization is an extension or outgrowth of patriarchal capitalism. Few ecofeminists have explored the problem of globalization head-on, challenging the thesis or rhetoric of its proponents, but many do explicate its real effects in the world and on women. Examples abound of women fighting patriarchal capitalism and globalization in grassroots women's organizations.

Ecofeminists are concerned about globalization because it represents the consolidation and concentrating of the power of patriarchal capitalism. They explore the impacts of globalization in a number of ways: the changing concepts of state, the neocolonization of patriarchal capitalism, globalization as damaging diversity, and the feminization of poverty.

The Changing Nation-State

Central to globalization is the changing role of the nation-state. According to globalization theorists, the nation-state as we know it will shrink in size and power until the state apparatus only exists to control rump functions such as police functions, tax collection, and so on. The state, as the primary mode of social organization, will be superseded by the market. The freedom of trade, information, and cultural flows will create a "global village" in which individuals are global citizens rather than nationals. Or so the story goes . . .

As many theorists have noted, it is important to untangle the rhetoric concerning globalization from the real changes that are occurring internationally. Although multinationals are becoming increasingly powerful and the role of the nation-state is changing, we must remember that globalization is a contested concept.

For ecofeminism the changing role of the nation-state has great significance. First, and perhaps most important, is that the state is argued to intrinsically be an institution of patriarchal capitalism. That is that historically the state was created as an institution in aid of the market and capital as an institution of control. "The economy cannot directly control women's sexuality, fertility and work capacity; to do this, the state, with its family policy, is necessary" (Mies 1993: 120). The "housewifization" of women, or the split between production and reproduction, was a requirement of capitalism and the state helped create this condition. As a diverse array of feminists have discussed, women were relegated to the private sphere and therefore denied equal access to participate in civil society (Mies 1993: 120). The continuing importance of public/private dichotomy is highlighted in the battles of the suffragette movement and the limitations of liberal feminism (Phillips 1987).

In the south the state as a mode of social organization has an even shorter history than in the north. Vandana Shiva explores the changing concepts of state in India as an example of the impacts of statism, capitalism, and globalization on subsistence communities in the south. Shiva states that the concept of motherland—rooted in the soil as an image of sacred life and creation, the feminine—was the traditional organizing metaphor in India. It was replaced by "Mother India" as a focus of resistance in the fight against colonization by Britain in the 1940s. The subsequent drive for development replaced the image of mother or feminine strength with the state itself as a patriarchal leader (Shiva 1993a: 108–9).

Yet the role of the state itself is changing. Shiva claims that at the economic level in India "the state has been totally subjugated to the superstate run by the transnational corporations (TNCs) and the Bretton Woods institutions—World Bank, International Monetary Fund (IMF) and the General Agreement on Tariffs and Trade (GATT)" (Shiva 1993a: 108). These institutions, she argues, are integrating India into a globalizing world economy at a great cost as people are forcibly removed from sacred soil, and female images of diversity are subsumed by the homogeneity and hegemony of a patriarchal capitalist market (Shiva 1993a: 109–11).

Again the state is explicated as an institution of patriarchal capitalism through its complicity in globalization in the guise of national interest. "When public interest is divorced from national interest, and national interest is predicated on international interests, then sovereignty is in crisis, along with democracy" (Shiva 1993a: 110). Shiva has great concern over the anger and violence that remain in the wake of national disintegration, loss of identity and self-determination through globalization. She identifies the rise of nationalism and internal ethnic conflict as a symptom of the dislocation of globalization, but challenges any idea that the creation of new nation-states will cure the illness (Shiva 1993a: 111–15).

Mary Mies also explores the link between the nation-state and the creation of globalization giving a Northern perspective. Mies utilizes Wallenstein's dependency theory to illustrate that the global orientation of capital and national self-interest are not in fact in contradiction to each other but "a precondition for both the nation-state and the market economy or capital-ism" (Mies 1993: 122). Capitalism requires both internal and external colo-nies to function, therefore in the guise of "free" trade and reciprocity globalization becomes the systematic use of the existing unequal global dis-tribution of wealth and power to further entrench relationships of depen-dency and exploitation. Northern states are fostering the processes of globalization in their own self interest, rather than their own dismantlement for a "global village" (Mies 1993: 121–22).

Ecofeminists are critical of both the institution of the state and its role in globalization due to its function in a patriarchal economy. As the state is so significantly tied to identity and political participation, the changing nation-state, never a holistic institution to begin with, has been important in the rise of nationalist disintegration and violence. Ultimately, however, ecofeminists are ambivalent about the future of nation-state, advocating new (or old) con-cepts of sovereignty in which people are economically, socially, and spiritu-ally embedded in the land that they live on, and therefore in nature (Van Zevern 1996: 91–93; Shiva 1993b: 106).

Neocolonization

Vandana Shiva and Maria Mies place great emphasis of the role of expand-ing international capitalism into the south and its interaction with subsis-tence modes of living. The expansion and neocolonization of capitalism into, over and onto other cultural/economic systems adds an important facet to ecofeminist discussion.

For Shiva, examining patriarchal capitalism is illuminating as "contempo-rary development activity in the Third World super-imposes the scientific and economic paradigms created by western, gender-based ideology on communities in other cultures" (Shiva 1989: xvii). The interaction between subsistence worldviews and institutions with capitalist ones illustrates the domination of both women and nature claimed to be inherent in the capital-ist system.

In subsistence economies the knowledge of women is highly valued and respected. The "feminine" is part of a web of belief that includes the imma-nent life force of mother earth or Prakriti, as it is called in India, but it is also reiterated in the socioeconomic position of women as providers of food and as mothers. In India, the spiritual dimension to the subsistence worldview is embedded in the material conditions of life (Shiva 1993b: 98–106). A "divorce of the spiritual and the material is incomprehensible to them" (Mies and Shiva 1993: 19). Due to their direct interaction with nature for day-to-day survival in a subsistence mode, women and men are materially embed-ded in nature. The split that materially and discursively characterizes West-ern societies is unknown (Mies and Shiva 1993: 16–20).

However, many traditionally subsistence-based communities have lost power and control over their lands and their practices, including women's knowledge and farming capacities, due to their interaction with capitalist economics and the dominant Western worldview. Ecofeminists argue that women, and children, are hurt most severely by this process, as women receive no equivalent position of power or self-determination in a patriarchal capitalist economy to what they had in a subsistence economy. Decision-making power, cash payments, and status are conferred to men in changing community structures, marginalizing women (Shiva 1992: xvi–xvii; Mellor 1992). Furthermore, the environmental degradation caused by fast tracked development and the removal of the ability of women to utilize their traditional knowledge in these new westernized systems are argued to be intractably linked.

Shiva's famous example is of the green revolution. She argues that the green revolution did not feed the hungry but perpetuated hunger through technological systems that took control out of the hands of traditional female farmers and placed it in the hands of multinationals through technological and hence economic dependence. The removal of local knowledge from decision making and the abstracted and reductionist qualities of Western science and the limited goals of the development paradigm created environmental degradation through poor land use, pest control toxic chemical use, as well as social dislocation of local residents. Shiva concludes that the devaluation of women in their political economic capacity and the devaluation of the soil as sacred and immanent are part of the same machination (Shiva 1989). Globalization requires the integration of local- and subsistence-based economies into a global market subsuming local interest to a global interest which is clearly specific interest and not a universal one at all (Shiva 1993b: 98–99).

Damaging Diversity

As an environmental ethic, spiritual ecofeminism is in a position to explore why capitalism and globalization are wrong morally. In particular it offers a critique of commodification in terms of loss of diversity, where diversity is a moral value. It provides a criticism of capitalism's ideology of competition as rhetoric in a world in which monopoly and oligopoly are norms.

For spiritual ecofeminists, globalization becomes particularly problematic due to its homogenizing effect on culture and nature through commodification and market mechanisms. Sometimes described as the "McDonaldization" of culture, globalization has been widely criticized for acting as a blanket culture that smothers difference and diversity in a sea of homogeneity and sameness (Norberg-Hodge 1999: 194–97; Ritzer 1996). And so we see "universal" fast food chains and beverages, and access to American television in countries where people starve.

Diversity is at the heart of an ecofeminist ethic and integral to ecological and spiritual health. Furthermore, the commodification of culture and resources to integrate it into the global marketplace overrides other social values leaving economic value as the global value. (Crittenden 1993: 53–54; Mies and Shiva 1993: 8–13). Commodification does not honor an ethic of the sacred which is central to an ecofeminist theology of the immanent divine. Furthermore, the atomization and reification of commodity does not respect the integrity of the webs of relationship in life and culture.

The Feminization of Poverty

Women today comprise the majority of the poor in the north and the south. Mary Mellor explores at length the impact that globalizing capital is having on the world's poor and particularly its women. The pressures of poverty make the exploitation of women and nature as cheap and disposable resources easy to achieve and highly visible. Mellor considers prostitution tourism and sweatshop labor examples of patriarchal capitalism resourcing women as "the ultimate cash crop" in the drive toward globalization (Mellor 1992: 171–74).

Prostitution has become a primary tourist attraction in Southeast Asia, with child prostitution and slavery also quite common. Yet the human rights and dignity that both poverty and prostitution steal are hidden behind masks. "By locating prostitution in the culture of poverty and the exotic, the question of human dignity becomes obscured and neutralised while Thai women become qualified as 'new pasture' in which local entrepreneurs can invest and make profits, and over which rich clients can exercise their sexual fantasies without guilt" (Mellor 1992: 176). The inequalities that have been created by capitalism are then exploited through the marketing and even active encouragement of prostitution as a tourist attraction in order for poor nations such as Thailand to keep a desperate toehold in the world economy. Mellor qualifies this, noting that red-light districts are also prevalent in the north, where sexual exploitation of women is also commonplace (Mellor 1992: 176).

Similarly, women are resourced by the imperatives of global capital to slave as outworkers and in sweatshops creating garments largely for sale in the affluent north. These women are mostly young and are valued for their nimble fingers and docility. This behavior is often derived from the desperation of poverty and the high exposure of the populations of poor nations to a military presence. This employment is paid pitifully if at all and conducted in poor conditions (Mellor 1992: 159–65). Like prostitution, sweatshop labor represents a net transfer of wealth both in commodities and capital from the south to the north (Mellor 1992: 178–79).

Yet even in the wealthy nations of the north, poverty is increasingly feminized. The work the women fill is largely part-time or casual, with poor status, low pay, and little security. This is compounded by the stigma associated with domestic labor and motherhood, leaving women with welfare handouts due to the nonvaluation of the daily labor (Selleh 1997: 88–91). "Men do one-third of the world's work for 95 per cent of its income, and own more than 99% of its assets" (Mellor 1992: 198). Ecofeminists take these trends as evidence of the patriarchal nature of capitalism. For ecofeminists, globalization is being created at the cost of women's welfare.

CAUSES

Ariel Salleh is one of the few ecofeminists to explicitly attribute the effects of patriarchal capitalism and globalization to causes stemming from gender differences. At the core of Salleh's material analysis of patriarchal capitalism is the gendered division of society as the predeterminant for the construction of duality in Western thought. Since ancient times the meaning of biological difference has been circumscribed by psychosexual assumptions and discursive constructions (Salleh 1997: 35–38).

Salleh claims that neither biology nor sexuality is polar, but a continuum of experiences so the categories of man and woman are artificial or at least overly simplistic. As the reproductive power of women could not be rivaled by men, it had to thus be controlled, and so children were "owned" by men (Salleh 1997: 38–41). "Ecofeminists conjecture that the identification of 'production' with 'masculinity' may arise because at some deep unconscious level men are mystified and alienated by women's unique potency in species reproduction" (Salleh 1997: 81). Therefore it is the psychosexual domination of men over women that has led to the valuation of masculine labor in the capitalist market as production and the nonvaluation of female child rearing and domestic labor as reproductive.

This has real consequences in the world that can be analyzed without reference to essential biological natures. It has placed woman as a mediator between man and nature. "Women's traditional positioning between men and nature is a primary contradiction of capitalism, and may well be the deepest, most fundamental contradiction of all. In anthropological terms—shaped by androcentric interests—women's bodies are treated first as if they were a 'natural resource', the uterus as organ of birthing labor bring the material origin of 'formal labor' as such" (Salleh 1997: 93).

The deepest contradiction, for Salleh, in capitalism is not the ownership of the means of production that is identified by Marxism, but the psychosexual domination of men over women and therefore over nature. That is the treatment of both women and nature as resources, and limitless commons to be exploited and as sources of externalities to be poisoned and discarded (Salleh 1997: 53–66).

According to Salleh, and also Mary Mellor, the psychosexual schism between men and women has come to inform the division of labor that is a precondition for capitalism. Capitalism is essentially patriarchal, according to ecofeminists, as it requires the duality of production/reproduction to function (Salleh 1997: 80–83). Production has become defined as the labor that is done primarily by men in creating commodities for the capitalist market. This is opposed to the unpaid and invisible work done primarily by women in child-rearing, domestic, caring, and volunteer capacities. This caring and domestic work is the auxiliary work that facilitates the operation of a capitalist economy. It provides emotional and structural support to allow a wage earner to perform his role (Salleh 1997; Mellor 1992: 194–206). "The basic character of this female exploitation remains unchanged by globalization and the workplace restructuring that comes with it" (Salleh 1997: 88).

LIMITATIONS OF ECOFEMINISM

Ecofeminism offers a useful theoretical framework to critique capitalism and globalization, but it is by no means the only framework. Other theoretical frameworks such as Marxism, deep ecology, social ecology, and inclusive democracy (Fotopoulos 1997) also enable people to critique capitalism and come up with analyses of its impacts that cover some of the same impacts as well as others not covered by ecofeminists. For example, similar analyses of the impacts of neocolonialism have been made by non-ecofeminists and the feminist angle is not that compelling, since the green revolution did not discriminate between male and female traditional farmers.

Ecofeminists also claim to offer a new system of values that makes them uniquely able to challenge patriarchal capitalist values. Mellor states, "Any interaction with the market must operate within its assumption that the only measure of value is price, and the only motivation for economic activity is profit. A feminist green socialism would challenge that proposition; it would show that some things are beyond price" (Mellor 1992: 194). But others have also challenged that position (Beder 1997: 90–106).

While materialist ecofeminists offer scathing appraisals of capitalism, they do not directly attack the institution of the market economy. It is often left unclear in their analyses how the market economy should be dealt with. In contrast the Inclusive Democracy project, which also challenges capitalism and its associated modes of domination, including sexism and naturism, stresses the role of the market economy and the ideology of growth.

The concentration of economic power and ecological destruction are shown as inevitable consequences, as well as fundamental preconditions, of economic growth [in capitalist growth economies]. . . . The crucial issue today is how we create a new society where the institutionalized domination of human being over human being and the subsequent idea of dominating nature is ruled out. The search for such a system will lead us to the conclusion that it is not just growth ideology which has to be abandoned but the market economy itself. (Fotopoulos 1997: 62–63)

Without directly addressing the problem of the market economy, ecofeminism leaves itself vulnerable to the charge of being reformist. Capitalist imperatives, realized in the market economy, are subsumed in ecofeminism by a preoccupation with gender relations.

CAPITALIST IMPERATIVES

Ecofeminist critiques of globalism are weakest where they seek to explain the causes of globalization in terms of feminist analyses. The domination of women by men has occurred in many precapitalist societies, but this domination and the dualities associated with it were not sufficient to create the sort of capitalist culture that seeks to expand its economic power globally.

The rise of modern capitalism from feudal societies has been more convincingly described by others. Max Weber's explanation emphasizes ideas and the role of religion. Weber described how work became a religious calling, a way of worshiping God (Weber 1930: 59–60). The idea of the moral value of work spread through Europe and to English Protestants. The English Puritans, in particular, embraced the gospel of work (Berstein 1997: 38, 69–71). The work ethic helped to supply the new entrepreneurs with "sober, conscientious, and unusually industrious workmen, who clung to their work as to a life purpose willed by God" (Tawney 1973: 177). From England, the Puritans took this idea of work as a calling to America where, as in England, preachers made it a topic of sermons.

Following the Protestant Reformation the acquisition of wealth became an approved and worthy goal, perhaps for the first time in history, and this was a major factor in the rise of capitalism in Western society. R. H. Tawney states in his *Religion and the Rise of Capitalism* that the significance of Calvinism consisted "in its admission to a new position of respectability of a powerful and growing body of social interests, which, however irrepressible in practice, had hitherto been regarded by religious theory as, at best, of dubious propriety, and at worst, as frankly immoral" (Tawney 1973: 90–91).

The Reformation provided moral support and legitimacy to a class of people who had an interest in raising the status and influence of commerce and industry. Protestantism provided a conducive environment for capitalism to flourish in and the moral high ground from which to pursue profit freely and with good conscience. Similarly the new businessmen supported a church and faith which told them that what they wanted to do was in keeping with what God wanted them to do.

The shrewd, calculating commercialism which tries all human relations by pecuniary standards, the acquisitiveness which cannot rest while there are competitors to be conquered or profits to be won, the love of social power and hunger for economic gain: these irrepressible appetites have evoked from time immemorial the warnings and denunciations of saints and sages. Plunged in the cleansing waters of later Puritanism, the qualities which less enlightened ages had denounced as social vices emerged as economic virtues (Tawney 1973:105).

In England, Holland, Scotland, Geneva, and America the combination of Protestantism and capitalism wrought social change of huge dimensions. In England it overturned the power of a feudal aristocracy "contemptuous of the economic virtues . . . more interested in maintaining customary standards of consumption than in accumulating capital for future production" (Tawney 1973: 99, 101).

Once the capitalist spirit took hold it was hard to resist or turn back. When businesspeople became capitalists, those in the same business either had to follow suit and give up their leisurely and relaxed way of doing business, or go out of business because they couldn't compete with the ever expanding capitalist entrepreneurs (Weber 1930: 68). The religious roots of the spirit of capitalism "died out slowly, giving way to a utilitarian worldliness" (Weber 1930: 176).

With the rise of capitalism, work came to be valued according to its productivity and wealth-creating potential. Success in business was measured solely in terms of profits. Wealth, as the supposed fruit of hard work, became an indicator of a person's worth and social standing. The emphasis on work as a religious calling was gradually superseded by a materialistic quest for social mobility and material success (Beder 2000).

As wealth came to symbolize the fruit of hard work, those who were wealthy gained status. They wielded power over others through being able to hire them or otherwise pay for their services and favors. And as wealth became a measure of worthiness and success, money became an even more effective means of inducement to manipulate and sway others (Beder 2000). Since the late nineteenth century business leaders have used their status, their control over employees, and their command over financial resources to make their influence felt in all realms of society, to exercise power and control over others, both men and women.

Globalization is a natural extension to the wealth- and power-acquiring tendencies of capitalism. The trend toward the concentration of economic power began in the United States at the end of the nineteenth century when a wave of business mergers created several very large corporations. Between 1898 and 1902 over 2,600 firms went out of existence as the result of mergers (Chandler and Tedlow 1985: 554). By the end of the 1920s giant corporations run by professional managers had come to dominate most U.S. industries, and with this economic life in general (Galambos 1975: 9).

A major purpose for these mergers was to overcome the uncertainty created by competition and so have more control over markets and therefore prices and sales (Galambos 1975: 9). This quest for control by avoiding competition led to the creation of trusts and holding companies to enable former competitors to combine. These trusts expanded horizontally to reduce direct competition but also vertically so that they could control their supply of raw materials and the marketing of their final products. They also expanded into foreign markets. In the United States this trend preceded a similar trend in other countries (Chandler and Tedlow 1985: 402).

In the past few decades the mergers of companies have taken place on a global scale. The economic muscle of transnational corporations is now formidable (Anderson and Cavanagh 1999: 26–27). Transnational companies account for most of the world's financial transactions and about 70 percent of the world's trade. The current trend toward large corporate mergers is likely to see corporations gaining considerably in economic power, compared to nation-states. While average world economic growth is around 2 to 3 percent per year, the largest transnational corporations are growing by 8 to 10 percent per year (Karliner 1997: 5).

The new supersize entities are not only able to control markets, prices, and sales but also to rival the economic power of nation-states and win freedom from the power of national governments to regulate their activities. The corporate push for free trade in particular, in the name of competition, has all the appearances of a push for corporate power over the nation-state.

Globalization clearly follows from the imperatives of capitalism. But the question we are addressing in this chapter is whether it is, as ecofeminists claim, the patriarchal nature of capitalism that provides its driving force and defines its essential nature? An alternative, more conventional explanation is that commerce and profit making, when they are raised above all other human activity, come to dominate all aspects of humanity and nature, so that all is subsumed in the drive for profits and economic growth.

PRODUCTION VERSUS REPRODUCTION

Salleh seeks to explain capitalism in terms of the dichotomy between the productive sphere of men and the reproductive sphere of women, rather than the more conventional explanation of a dichotomy between capital and labor. Salleh's difficulty is that it is not so easy to pigeon-hole women into the reproductive sphere. Early capitalism depended on women and children as workers—productive units—and power was exercised over them through economic and religious domination. And this form of domination was far more central to capitalism than the domination of husbands over wives, or production over reproduction.

Getting skilled workmen to submit to factory discipline was particularly difficult, and manufacturers looked for mechanical ways of replacing their labor so that most factory tasks could be reduced "to the exercise of vigilance and dexterity,—faculties . . . speedily brought to perfection in the young" (Thompson 1980: 396). Women and children were favored for such work because "their slender and more pliant fingers were better adapted to the tasks required of them; their shorter stature made it possible to place them in corners, and underneath machines" (Halèìvy 1960: 279). Also, children and young women were considered to be more "timid and easier to rule" (Halèìvy 1960: 279). However, with time men too became submissive in their work roles. Industrialization depended on "a process of socialisation which aimed at stabilizing and inculcating fidelity among those whose labor was being conscripted" (Ewen 1976: 6).

This was achieved in many cases through religion, which taught a work ethic. The ideal solution was a workforce that was motivated to work for work's sake. Many factory owners, despairing of the traditional lackadaisical attitudes of their workers, "launched 'moral crusades' and attempted to convert whole sections of their labor force" to Protestantism in the hope of creating "an efficient, diligent, and reliable" workforce (Marshall 1982: 125).

For many such factory owners, the new evangelical branches of Protestantism such as Methodism seemed to serve the purpose well. Methodists tended to have "methodical" habits, to pay careful attention to instructions, to fill contracts on time, and not be inclined to embezzle materials (Thompson 1980: 395). They were imbued with a work ethic and were generally sober, hard-working, obedient employees. The following directive was issued at the Methodist Conference in 1766: "We must never forget the first rule, Be diligent. Never be unemployed for a moment. Never be triflingly employed. Never 'while away time; neither spend any more time at any place than is strictly necessary" (Jones 1997: 762).

Methodist preachers taught their followers to submit to authority and be obedient: "Even if those in authority are evil or without faith, nevertheless the authority and its power is good and from God" (Thompson 1980: 399). Elie Halèìvy notes that Methodist leaders had declared their intention of "promoting loyalty in the middle ranks as well as subordination and industry in the lower orders of society" (Thomis 1974: 166).

Thompson argues that workers accepted Methodism in part because they were indoctrinated. The Methodist Sunday schools were very active and often the only source of education for poor children. These schools were more concerned with teaching good behavior and submission than teaching reading and writing. In fact, Methodist Sunday schools, like Anglican Sunday schools, discouraged the teaching of writing. Methodists believed children were naturally sinful and education tended to be aimed at their moral rescue. They were not allowed to play freely; their play had to be channeled into useful activities such as chopping wood and digging (Thompson 1980: 412–15; Thomis 1974: 173–75).

> Break their will betimes. Begin this work before they can run alone, before they can speak plain, perhaps before they can speak at all. Whatever pain it costs, break the will if you would not damn the child. Let a child from a year old be taught to fear the rod and to cry softly; from that age make him do as he is bid, if you whip him ten times running to effect it . . . Break his will now, and his soul shall live, and he will probably bless you to all eternity. (Thompson 1980: 412)

This domination and socialization of children so that they would grow up to be subservient adults had little to do with the dichotomy between production and reproduction. The domination of women was only one of the forms of domination that occurred in early capitalist societies.

When religion had run its course the work ethic continued as a motivator, reinforced through propaganda, socialization at home and school, and popular culture. The active stigmatization of unemployed and poor people as being to blame for their fate also contributed to the reinforcement of the work ethic (Beder 2000).

The irony is that having made productive work the center of life, both material and spiritual, capitalism then proceeded to destroy work as a satisfying, meaningful activity for millions of people by fragmenting it and reducing some jobs to activities better suited for animals or machines. Unable to rely on a work ethic to motivate manual workers in such jobs, employers have used the services of engineers, psychologists, sociologists, and others to find ways to increase productivity and motivate workers.

Frederick Winslow Taylor's scientific management was one such method. Taylor sought to separate the thinking part of the work from the physical part and give it to managers who would then tell the workers exactly what to do and how to do it. Taylor's views of workers were not particularly enlightened: "Now one of the very first requirements for a man who is fit to handle pig iron as a regular occupation is that he shall be so stupid and so phlegmatic that he more nearly resembles in his mental makeup the ox than any other type" (Taylor 1911: 59). It was Taylor's separation of mental and manual labor that became characteristic of mass production methods in the twentieth century.

While both women and men work and are therefore part of the production apparatus of capitalist society, it is difficult to agree with Salleh that the female social experience is one in which time is not commodified but filled with life-affirming and organic practices such as child raising, caring, creating home and community. Salleh also argues that due to the necessary exclusion of women's reproductive labor from the formal economy, women experience a different reality. However, reproduction is increasingly being incorporated, through new technologies, into the capitalist realm of production (Clonaid 2001). Her conclusion that our different life experience allows women the privilege of *embodying* the aspects of culture that are still firmly rooted in nature is therefore somewhat debatable.

Mellor recognizes that women have now become highly integrated into the workforce rather than simply being housewives, yet suggests that women workers still display an "immediate altruism" or sense of duty for domestic caring work in addition to their wage labor, when many men may not. Mellor has reservations over giving a biological explanation to this phenomenon but is uncertain of an alternative (Mellor 1992: 252–54). Her implication is that women are more altruistic because of their upbringing or life experience as mothers. Yet this unproven tendency in women, or its lack in men, hardly qualifies as a major social determinant of globalization.

RULING ELITES

Ecofeminists also point to the predominance of men in the ruling elites and capitalist ranks as significant. But gender is only one of the criteria for success in a capitalist society and an increasingly less important one. Ralph Miliband (1982: 7) noted in his book *Capitalist Democracy in Britain* that

> there is a high degree of homogeneity among the members of the dominant class, much of it based on a marked similarity of social background, education, and 'life-styles'. A majority are of middle- and upper-class origin, and have had a public-school and Oxford or Cambridge education. Many of them are linked by ties of kinship. . . . They constantly cross each other's paths in an incessant round of meetings, lunches, dinners, functions, and ceremonies, and as members of boards, commissions, councils, committees, and institutions of the most varied kind.

Miliband (1982: 7) notes that these people shared similar ideologies and political views and that those who joined the power elite from outside soon learned to take on the values and behavior of the elite, as an essential requirement of success.

The alternative route to wealth, by rising up the corporate hierarchy, is just as restricted. The hierarchical structure of business organizations mirrors the class structure of the society they are in. In Britain, those at the top of the organizational hierarchy tend to be those of higher class. Because of their education and upbringing they fit in with the company power brokers better: for a man to be promoted to the top ranks of a company "he must be like those who are already in, and upon whose judgments his own success rests. . . . To be compatible with the top men is to act like them, to look like them, to think like them" or at least to give that impression. Upper-class men possess a cultural capital which includes a manner and style and way of speaking that enables them to fit in with ease and tends to give them authority with subordinates, a quality expected of senior executives (Watson 1987: 189; Mills 1956: 141).

Similarly in the United States, when Mills studied the top chief executives of the largest companies in each generation from 1900 to the 1950s, he found that they too were "a quite uniform social type which has had exceptional advantages of origin and training." They were mainly American-born of American-born fathers, college-educated, Protestant, white, and from upper- or upper-middle-class families. Seven out of ten had fathers who were businessmen or professionals. And the proportion coming from working-class families was falling over time, with only 2.5 percent of chief executives under fifty in 1952 coming from such families (Mills 1956: 127–28).

There is no doubt that sexism exists in capitalist societies and plays a role in preventing women from reaching the top positions in corporations. But class, race, ethnicity, and sexual preference can also limit one's chances. Are these prejudices actually necessary to capitalism, as ecofeminists argue?

The work ethic provides the legitimation and justification for inequality in our society because it teaches us that those who have wealth deserve it and those who are poor have themselves to blame. It also provides a mythical means by which individuals can climb to the top through talent, perseverance, and hard work. In many ways sexism and other "isms" provide obvious counters to this myth making and it is in the interests of an all-encompassing capitalism to break them down, which is slowly happening. Although more women and homosexuals and blacks and non-Christians are seeping into the ranks of the elites, the values of those elites remain unchanged. Women who become top executives do so by accepting corporate values and excelling at them. They take on the corporate culture and become thoroughly integrated into the capitalist culture.

Is the problem that the top ranks of corporate executives and owners are singularly unrepresentative of the broader population, or does the problem lie more deeply within a capitalist culture that prioritizes profits over other human values, including environmental protection. Would a more representative corporate elite behave any differently?

CAPITALIST CULTURE

Salleh claims the project of ecofeminism is to use the experience of women to pull men out of patriarchal capitalism, rather than integrate women into it. She points out that a system of domination, such as patriarchal capitalism, hurts men just as it hurts women, leaving them fundamentally unhappy. But Salleh argues that women have a freedom from the system that men do not have because they do not receive the ego gratification that men do from the system (Salleh 1997).

But is this true? Western women are deeply embedded in most aspects of capitalist culture, and even women who are not corporate executives receive some measure of ego gratification from it. Women living in affluent countries are not separated from capitalist culture any more than men, despite their reproductive capacity and cycles. Perhaps this is most evidenced in their acceptance of consumerism and the work ethic, whatever their roles as mothers or workers.

Capitalist culture depends not only on the capitalists at the top but also on a degree of acceptance by the wider society that capitalist culture delivers a quality life to everyone who deserves it. Gramsci used the term "hegemony" to describe the phenomenon by which the majority of people accept the values and political axioms that ensure their own subordination to the ruling elite. Earl Shorris (1994: 17–18), in his book *The Oppressed Middle*, discusses how:

> The most insidious of the many kinds of power is the power to define happiness. It is the dream of merchants, despots, managers, and philosophers, because whoever defines happiness can control the organization and the actions of other men: he not only assigns aspirations and desires, he constructs the system of morals by which the means of achieving happiness is judged.

A merchant in an affluent society defines happiness in ways that encourage acquisitiveness, wastefulness, "and social competition through displays of material wealth" (Shorris 1994: 22, 25). In such a society, many people participate in this definition of happiness so that they can sell their own services and goods. Managers "prove the system" by enjoying "more of the signs of happiness" than those beneath them and by the status and power they have over their subordinates. Each step up the social hierarchy offers the aspirant a small reward in terms of status, power, and income, a proof of the eventual happiness in store for those who keep climbing (Shorris 1994: 26–27).

In order to sell its products, capitalists feed on profitable aspects of patriarchal domination. Capitalist commodities such as women's magazines, to use a very crude example, are socializing agents of women. The underlying drive of these magazines is consumerism—they tap into patriarchal behavior as a selling point. Beauty is narrowly defined and fetishized in order to sell products, and the early sexualization of girls is promoted to expand markets, both in readership and products (Adorno 1991:86; Keane 1991:81–82). But is it the relationship between men and women that creates a capitalism that exploits women or, as seems more likely, is capitalism simply using patriarchal values to its own advantage?

The degree to which women have internalized consumerism cannot be downplayed or dismissed. Although consumerism is addressed by ecofeminists as a problem for women of the north created by patriarchal capitalism, they do not adequately take account of the power of consumerism to acculturate women and shape individual self-actualization. Although ecofeminists maintain that it is the social experience of women participating in community outside commodified time and necessity in the realm of reproduction that allows them to experience or "know" an embeddedness in nature, is it possible to conjecture that this removes women from their lifetime of culture and socialization to the contrary? Certainly not in the north. In the south, as Shiva and Mies note, people have the raw experience of capitalism subsuming their traditional ways of life and worldviews but this is true of both men and women.

By effectively removing women from culture—the acculturation and socialization processes entailed in the work ethic, and corporate and consumer cultures—materialist ecofeminists actually fail to break apart the dualism of culture/nature. The implication that men are subject to culture and women aren't is a form of essentialism, the very problem material ecofeminism attempts to address.

CONCLUSION

Ecofeminism has strengths in its ability to highlight the impacts of globalization and their significance, particularly with respect to its impacts on women and children and on cultural and biological diversity. However its weakness is in analyzing the causes of globalization and this is because of its focus on only one of the characteristics of capitalism, and perhaps one of the less important when it comes to the capitalist drive to globalism.

Another problem with ecofeminism is its tendency to alienate men. Men are also exploited and damaged under capitalism. Even when ecofeminists address essentialism that may linger in their dialogue so that men are not simply bad or destructive by their nature, ecofeminists imply that men are spiritually marginalized and separated from nature through their experience. The generalizations and uniform assumptions that ecofeminists make about men are alienating: "Men never think of life. They only want to conquer nature and the enemy" (Shiva and Mies 1993:15). These sentiments and blanket statements may arise from a rage that should not be devalidated but the experiences of men have variety just as women's do. Men, like women, are divided by class, ethnicity, and so forth. Many suffer poverty and human rights abuses as do women.

Ecofeminists argue that truth is contextual and plural (Hicks 1996: 3; Howell 1990: 235) and reality is like a patchwork quilt with no absolute story within. Perhaps this is how we should view ecofeminism itself. Not as *the* truth but as a contribution to understanding that can be augmented from other sources with different viewpoints. Viewing ecofeminism in such a way moves its project toward compatibility with an inclusive democracy that synthesizes democratic and socialist, radical green, feminist, and libertarian traditions (Fotopoulos 1997: x).

REFERENCES

Adorno, Theodor. 1991. "Culture Industry Reconsidered." In J. M. Bernstein, ed., *The Culture Industry: Selected Essays on Mass Culture.* London: Routledge.

Anderson, Sarah, and John Cavanagh. 1996. "Corporate Empires." *Multinational Monitor,* December 1996, 26–27.

Barry, John. 1997. "The Emergence of an Ecofeminist Political Economy." In Ariel Salleh, ed., *Ecofeminism as Politics: Nature, Marx, and the Postmodern,* 150–55. London: Zed.

———. 1998. "The Emergence of Ecofeminist Political Economy." *Environmental Politics* 7, no. 3.

Beder, Sharon. 1997. "The Environment Goes to Market." *Democracy and Nature* 3, no. 3.

———. 2000. *Selling the Work Ethic: From Puritan Pulpit to Corporate PR.* London: Zed.

Bernstein, Paul. 1997. *American Work Values: Their Origin and Development.* Albany: State University of New York Press.

Chandler, A. D., and R. S. Tedlow. 1985. *The Coming of Managerial Capitalism: A Casebook History of American Economic Institutions.* Homewood, Ill.: Richard D. Irwin.

Clonaid.com. 2001. www.clonaid.com/english/pages/home.html.

Crittenden, Chris. 1993. "Ecofeminism Meets Business: A Comparison of Ecofeminist, Corporate, and Free Market Ideologies." In Maria Mies and Vandana Shiva, eds., *Ecofeminism.* London: Zed.

Ewen, Stuart. 1976. *Captains of Consciousness: Advertising and the Social Roots of the Consumer Culture.* New York: McGraw-Hill.

Fotopoulos, Takis. 1997. *Towards an Inclusive Democracy: The Crisis of the Growth Economy and the Need for a New Liberatory Project.* London: Cassell.

Galambos, L. 1975. *The Public Image of Big Business in America, 1880–1940.* Baltimore: Johns Hopkins University Press.

Gray, C. 1999. "Corporate Goliaths: Sizing up Corporations and Governments." *Multinational Monitor*, June 1999.

Haleìvy, E. 1960. *England in 1815*. Trans. E. I. Watkin and D. A. Barber. Paperback ed. London: Ernest Benn.

Hicks, D. 1996. "Identifying Sources of Hope in Postmodern Times." In R. Slaughter, ed., *New Thinking for a New Millennium*. London: Routledge.

Howell, Nancy R. 1997. "Ecofeminism: What One Needs to Know." *Zygon* 32, no. 2.

Jones, H. B. 1997. "The Protestant Ethic: Weber's Model and the Empirical Literature." *Human Relations* 50, no. 7.

Karliner, J. 1997. *The Corporate Planet: Ecology and Politics in the Age of Globalization*. San Francisco: Sierra Club Books.

Keane, John. 1991. "Deregulation." In John Keane, ed., *The Media and Democracy*. Cambridge: Polity.

Marshall, G. 1982. *In Search of the Spirit of Capitalism: An Essay on Max Weber's Protestant Ethic Thesis*. London: Hutchinson.

Mellor, Mary. 1992. *Breaking the Boundaries: Towards a Feminist Green Socialism*. London: Virago.

Merchant, Carolyn. 1980. *The Death of Nature: Women, Ecology, and the Scientific Revolution*. San Francisco: HarperSanFrancisco.

Mies, Maria. 1993. "Women Have No Fatherland." In Maria Mies and Vandana Shiva, eds., *Ecofeminism*. London: Zed.

Mies, Maria, and Vandana Shiva. 1993. *Ecofeminism*. London: Zed.

Miliband, R. 1982. *Capitalist Democracy in Britain*. Oxford: Oxford University Press.

Mills, C. W. 1956. *The Power Elite*. Oxford: Oxford University Press.

Morgan, Robin. 1982. *The Anatomy of Freedom: Feminism, Physics, and Global Politics*. Oxford: Martin Robertson.

Norberg-Hodge, Helena. 1999. "The March of the Monoculture." *Ecologist* 29, no. 2.

Phillips, A. 1987. Introduction to *Feminism and Equality*. Oxford: Basil Blackwell.

Plant, Judith. 1989. "Toward a New World: An Introduction." In *Healing the Wounds: The Promise of Ecofeminism*. Philadelphia: New Society.

Plumwood, Val. 1995. "Nature, Self, and Gender: Feminism, Environmental Philosophy, and the Critique of Rationalism." In Robert Elliot, ed., *Environmental Ethics*. Oxford: Oxford University Press.

Ritzer, George. 1996. *The McDonaldization of Society: An Investigation into the Changing Character of Contemporary Social Life*. Rev. ed. Thousand Oaks, Calif.: Pine Forge.

Salleh, Ariel. 1997. *Ecofeminism as Politics: Nature, Marx, and the Postmodern*. London: Zed.

Shiva, Vandana. 1989. *Staying Alive: Women, Ecology, and Development*. London: Zed.

———. 1993a. "Masculinization of the Motherland." In Maria Mies and Vandana Shiva, eds., *Ecofeminism*. London: Zed.

———. 1993b. "Homeless in the 'Global Village." In Maria Mies and Vandana Shiva, eds., *Ecofeminism*. London: Zed.

Shorris, E. 1994. *A Nation of Salesmen: The Tyranny of the Market and the Subversion of Culture.* New York: Norton.

Tawney, R. H. 1973. "Religion and the Rise of Capitalism." In Robert W. Green, ed., *Protestantism, Capitalism, and Social Science: The Weber Thesis Controversy.* Lexington, Mass.: D. C. Heath.

Taylor, F. W. 1911. *The Principles of Scientific Management.* Westport, Conn.: Greenwood.

Thomis, M. I. 1974. *The Town Laborer and the Industrial Revolution.* London: B. T. Batsford.

Thompson, E. P. 1980. *The Making of the English Working Class.* London: Penguin.

Van Zevern, Claire. 1996. "Land, Ecology, and Women: Global Implications for Hawaiian Sovereignty." In Jennifer Turpin and Lois Ann Lorentzen, eds., *The Gendered New World Order: Militarism, Development, and the Environment.* New York: Routledge.

Warren, Karren J. 1990. "The Power and the Promise of Ecological Feminism." *Environmental Ethics* 12, no. 1.

Watson, T. 1987. *Sociology, Work, and Industry.* 2nd ed. London: Routledge & Kegan Paul.

Weber, Max. 1930. *The Protestant Ethic and the Spirit of Capitalism.* Trans. Talcott Parsons. 2nd ed. London: George Allen & Unwin.

Endnotes

INTRODUCTION

1. These facts, and many others, can be found at the Networld-Project at www .green-networld.com/facts/facts_fr.htm.

2. In 1991 the GNP (gross national product) was turned into the GDP (gross domestic product). With GNP the earnings of a multinational firm were attributed to the country in which the firm was owned and where most of the profits would eventually return. With the change to GDP, however, the profits are attributed to the country where the factories or mines, or other corporate assets are located, even though most of the profits won't stay there. Thus GDP excludes overseas profits earned by U.S. firms, but includes profits earned in the United States by foreign firms. Although it makes little difference in the index of economic growth in wealthy countries, this accounting shift does raise the measure of economic growth in the poor or peripheral countries. However it tends to hide the fact that profits extracted from the periphery are generally going to core countries.

3. Some of the more up-to-date information is contained in the Intergovernmental Panel on Climate Change (IPCC) and can be accessed at www.ipcc.ch.

CHAPTER 1: THE ECOLOGICAL FOOTPRINT

1. A report from the Redefining Progress Sustainability Indicators Program, www.rprogress.org/publications/2006/Footprint%20of%20Nations%202005.pdf.

2. A draft manuscript was presented to outside academic reviewers from Stanford University, Claremont College, University of California–Berkeley, University of Illinois, University of Texas–Austin, and Illinois Natural History Survey. Feedback was given due consideration in the final analysis. The findings have been submitted for peer review consideration in an academic journal.

CHAPTER 2: ENERGY

1. Reprinted from *Social Justice* 23, no. 4 (1996): 87–99.

2. Data for this article were collected while conducting anthropological fieldwork in Oloma Village, Bonny, for twelve months between 1983 and 1984.

3. For a model of an eastern delta fishing community before European contact, see R. Horton (1969): 37–58. See also E. J. Alagoa (1970): 319–29; (1971): 269–78.

4. See A. Jewett, "Change and Continuity among the Ibani" (Ph.D. diss., Cambridge University), chap. 2, for an overview of the decline of Bonny in the twentieth century.

5. See Tumini Dagogo Waribor, June 1976.

CHAPTER 3: WATER

1. *Oprah Winfrey Show*, "What's Happening in Africa?" www.oprah.com/tows/pastshows/tows_2002/tows_past_20020920_c.jhtml.

2. Reprinted from *The Ecologist* 34, no. 2 (2004): 52–58.

3. Reprinted from *Mother Jones* 27 (2002): 38–47.

CHAPTER 4: GLOBALIZING THE EARTH'S CRUST

1. Reprinted from *New York Times*, October 24, 2005.

CHAPTER 5: THE SEAS AROUND US

1. Reprinted from *Mother Jones* 31, no. 2 (March–April 2006): 32–48.

CHAPTER 6: CONSUMING THE CULTURE OF SUVS

1. Reprinted from *Environmental Politics* 15, no. 1 (2006): 1–22.

2. Thanks are due in particular to Heidi Anderson and Dale Armstrong for research assistance, and to two anonymous referees and Andy Dobson for constructive comments and advice.

3. The SUV in particular has received a fair bit of critical attention. In broad lines with some of what we say below, see Gunster (2004), or Luke (2001). Gunster (2004) analyses specifically SUV advertising, while Shukin (forthcoming) examines car advertising more generally, in terms of the complicated constructions of nature in these ads. We concur with many arguments here but emphasize in our analysis that such an account of nature is always implicated with an imperial politics.

4. The reading is thus carried out in the spirit of analyses like Wernick (1991) or Williamson (1981), or in the similar analysis of the film *The Big Lebowski* by Martin-Jones (forthcoming).

5. This ad appeared, among other places, in *Canadian Geographic*, May–June 1999, 16. For further information, please contact the authors.

6. Such an image was intentional: "Our new SUV 'No Boundaries' umbrella strategy communicates to consumers that there are no limits to where a Ford SUV can take them," states Ford's 2000 Annual Report (Ford Motor Company 2000:10, as cited in Luke 2001:316). It is perhaps worth noting that Ford's ads are relatively less militaristic than those, say, for the Cadillac Escalade or the Hummer. In part, this is because of the contradictions brought about by Ford's attempts to present itself as a "green" car company, while still developing new and bigger SUV models. On this, see Luke (2001). Nevertheless, the no boundaries tag line implicates it closely in a politics which is about avoiding spatial constraints, a trope which implicates individual consumers in the mode of existence of U.S. imperialism.

7. Bradsher gives similar examples of imagery used in marketing the Escalade, with an ad where the main slogan is simply the injunction "Yield." See Bradsher (2001: xix).

8. Heads-up display refers to elements of the display projected from the dashboard onto the windscreen so it is visible at eye level.

9. Note for North American readers: The Honda Jazz in Europe is a midsize family car, not a small motor scooter.

10. Although this is a long series of ads, the one specifically discussed appeared, among other places, in the *Guardian* weekend magazine, February 22, 2003.

11. It is also perhaps worth reflecting on the way that SUVs in many parts of the developing world come to figure as symbols of the new colonialism of aid workers, the UN, as they are typically driven by such workers. In Nepal, for example, such a culture is known as Pajero culture, given the frequency with which Mitsubishi Pajero SUVs are chosen by aid agencies. See Shah (2002).

CHAPTER 7: ECOTOURISM

1. Reprinted from *American Anthropologist* 107 (December 2005): 654–65.

CHAPTER 8: TECHNOLOGY AND THE GREEN REVOLUTIONS

1. Reprinted from *The Violence of the Green Revolution: Third World Agriculture, Ecology, and Politics* (London: Third World Network, 1991).

CHAPTER 9: GLOBAL TRADE OF ELECTRONIC WASTE

1. Printed from *Salon*, April 10, 2006 www.salon.com/news/feature/2996/04/10/ewaste.

CHAPTER 10: GLOBALIZATION AND
THE CHANGING CLIMATE

1. Reprinted from *Boston Review*, January–February 2007.

CHAPTER 11: THE PROBLEM
OF A RISING SEA-LEVEL

1. Reprinted from *Mother Jones* 28, no. 4 (July–August 2003): 50–55; 92–93.

CHAPTER 12: WAR AND MOBILIZATION

1. A report prepared for the Sierra Club of Canada by Jessica Adley and Andrea Grant, (August 19, 2003) www.sierraclub.ca/national/postings/war-and-environ ment.html.

2. Quoted in Richard W. Fisher, "The Environment and Military Strategy," *Air & Space Chronicles*, June 2003, www.airpower.maxwell.af.mil/airchronicles/cc/ fisher.html.

CHAPTER 13: ENVIRONMENTAL JUSTICE AND
GRASSROOTS GLOBALIZATION IN THE
NUCLEAR PACIFIC

1. Reprinted from *The Environmental Justice Reader: Politics, Poetics, and Pedagogy* (Tucson: University of Arizona Press, 2002).

2. This assessment of the NFIP comes from my own interviews with members of the movement, as well as from correspondence with representatives at the Pacific Concerns Resource Center, which is the NFIP secretariat in Suva Fiji. The quotations are taken from NFIP informational materials.

3. By "globalization from below" I mean to call attention to the way in which the NFIP forms a coherent and relatively recent regional bloc (made up mostly of minor economic players) in order to address both colonialism and the new power blocs usually associated with transnational markets and "globalization from above."

4. In 1999 I traveled to Tahiti, the Republic of the Marshall Islands, and Guam to research postnuclear economies and cultures, as well as the NFIP. The information in this chapter on both Tahiti and the Marshalls is, in part, the result of my interviews and observations in the field.

5. This suggestion appeared in a report presented on December 17, 1997 by Socialist Party member of parliament Christian Bataille. Report 541 to the French National Assembly.

6. Such focus on nuclear weapons has been required by the urgency of cold war nuclear politics. Consequently, because of the cold war spectacle of apocalypse, the serious problem of mounting nuclear wastes has taken a backseat in nuclear studies. However, not all scholars focus on weapons to the exclusion of waste.

7. The term "nuclearism" is a way of designating various aspects of nuclear or radioactive activities in one word, so as not to have to list nuclear testing, radiation experiments, nuclear development, waste burial, and uranium mining (or any combination of the above) each time I refer to more than one aspect of nuclear activity. The term also implies the structures—administrative, military, political, scientific—that surround and support nuclear activities of various kinds.

8. This quote from the NFIP Peoples Charter can be found on the NFIP website at www.pcrc.org.fj/index.cfm.

9. This quote is from an unidentified U.S. news segment videotape and is cataloged in the Department of Geography at the University of Canterbury, N.Z.

CHAPTER 14: MULTINATIONALS, CHINA, AND THE ENVIRONMENT

1. Reprinted from *Environmental Politics* 15, no. 2 (April 2006): 310–29.

2. Notable exceptions include Ferris and Zhang (2002), Oberheitmann (2002), CCICED (2004), and a special issue of *Sinosphere* 3.

3. For a counterargument, see Jahiel (2002).

4. Chai's data is based on SEPA statistics that do not generally include data from private firms and small rural enterprises.

5. For foreign-funded projects, see "Inventory of Environmental Work in China," in Woodrow Wilson International Center for Scholars, *China Environment Series* 5 (2002): 137–227.

6. Between 1985 and 1996, foreigners invested US$2.18 billion in 1,004 ODS-related enterprises (CCICED, 1997).

7. One of China's concerns was that environmental laws in other countries would increasingly be used to restrict trade, at great cost to the economy. In May 2002. the issue of protectionist green trade barriers was brought up repeatedly by environmental officials and policy analysts I spoke with in Beijing, and by presenters at the International Conference on China's Entry into the WTO: Economic and Ecological Challenges and Opportunities, in Kunming. SEPA's 2002 report *Jiaru WTO* noted that environmental labeling laws in fifty countries had already affected Chinese products worth US$4 billion.

8. Tariffs have been falling from the original 80–100 percent in 2001 to the required 25 percent in 2006, while import quotas for foreign automobiles have increased by 15 percent each year (Panel et al. 2004).

9. In 2003, small coal mines, representing 17.6 percent of the nation's coal output, accounted for over 46 percent of the increase in production over the previous year (Jiang et al. 2004).

10. These include "Criterion for the Formaldehyde Content of Textile Products," "Water Consumption Quota for Printed and Dyed Cotton Products," and "Textile Requirements on Environment-friendly Textile Products."

11. In 2003, the area sown to cotton grew by 22 percent (Asia Pulse Analysts, 2004).

12. At the time of WTO entry, various pesticides used in China were prohibited

in other industrialized countries. China had maximum toxicity levels for only 62 types of pesticides, compared to Japan's 96 and the U.S.'s 115; in addition, other countries had adopted fruit- and vegetable-specific residue and use standards, but China had not (Wang 2001; Hamburger 2002).

13. According to a World Bank study, China's rural poor have suffered a 6 percent decline in living standards since WTO entry (*Agence France Presse*, February 21, 2005).

CHAPTER 15: GLOBALIZATION AND THE BURDEN OF CRITICAL THEORY

1. See Jeanne Kay, "Human Dominion over Nature in the Hebrew Bible," *Annals of the Association of American Geographers* 79, no. 2 (June 1989): 214–32.
2. Reprinted from *Democracy and Nature* 7, no. 2 (July 2001): 281–302.

Index

About the Editors

Richard Robbins received his PhD in anthropology from University of North Carolina and has spent his entire teaching career at the State University of New York at Plattsburgh. His most recent publications include *Cultural Anthropology: A Problem-Based Approach* (5th edition 2009) and *Global Problems and the Culture of Capitalism* (4th edition 2007). He is co-editor with Mark Nathan Cohen of *Darwin and the Bible* (Penguin Academic 2008). He is the recipient of the SUNY Chancellor's Award for Excellence in Teaching and the American Anthropological Association/McGraw-Hill Teacher of the Year Award. He appeared also in the hit anti-globalization documentary *The Yes Men*. He is currently SUNY Distinguished Teaching Professor at Plattsburgh, and maintains a global problems website at www.plattsburgh.edu/legacy and a general website at faculty.plattsburgh.edu/richard.robbins. He can be contacted by email at richard.robbins@plattsburgh.edu.

Gary Kroll received his PhD in the history of science from the University of Oklahoma and now teaches U.S. environmental history and the history of U.S. science, technology and exploration at SUNY Plattsburgh, where he has been since 2001. He was recently awarded the SUNY Chancellor's Award for Excellence in Faculty Service, is the author of *America's Ocean Wilderness: A Cultural History of Twentieth Century Exploration* (Kansas 2008), and is co-author of *Science and Exploration: Social Impact and Interaction* (ABC Clio 2007).